THE INVESTING GUIDE

INVESTING USING TECHNICAL

AND FUNDAMENTAL ANALYSIS

THE INVESTING GUIDE

INVESTING USING TECHNICAL AND FUNDAMENTAL ANALYSIS

JIM VICKERY

Founder and Editor of InvestProfits.com

DEDICATION

This book is dedicated to all those who have inspired me to include but not limited to my brothers John, Tim, my sisters Cindy, Christy (in memory) and Michelle. Also to Emma for her meticulous editing of the content.

TABLE OF CONTENTS

7

8

PREFACE

This book is intended for those with some basic knowledge and understanding of investing. While this book does cover complex concepts like Capital Asset Pricing Model (CAPM) and economics, and can be beneficial to MBA students and CFA students, it is not limited to this audience. Even the novice investor can benefit from the technical and fundamental concepts covered in this book.

While investing can be a very profitable endeavour, some investors have success while others have poor results. Some of those leave investing forever. This book will discuss ways you can become a better investor using methods that make it easier to find stocks that are most likely to increase in value.

There is unlimited opportunity to invest in the stock market. And with all the technology and internet capabilities, there are unlimited opportunities to research and analyze stocks, bonds and mutual funds. However, I am going discuss methods of investing in individual stocks. However, this book is not limited to short term traders. It also covers methods to invest for the long term assets like mutual funds, ETS's and bonds.

Some of the shorter term examples include details of stocks that had impressive growth resulting in substantial profits. For example:

* Learn to find stocks like Dollar General before it doubled in price from $28 to over $55 after having several RSI buy signals back in February 2011. By using indicators like moving average and RSI, investing can be more profitable.

* Learn how to identify stocks like Buffalo Wild Wings before it had a 225% increase in 2 ½ years by using technical indicators such as Relative Strength Index and other technical indicators.

Further, discussions involving opportunities that benefit short-term traders and long-term investors are detailed. For example, how a stock investment of $10,000 could have turned into $30,000 in one year. Technical analysis indicators such as RSI, MACD, and moving averages were used to find that stock. Conversely, analysis of fundamental analysis and its implications are discussed. Additionally, the economy and its impact to the markets and investing are covered.

Getting better investment returns over the short-term and long-term can be accomplished. *Both traders and investors can gain insight into buying and selling stocks for profit by using the methods in this book.* This book covers both technical analysis indicators and fundamental indicators in ways that make evaluating stocks easier. All of this is done to allow an investor or trader to have solid risk management and better trade execution. While these methods are discussed, it is not exhaustive; some methods are discussed in brevity.

Investing can be very profitable for diligent and patient investors. Take this example: the 10 year stock return for Apple going from February 2003 to February 2013 was up more than 4000% in September 2012, while the S&P 500 was up only 86% during the same period.

Furthermore techniques are used to examine stocks that have performed well in the past using back-testing, while revealing ways to identify stocks with similar attributes that have a high probability to outperform the market. This book is about the various concepts of investing, including economics, stock picking strategies, and using fundamental and technical analysis. I will delve into the best ways to find the best methods to buy and sell a stock. This book will cover a vast amount of information; however, it is not exhaustive. Nonetheless, every effort has been taken to cover the subject matter thoroughly enough to benefit investors and traders. All of this is done while trying to maintain brevity of subjects when possible.

Chapter 1: Investing Basics

First, let me begin this book by telling you that I have been an investor for over 10 years and in that time, I have encountered many up and downs in the market. Some occurred in the mutual funds I owned and others in individual stocks. And during those ups and downs, I have learned many lessons: some good and some bad. It is really difficult to know which way the market is going at any given time. Then, as I researched better investing techniques, I finally found ones that worked. Thus, I came up with some sound investing techniques many of them will be discussed in chapter 2 and chapter 3. However, before beginning it is imperative to discuss some of the history of the stock market. This is imperative because the stock market is like the rest of

15

history: If we are not familiar with the past, we are doomed to repeat it. Many intelligent investors have failed to succeed in the market by failing to study the past...some of them were Noble prize winning economists, like those of Long Term Capital Management (LCTM).

No Investor is perfect

No investor is perfect nor is every investment is perfect. Sometimes an investor will apply all the necessary due diligence to research a stock only to lose money on a stock pick. Even Warren Buffett has often said that his picking 3 winners out of 10 can give him a sizable gain in the market. Furthermore, no analysis can be infallible when choosing which stock to pick. Therefore, an investor can only be sufficiently prepared when making investing decisions using diligent analysis and research. Then, when three or four stocks out of 10 perform better than the market, he can be confident of prospering in the market.

The reasons so many investors do poorly are many. But these are some of them: many times investors will not use careful analysis in choosing which stocks to buy and as a result end up with diminished returns. The astute investor should not fall to these lethargic methods. Nonetheless, the investor would be wise to not time the market, not unless risks are mitigated with diversification.

Timing the Market

It can be very hazardous to one's wealth (and possibly health) when they try to time the market. Many of the best days to be invested in the market are often lost by those who time the market. Many studies have concluded that those who time the market usually perform worse than the average of the S&P 500 over time.

While it is not recommended for anyone to try to time the market, it's not entirely impossible to get better returns by buying and selling at the most opportunistic time possible. That's what the role of technical and fundamental analysis can provide.

Key Steps to Investing

1. Define your Goals- The best plans in life happen from well defined goals. Find investing goals and go after them; it could be saving for retirement, planning for financial independence, or money for college, but define your goal first.

2. Find your Risk Tolerance - If you have a low threshold for risk, you should only invest in bonds, or money market funds. If you have a moderate risk tolerance, then index funds and individual stocks are more suited for you.

3. Research Stocks, Bonds, and Mutual Funds - After you know your investment goals, risks, it is time to research the best places to park your money so that your returns are not diminished.

4. Keep Costs Low- If you decide that you want a mutual fund in your portfolio, keep the fees low. Many times a mutual fund will have a high expense ratio. This is a

17

method of giving away your hard earned money, especially if the fund performs no better than the stock market as a whole. Therefore, it is wise to read the mutual fund's prospectus beforehand. This is a good way to find hidden fees and other expenses. Or at least look up the expense ratio online. Otherwise, your money could be at risk.

As seen in Figure 1-1, a mutual fund with an expense ratio of 3.6, would reduce an investment of 10,000 (and 300 contributed monthly) over 20 years from $355,211 down to $343, 041. That's a difference of over 12,000. See Fig.1-1 for an example of how expense ratios can cut into future returns.

Mutual Fund Expense Ratio Comparison Chart					
Amount Invested	-10,000	% Return		12.00%	
Amount /Month	-300	See how Expense Ratios Affect Returns- In Difference Columns			
Expense Ratio	0.18%	3.60%	Difference	2.00%	Difference
1 Year	$14,773	$14,267	$506	$14,504	$269
2 Year	$20,140	$19,450	$690	$19,772	$367
3 Year	$26,150	$25,254	$896	$25,673	$477
4 Year	$32,881	$31,755	$1,127	$32,282	$600
5 Year	$40,421	$39,036	$1,385	$39,684	$737
6 Year	$48,865	$47,191	$1,674	$47,974	$891
7 Year	$58,322	$56,324	$1,998	$57,259	$1,063
8 Year	$68,914	$66,553	$2,361	$67,658	$1,257
9 Year	$80,777	$78,010	$2,768	$79,305	$1,473
10 Year	$94,064	$90,842	$3,223	$92,349	$1,715
11 Year	$108,946	$105,213	$3,733	$106,959	$1,986
12 Year	$125,613	$121,309	$4,304	$123,322	$2,290
13 Year	$144,280	$139,336	$4,943	$141,649	$2,631
14 Year	$165,187	$159,527	$5,660	$162,175	$3,012
15 Year	$188,603	$182,141	$6,462	$185,164	$3,439
16 Year	$214,828	$207,468	$7,360	$210,911	$3,917
17 Year	$244,201	$235,835	$8,367	$239,749	$4,452
18 Year	$277,099	$267,605	$9,494	$272,047	$5,052
19 Year	$313,944	$303,188	$10,756	$308,220	$5,724
20 Year	$355,211	$343,041	$12,170	$348,735	$6,477

Fig 1-1 (How Expense Ratios Affect Returns)

5. Read financial magazines and watch Business News with caution- Many of these finance magazines and business news channels will give hyped up buy and sell recommendations...sometimes at the worst time. Therefore, when listening to these media resources, you should use your own research. Especially since many analysts will like a stock one day only to not like it the next day, week, or month. Furthermore, many analysts

19

will like a stock after it has risen substantially, only to "not like" it when it falls. As a result, the investor is left with buying the stock high and selling low. Other times, an investor will follow an analyst recommendation only to end up buying high and selling higher; this method can work, but with diminished returns and very high risk.
6. Stay the Course- You should stay the course and not change your investing methodologies. For example, if your goal is to invest for the long-term and also hold some individual stocks, then you should stick with those goals and not change them repeatedly.

Be aware that staying the course is difficult even for the disciplined. Think about it! When you buy and hold a stock or mutual fund, the bankers and brokerage firms don't make money. They make money from trading activity. How? When you sell or buy a stock (and in some case a mutual fund) the banks and brokerages get paid for the transaction. That's why on even a down day in the market; the bankers and Wall Street executives are clapping at the ringing of the closing bell. They are not clapping when the market closes because the market was down, and now that it's closed they no longer have to be concerned with falling stock prices. For them, the falling stock prices were never a concern to begin with. In fact, the wild descents and ascending of the market is what they like. The more volatile the market, the better is for the banker and Wall Street brokerage houses. So when you trade excessively you will help fatten their bank account, whether you make money or not.

A Short History of the Stock Market

Beware of Hot Stocks / Hot IPO's

A stock that is hot is comparable to a burning match being passed around the room. The first person who gets the match burning then passes it to the person next to him. The next person to get it does the same thing as the flame is burning down, until the last person to get it gets burned. Buying a hot stock can be similar to this burning match metaphor: the last person to get a hot stock may be the one to get burned. Therefore, an investor is wise to avoid hot stocks as this can include new issues of stock.

An initial public offering is a new stock offering by a company. The first of these offerings is often covered by intense media coverage and attention from investing professionals like mutual fund managers. This attention can lead to over hyping a stock; remember Netscape? Its stock price doubled in the first week, and then soon fizzled. Sometimes, the stock will go public and crash on the first day; remember Facebook? At its initial offering, Facebook's IPO was overpriced and quickly crashed. Its stock went public at $38 on May 18, 2012 and fell all the way down to $17.73 on September 4, 2012, dropping a whopping 54% in value (see Fig 1-2).

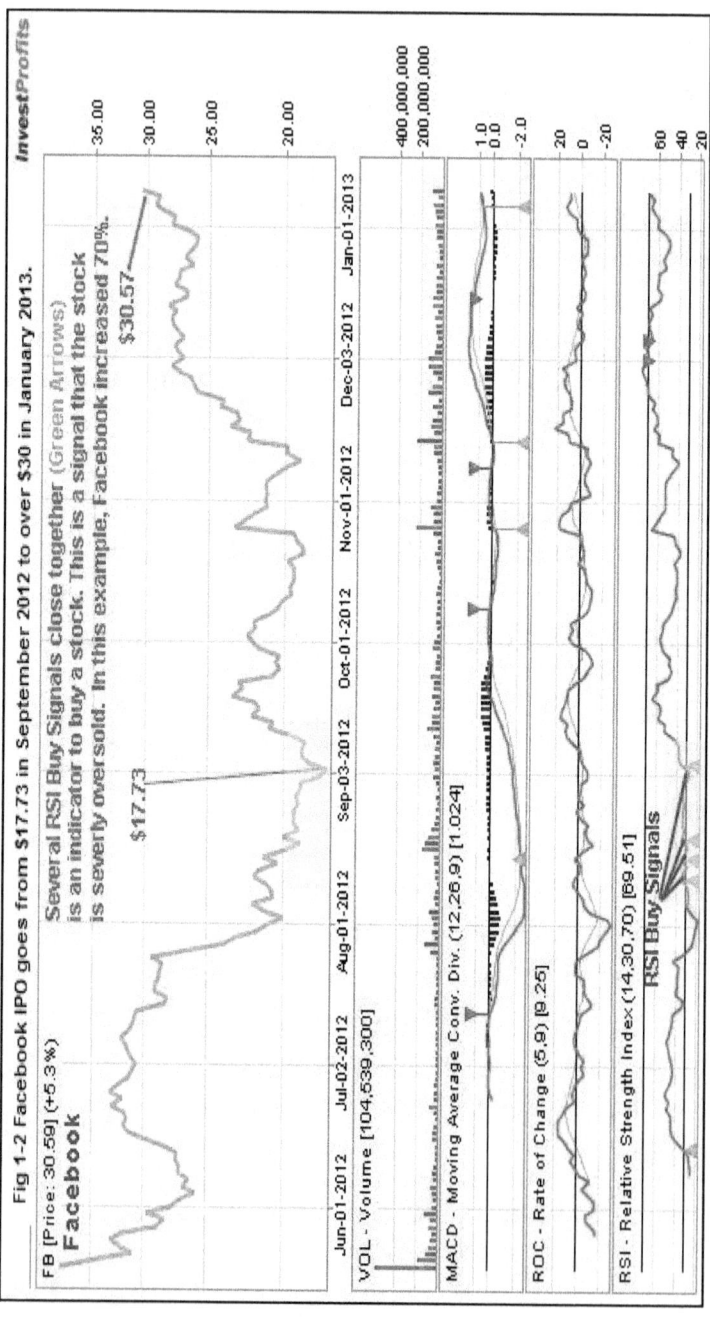

Fig 1-2 Facebook IPO goes from $17.73 in September 2012 to over $30 in January 2013.

Several RSI Buy Signals close together (Green Arrows) is an indicator to buy a stock. This is a signal that the stock is severly oversold. In this example, Facebook increased 70%.

However, some IPO's have worked out well: On March 27, 2000, Cisco Systems stock hit a price of $548 making it the most valuable company in the world. Had you bought the stock 10 years earlier during its IPO, and sold it on March 27, 2000, you would have made an average of 217% annually during the 10 years.

Many have tried to become sound investors and some have exceptional track records. Warren Buffett, Peter Lynch, and others have done very well. But others have done poorly, like the group of economists who started a LTCM. These individuals had won a Nobel Prize in economics. There was no way it could fail...right? Wrong! It did fail. In 1998 Long Term Capital Management (LTCM) went down in flames and almost took the entire financial system with it. But how could well educated individuals and Nobel Prize winners in economics do poorly managing a mutual fund? Well it's easy! They made some simple mistakes, one of which was that they failed to understand the history of the stock markets. This oversight caused them to mistakenly put their own intellect above that of the market...big mistake especially the madness of crowds makes markets to behave irrationally. Sir Isaac Newton once proclaimed this notion in saying, "I can calculate the movement of the stars, but not the madness of men." And with this kind of bravado the Nobel Prize winning economists of LCTM failed to realize that markets are highly unpredictable. Therefore an investor should not discount this financial tenet. Furthermore a great saying about history goes something like this, "Those who fail to study the past are bound to repeat it." This is especially true of financial history and it's especially true of inflated bubbles.

Bubble Mania

Many bubbles have occurred throughout history. The tulip blub craze where investors paid exuberant amounts of money for tulip bulbs that had a virus that gave them vibrant colors. The more variant the colors, the more valuable the bulbs were perceived to be. This craze lasted until several investors got burned and lost their money after the tulip bulb bubble burst.

The South Sea Bubble is another manic craze that left investors with huge losses. The Internet Bubble that happened in the late 1990's and had investors buying stocks in internet companies that did not even have a profit...or any revenue in some cases. Take for example theglobe.com. Its stock price grew in the first few days and when as high as $ 37.50 and then crashed all the way down to a penny stock. Figure 1-2 depicts the monthly prices of theglobe.com from Jan 1998- February 2004...notice the huge decline in the stock price. This stock climbed high in price and the company didn't any revenues; the price of the stock was bid higher based on its prospects a definite bubble was occurring at the time. Internet and technology stocks were all the rage. This artificial value lifted stocks to an all-time high at the time.

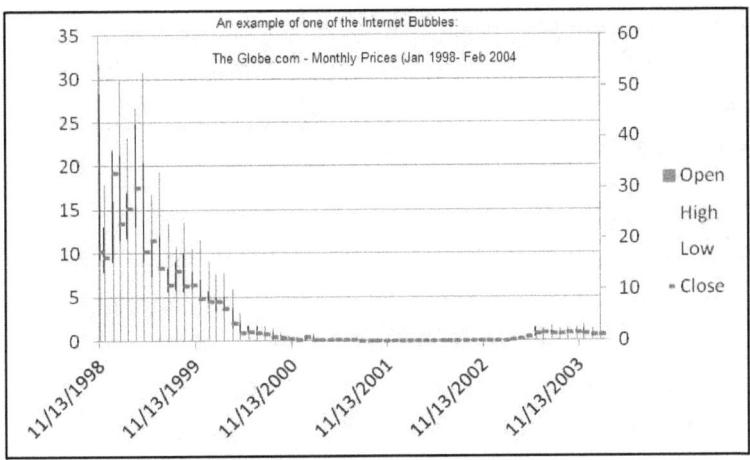

Fig 1-3 (The Globe Monthly Price Chart)

Avoid Hot Tips

The tips you get at a cocktail party or golf game should be avoided. The tips usually turn out to be speculative and almost never pan out....usually leaving you wondering what happened and wishing you hadn't listened to the tip in the first place. Hot stock tips are usually hyped up by someone else who owns the stock(s) and is trying to hype them up in order to sell it at a higher price; this is typically known as pump and dump. This type of investing is best left to gamblers because they are the only ones who should take a big risk like this. If you are going to speculate which is nothing more than gambling, then go to Las Vegas or buy a lottery ticket. But stay away from hot stock tips; they are a good way to lose money and the only people making money are the ones hyping them. If you must buy on a hot stock tip, then buy a small amount and watch the fundamentals and technicals of the

25

stock. If the stock should lose money, at least you will have had an opportunity to learn a lesson at a cheap price. This is a famous saying in learning a lesson the hard way that applies to hot stock tips: sometimes the only way to learn that stoves are hot is to touch it one time.

Copycat Craze

Sometimes companies that are on top will not stay there forever and the company's stock price will come down as a result. Sometimes this happens due to something known as the "copycat craze." However, many companies will refer to it as benchmarking, a form of copying another company's products for services. This usually happens when a product is so popular that many competitors will copy it, and thus take away market share from the original producer of the product. This has happened many times in the technology sector. That's a good reason the investor should NOT hold a stock too long; look at phone maker Blackberry as an example of how a dominant product can lose its market share.

Avoid the Herd Mentality

Many times investors will follow the herd as a way to invest. They will simply buy what others are buying and sell when others are selling. This type of behavior usually leads to poor results due the incorrect timing of the market. Many times this type of investing will lead to buying high and selling low. It is the noise from all the media outlets that lead to this irrational exuberance. Following the herd when investing can lead the investor to the poor house. This behavior is only amplified when more investors are doing the same thing, giving a false sense of security. As a result of the herd mentality, sometimes investors will think that they are doing much better than their actual results. A good example would be the well known investment club from Pennsylvania known as the Bardstown Ladies. *The Bardstown Ladies* is a book about this investing club of grandmothers that stated that the members investing club returns had beaten the S&P 500 over several years. However, during a thorough analysis, it was determined that the returns were much lower than originally reported and that the investing club had underperformed the S&P 500 by a wide margin. It was found that the error occurred from the fact that the members of the club were counting their new investment funds to the returns leading to false return on investment calculations. Bottom line: it is wise to avoid the herd mentality when investing.

Profiting from Market Fluctuations

Since common stocks are subject to market fluctuations, even investment grade stocks, an investor can profit handsomely from these pendulum swings. Be aware that an investor needs to be prepared both financially and psychologically for this erratic swing: financially prepared by being able to leave the money in the market, and psychologically prepared by not getting spooked and pulling money out of the market during wild moves down. If an investor can be prepared both financially and psychologically, then they can profit during the pendulum swings and reap nice profits. This can be done in two ways, through timing or pricing.

It can be done by timing by anticipating the direction the market may go and buying when it is expected to go higher, and selling when it is expected to go lower. An investor should think about technical analysis, especially RSI and moving averages for an advantage when attempting to time the market.

Pricing refers to buying a stock when the price of the stock is selling lower than its perceived value and selling when the stocks' price is higher than its perceived value. This is considered value investing and implemented using fundamental analysis. Particular attention should be applied to high ROE, and a low P/E ratio.

I am convinced that an investor can reap profits from using either method. The timing method can be beneficial because it is similar to forecasting...something done in many of the physical sciences with more accuracy than inaccuracy. Timing the market can be difficult, but using forecasting methods described in chapter 2 can prove beneficial for the astute investor.

The pricing method helps the investor who is patient by allowing him to ride the lows and highs of the stock market by holding tight even in the most erratic of markets. Many long-term investors have performed well by holding onto their investments when the market collapsed. For example, during the market decline in 2008-2009, the S&P 500 declined over 40% down to 678.

Then in less than three years it more than doubled to over 1,400 by 2012. Those investors who held on to their investments...even better results for those who added more money to their equities...had a better than 100% gain in 3 years (see Fig 1-4), doubling an investors' money in that time. This type of patience is not without its anxiety. Many investors may find it difficult to hold when they see the market in free fall, but patience is definitely a virtue in markets like those seen in 2009 through 2012.

This patience was even more complicated when some analysts were expecting the market to decline, or go into a correction. As you will notice in Fig. 1-4 the market has been on a steady incline and those who waited on the sidelines missed out on the growth of the market. That is why it's best to do your own analysis before taking the recommendation of the analysts and so called experts.

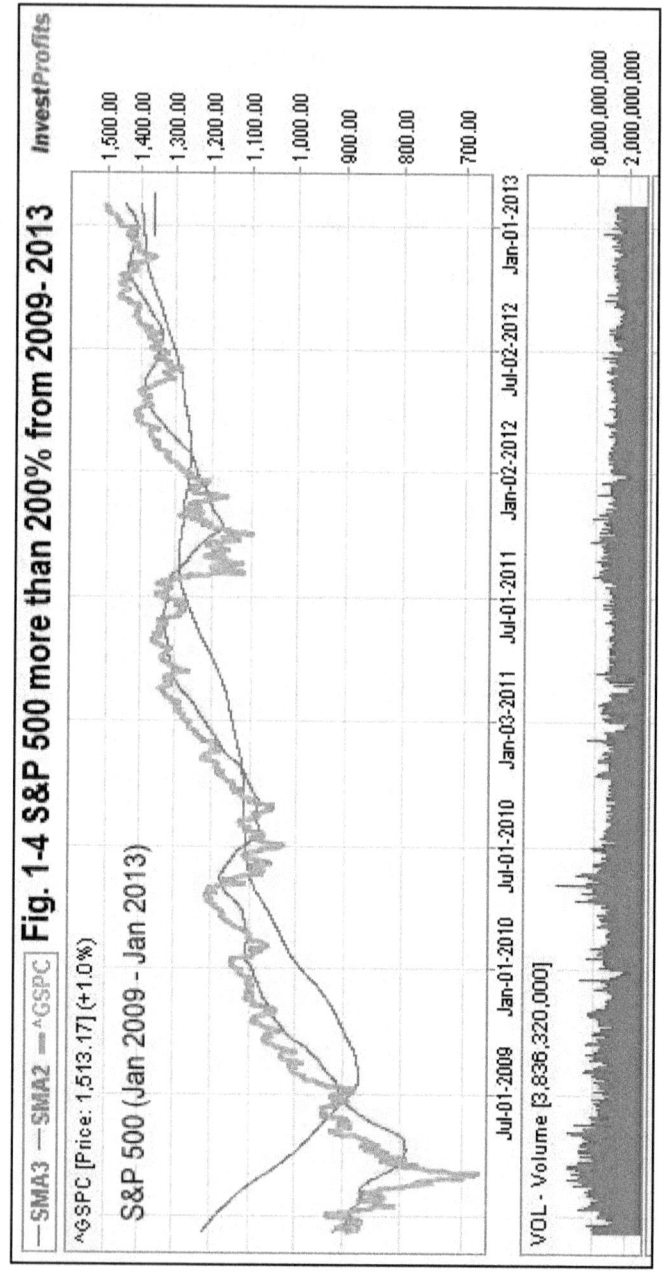

Fig. 1-4 S&P 500 more than 200% from 2009- 2013

Many times the general public is referred to as a retail investor...not in a negative sense...it's just that the mutual fund and hedge fund investors and others on Wall Street are considered the big money investors. As a result, they usually get to buy their equities at a discount. It is not absurd to think that the retail investor can make big money in the stock market. However, due diligence is required in order to pull this off. That is exactly what this book intends to do: make is easier for the retail investor to profit in the stock market.

Low PE Ratios and Future Returns

During the early part of the 1980's, P/E ratios were unusually low and bond yields were very high. Yet, during the next 20 years, stocks had one of the best 18 year market inclines ever. Conversely, bonds performed poorly. Many studies have been done and found that stocks with low P/E's relative to the market produce higher rates of return over the long run.

Individual Retirement Accounts

Regardless of which type you are everyone should have a retirement account in their portfolio. They come in many types such as Traditional IRA, and Roth IRA. Both of these have tax benefits...one grows tax free (the Roth IRA) and the other is tax deferred (Traditional IRA). All individuals can participate in an individual retirement account, provided they meet the income requirements. The type and amounts that can be added to these accounts vary depending upon the income earner's amount of adjusted gross income. The amount of money allowed to be added to an IRA has been growing since 1998. The four types of IRA's I will cover are Traditional, Roth, SEP, and Educational.

Roth IRA

Individuals and couples that are eligible for the Roth IRA can convert their traditional IRA to a Roth IRA. You will have to pay income taxes on the amount converted, but there will NOT be a tax penalty. The Roth IRA is a retirement account that grows tax free. This means that if you earn $50,000 and invest $5,000 into a Roth IRA, you would have already paid tax on your earnings at tax time, before or on April 15 of the following year.

The $5,000 Roth investment can grow into any amount in the future, for example, like the $640,000 described below. All of the money could be taken out of your account at 59 1/2 years of age tax-free. In other words, the 635,000 growth will not be taxed...and the other $5000 was already taxed years ago when it was deposited into the Roth IRA. This could happen through the power of compounding if you averaged 12% annually (the market's average over the long term). At 12% the investment would double every 6 years....so with a 42 year time period, the amount would double 7 times. For example, first time it doubles: $5,000 X 2 = 10,000; second time would be $20,000, third time = $40,000 and so on... eventually reaching $640,000. The other individual retirement, the Traditional IRA, works in an opposite way when it comes to taxes.

Traditional IRA

This individual account is tax deferred which mean that an investor who earned $50,000 and invested $5,000 into your IRA, your tax burden for the year would be lower by $5000 due to the IRA contribution not being taxed when you earned it. It will be taxed when it is taken out, but so is the growth of $5,000. Also it can't be taken out until you are 59 ½ years old. Therefore, if your account grew to $640,000 (like in the Roth example) your entire $640,000 would be taxed at 15% capital gains (at least according to current tax laws). It is for this reason many investors like the Roth IRA over the Traditional IRA...and I am no different. The Roth IRA is best retirement account for most investors.

Simplified Employee Pension IRA (SEP IRA)

A SEP IRA is used by small companies and self employed individuals as a retirement plan. The contribution limit for SEP is far greater than that of a traditional IRA. The amount changes over time and continues to increase every few years. Investors in a SEP are eligible to withdraw money at 59 1/2 years of age.

Educational IRA

An educational IRA allows individuals to contribute up to a set amount in after tax dollars to an educational IRA for each person that is less than 18 years of age.

33

This is a good investment as it allows the money to grow tax-deferred. Then, as long as the money is withdrawn for educational purposes, the money is not taxed.

Buying Options

Many times investors will try to increase the return on your investment by using leverage as a form of investing to increase their return on investment using a small amount of money. Options typically come in two forms: one type is a put option and the other is a call option. One way to remember the difference is to think of a call in this way: "You CALL UP someone on the phone." Hence, a call option is bought with the investor making money if the stock goes up in price. On the other end is the Put Option. The best way to remember the concept of a Put option would be to associate it with, "PUT DOWN", as in "put down the phone." Hence, an investor that buys a Put Option makes money if the stock goes down. Options are nothing more than an option to buy or sell a security/stock at a specific price. More of the differences between Option sellers and buyers are noted in figure 1-5.

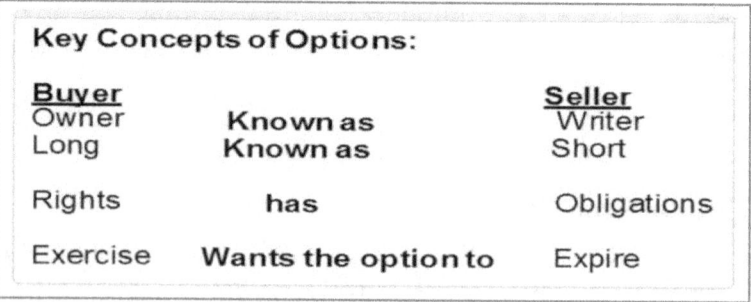

Key Concepts of Options:		
Buyer		**Seller**
Owner	Known as	Writer
Long	Known as	Short
Rights	has	Obligations
Exercise	Wants the option to	Expire

Fig 1-5 (Features of Options)

Options can be very risky, but they do offer a greater return on an investment by using leverage. However, new investors should be aware that selling (also known as "writing") options is more risky than buying them. As options can get very complex, this book will not go into comprehensive details about options. If you decide to buy them, remember the increased risk involved as many options expire worthless leaving the buyer with a loss and the seller with a profit. However, they can be used in a way that's similar to the way insurance is used.

Using Options as a Hedge

Sometimes investors will buy options as a way to hedge against a loss. One way this is done would be to buy a put position in a stock that the investor already owns. Let's say that John owns a position in Netflix (NFLX). After the stock has risen significantly, he wishes to keep his position but is concerned that the price may fall. He could buy a put option on Netflix (NFLX). This way he can have an unrealized gain that is protected from the downside risk by paying a put option premium. This is a win-win situation: if the stock goes up he makes money from the price increase; if the stock price goes down, he locks in his gains with the put option. The only loss John incurs would be if the stock price goes up and his put option expires worthless, which is not a total loss because his option loss would be offset by the increase in the stock price. A put option on a stock already owned by John is comparable to having insurance on a home. If he never uses it on a claim, that's good, but the insurance premium he paid is never given back to him; in other words it expires and has to be renewed at regular intervals. The same thing is true of buying a put option. Conversely, if his house is ruined by fire, having the insurance is worthwhile as it would pay his claim and help him recoup his home. Buying put options on a stock you already own is no different than buying insurance on a home or auto.

Many factors can affect the direction of an individual stock and the market as a whole. Some of them include legislative risk, market risk, inflation risk, and of course fraud. As a result, taking precautions to reduce risk such as using options as a hedge can be prudent.

An investor may purchase a stock and buy a put option on the stock. As a result, the investor has locked in, or set a minimum sale price that they will receive in the event the stocks should decline. In other words, buying a stock and a put on that stock will guard against a loss and protect an unrealized gain. This is known as a married or protective put.

> "Wall Street is the only place that people ride to in a Rolls Royce to get advice from those who take the subway."

Stock Investing Methodology

I have invested in stocks that went up, like when I bought Select comfort at $14 and watched it go to $24....only to hold on and watch it drop back to $15, before selling it with a marginal gain. Another time, I bought Valero Energy and watched it go down, before, finally selling at a 20% loss. All of this happening while I was still doing dollar cost averaging in Index mutual funds...as a long-term investment. And those index funds were doing great, after all it was 2003. When I bought the mutual funds, they prospered until 2008. Then the bursting of the housing bubble decimated the stock market. Then, something really bad happened...

Stocks are good investments! You should invest in stocks and the stock market because they tend to return higher rates of return than any other single investment including bonds CDs and even homes.

The Great Recession hit, dropping the S&P 500 more than 50% from over 1400, down to below 700, 672 to be exact. It was that that moment, I realized that it was time to add more money into the stock market: the S&P 500 index fund. This was March 2009, and I had just some purchased real estate and was short on funds. Nevertheless, I added as much money as I could to the S&P 500 index fund expecting it to climb in the long-term.

I did have doubts! What if it goes down even further...I was concerned. Thankfully it didn't. Instead in less than 3 years, it climbed to 1429 by the spring of 2012. Moving from 673 in March 2009 resulted in an annualized gain of 32%. This quick doubling of my money had me feeling exhilarated. However, I had lost some money in the market in the past...mostly buying individual stocks. Therefore, the benefit of this recent gain was less enthusiastic than it could have been. Then, I realized a better way to research individual stocks was needed. I searched and searched and searched, but nothing seemed to work accurately.

I tried one investing method after another, including ones that involved trading stocks and ones involving buying value stocks, like Benjamin Graham and Warren Buffett do, based on value investing. While good for long term investors, value investing has its own pitfalls: even value stocks can decline in value. By using value investing methods in the past, I had both good and bad results. Remember that all my individual stock picks have been mediocre at best. Then, after researching several investing methodologies, I found one that worked better than the rest.

The method I am referring to involves using both technical analysis and fundamental analysis together. However, a little disclosure is needed. Primarily, I use technical analysis for shorter term investing, one to three years (or perhaps as little as six months). Then, for long-term investments...say three to five years or more... I will combine both technical and fundamental analysis together to find the best stocks to buy. Deciding on which method to give more weight depends on the situation of the individual stock and the current state of the economy. That is, which one presents the most significant opportunities to buy and sell at the best profit? I found that this can be done by using an investing methodology that is easy to use. Furthermore, the tools and information to implement these strategies can be found online.

However, never forget that it is difficult to predict the madness of crowds...and nothing can be more maddening than the stock market with its wild upward and downward swings. Another thing that can influence the market is investor sentiment, and you never know how it will affect the market. For example, the credit rating agencies could lower the U.S. credit rating like they did in 2012. Or, the debt ceiling may get too high. Things like this and other sentiments can affect the direction of the overall market, as well as those of individual stocks. However, that same madness results in volatility that can be beneficial for investors and traders alike. One of the ways to find this "volatility advantage" as I like to call it, is using technical indicators that are good at finding oversold stocks. More on this in a moment, but first a point needs to be made about money managers and brokerage firms.

It seems that bankers, lawyers, and accountants all have

fiduciary responsibilities for their clients but that's not the case with stock brokers. They may be out to sell a product, service, stock, or bond... but with the sole intention of making a commission. Therefore, beware when looking for a stock broker or brokerage firm; it is highly recommended to avoid full service brokers. This is one of the more diligent duties an investor should implement. Their fees are extraordinary. Therefore, it is best to choose a discount brokerage. This will prevent you as an investor from allowing full service brokers to fill their pockets with commissions and fees from your money. That's why investors should use discount brokers. However, many of them have limited charts and research tools. This will not be a problem as I will cover tools that include free stock charts to help your investment research...so let's begin.

The method I use most often, and have found the most success with by the way, is Relative Strength Index (or RSI, for short). RSI is a technical indicator that shows when a stock is overbought or oversold. I use it more for the overbought indicator as you will soon see. This indicator can be beneficial when looking for a stock that may be severely oversold, meaning that it is usually undervalued and a good bargain. Anything that is a good bargain, especially an asset like a stock or house, can be a profitable endeavor. Just look at Chipotle Mexican Grill (CMG) trading at $50 in March 2009 then moving above $440 in April 2012. While technical analysis is usually used by traders and fundamental analysis is usually used by investors, combining them can prove most beneficial. Let's start with technical analysis.

Chapter 2:
Technical Analysis

Technical analysis is the study of time, price, volume, and sentiment as it relates to the financial markets. This stock picking method is used primarily by traders, but not only traders. Many times short-term and longer-term investors will use it. As a result, some investors use charts and other technical indicators when they're investing. These types of investors are considered to be technicians or chartists. Investing using stock charts can be beneficial in many ways. For example, it helps you find trends and spot other indicators that may not be obvious in a stock. Additionally, charts can help the investor know when a stock is trending upward or downward. Many times an investor will use both technical and fundamental analysis together when deciding on which stocks to buy or sell. Therefore, it's essential to understand some of these technical indicators

Technical Analysis Overview

Short interest: This happens when a short seller who sold the stock short because they are betting that the stock price will fall . In order to close out their position, they must repurchase the stock. All the investors who bought the stock short must eventually repurchase the stock because of all the short sellers becoming potential buyers for the stock. A high short interest is considered a bullish indicator; the demand from their buying can bring the stock price higher.

Odd lot trading: This is a theory that believes that smaller investors, who cannot afford to buy in round lots, will invariably buy and sell at the wrong time. Therefore, a high level of odd lot purchases is indicative of a market top. A high level of odd lot selling would be indicative of a market bottom.

Efficient Market Theory (EMT): The efficient market believes that all of the available information is priced into the stock price at any given time and therefore it is impossible to beat the market. EMT is something that some investors believe in while others scoff at it. Warren Buffett is one of the many investors who believe that efficient market theory does not exist. He feels that if it did exist, no investor would be able to make substantial gains in the market. He feels that if it did not exist, it would be impossible to make money in the market. His proof for this is the fact that his investments have been extremely prosperous. According to the Berkshire Hathaway 2012 letter to shareholders, Buffett has outperformed the S&P 500 by 10.3 percentage points from 1965-2012.

The Discount Rate: The Federal Reserve Board can change the discount rate in an effort to guide the economy through the business cycle. The discount rate is the rate that the Fed charges member banks on loans. If the Fed wanted to increase the rate of the economy, it would reduce the discount rate. As the discount rate falls, all the other interest rates fall, making the cost of borrowing lower. This would encourage borrowing and demand of products and services which would stimulate the economy. Conversely, when the discount rate is increased, the other rates increase. As the cost of borrowing increases, consumers and businesses are less likely to borrow and the economy slows down.

Federal Open Market Committee (FOMC) is a method used by the Fed to buy and sell Government Securities in a way to control the economy by stimulating it when it's slow and cooling it when inflation is on the rise. To stimulate the economy, the Fed can buy government securities. When the Fed buys these securities, money is instantly sent into the banking system. As the money flows into the economy, more money is available to lend. Because there is money available, interest rates go down and the economy will thrive from the increased borrowing and spending from consumers and businesses.

Chart Patterns

Support: Support happens when there is a situation where the stock falls to a point that it will attract buyers. The new buyers that are brought into the market end up creating demand for the stock, and thus prevent it from falling further.

Resistance: Resistance is created when a stock price has risen to the point that it brings in more sellers and the new selling produces a resistance in the stock price, preventing it from going higher.

Consolidation: A consolidation is characterized by a horizontal movement in the stock price. Buyers and sellers are willing to trade the stock at almost the same prices.

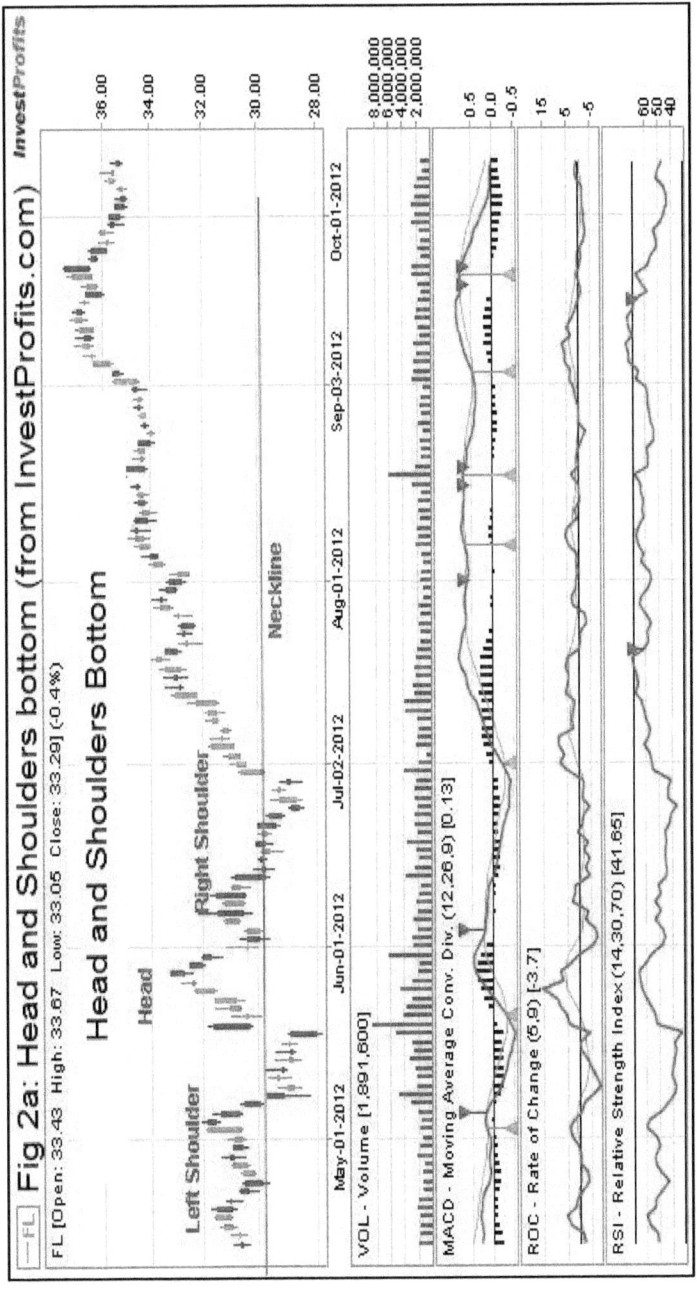

Fig 2a: Head and Shoulders bottom (from InvestProfits.com)

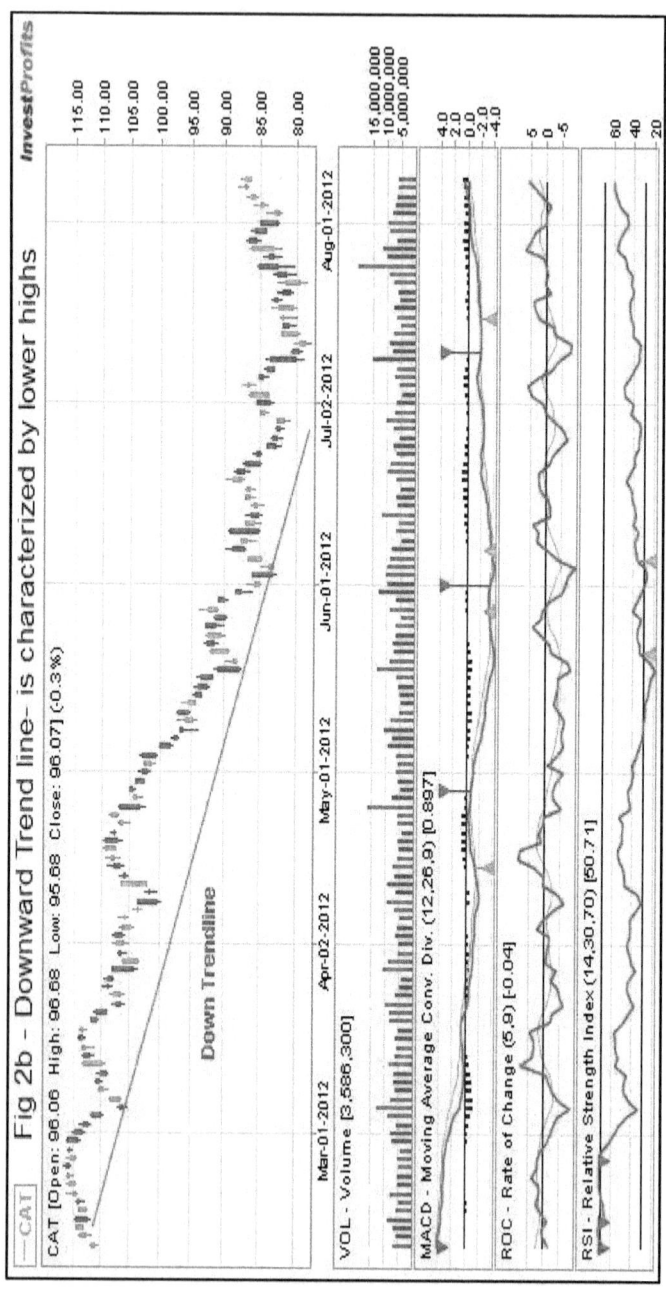

Fig 2b - Downward Trend line- is characterized by lower highs

A head and shoulders bottom- is a chart pattern that is typically a bullish signal, like the one seen in figure 2a. Conversely, a head and shoulders top is a bearish indicator.

Downward Trend lines- are downward lines that are characterized by lower highs. The line is drawn at the lower ends of the descending line as seen in figure 2b.

Upward Trend lines- are upward lines that are characterized by higher highs. It is a line drawn connecting the series of higher lows on the trend line as seen in fig 2c.

A common trading technique involves the intersection of the trend-line with the most recent prices. If the trend-line for a downward trend crosses through the most recent prices, then a sell signal is generated.

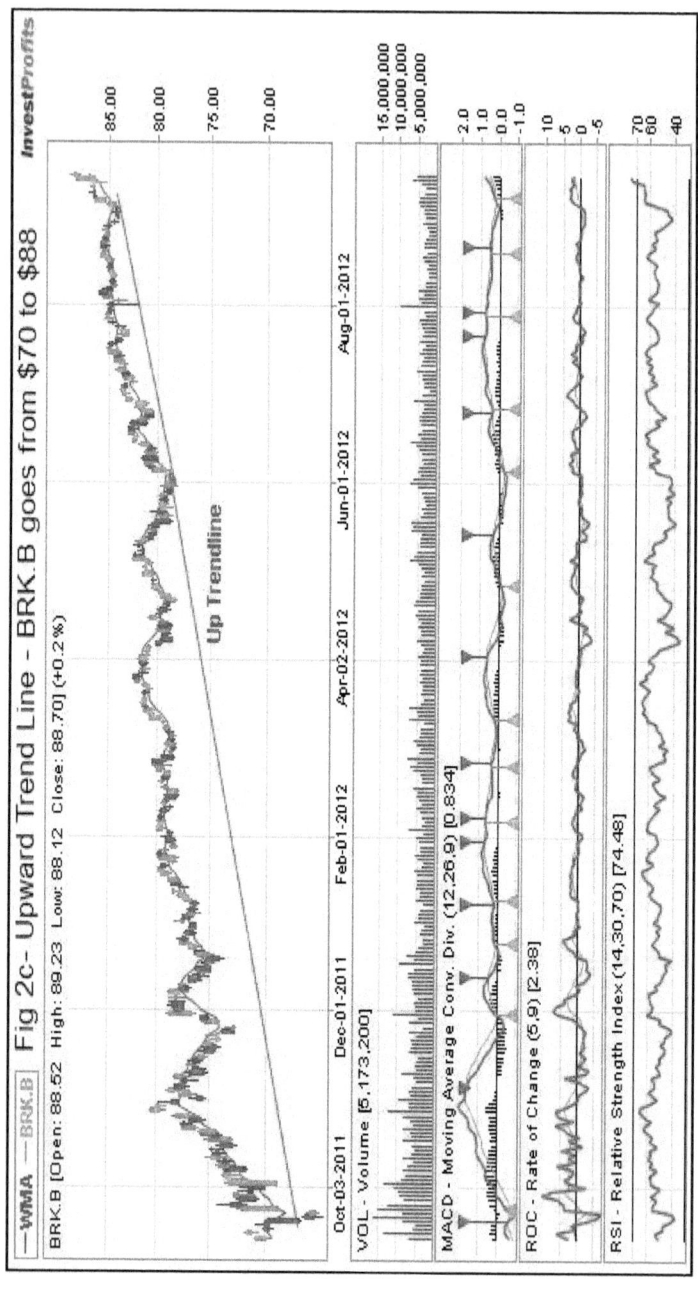

Fig 2c- Upward Trend Line - BRK.B goes from $70 to $88

While chart patterns such as head and shoulder formations along with upward and downward trend lines, are discussed briefly, the focus of this chapter will concentrate on the technical indicators such as RSI, MACD, and some of the moving averages. The charts used here can be found at www.investprofits.com. The charts are interactive and memberships are free.

Investing in Stocks using Relative Strength Index (RSI)

RSI normal range is between 30 and 80. When it goes below 30 a stock is considered to be oversold and is a bullish signal after it returns back to 30 or higher. If it goes above 80, it is considered overbought and is a sell signal after it comes back down to 80.

After extensive research of stocks and their charts, I noticed that stocks with several RSI buy signals indicate a buying opportunity. For example, when a stock has 2 or more RSI buy signals very close together (as seen in the triangles at bottom of the charts), the stock is considered oversold and is usually a good time to buy as the stock price is very low. Conversely, when the stock is severely oversold, it will have 2 or more buy signals (downward triangles in the charts) very close together. Once, again, it should be noted that these same charts are available free at investprofits.com.

51

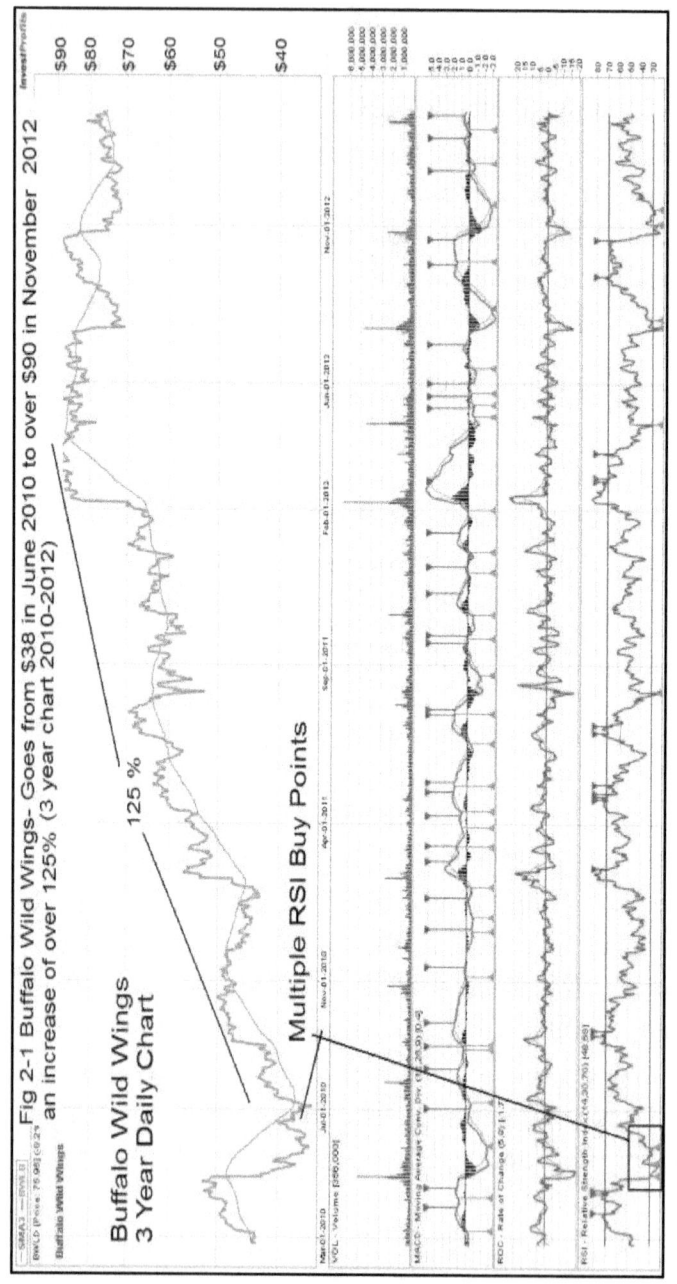

Fig 2-1 Buffalo Wild Wings– Goes from $38 in June 2010 to over $90 in November 2012 an increase of over 125% (3 year chart 2010-2012)

Buffalo Wild Wings
3 Year Daily Chart

125 %

Multiple RSI Buy Points

Buffalo Wild Wings up 225% -RSI Example #1

In this RSI example, Buffalo Wild Wings (Fig 2-1) had an exceptional run from $38 back in June 2010 to over $90, giving it over 225% increase. This occurred after the stock had three RSI buy signals (at bottom left of chart) close together as seen in this three year daily chart. Conversely, when several sell signals occur together, the investor should sell.

> "If you want to have a better performance than the crowd, you must do things differently from the crowd."

Don't follow the Crowd

Some investing methodologies will have you buy high and sell higher. One of them is Investor's Business Daily (IBD). While this investing technique does have its merits, it should be noted that gains can be modest. Typically, this method will result in smaller returns because most of the big gains have already occurred. It is a useful method for gaining 15 to 20 % (most of the time); but don't expect big gains with this method. Nevertheless, it does have its benefits: those returns can come in very short periods, as soon as 3 months or as little as 3 weeks. Just know that the returns are moderate at best due the fact that the investing is down by jumping into stocks after they have reached great momentum.

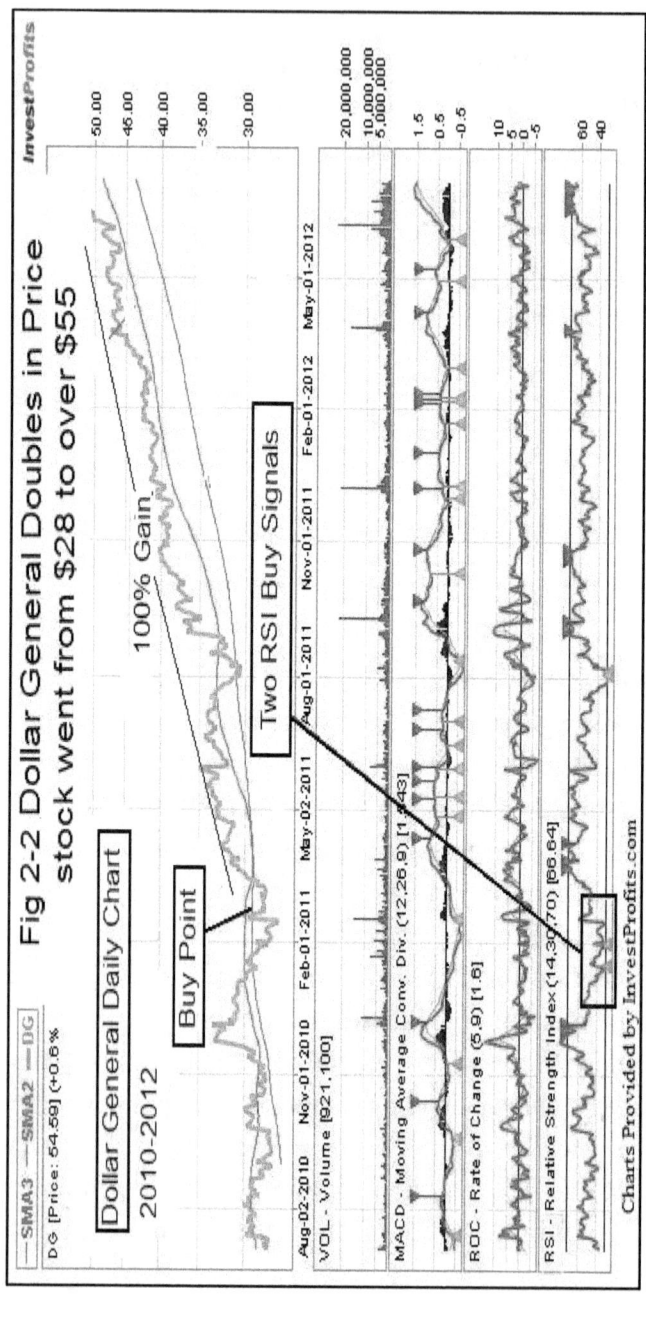

Fig 2-2 Dollar General Doubles in Price stock went from $28 to over $55

Dollar General Doubles in Price – Example #2

As seen in Fig 2-2, Dollar General (DG) reached several buy signals and doubled in price. Two different buy indicators, RSI and Moving Average, indicated a buy. Furthermore, the RSI buy point had several buy signals, not just one. As seen in the daily chart covering two years (2010-2112), the stock went from $28 to over $55 after hitting an RSI buy signal back in February 2011. With two technical indicators indicating a buy and with a low P/E, Dollar General had several reasons an investor should use to see that this would have been a good time to buy.

Key Points

- RSI Buy Signals are key points for buying, the more the stronger the buy signal
- Stocks trending above a moving average, like the 50, or 200 day is a buy indication
- Stocks with a low P/E are less risky, the lower the better

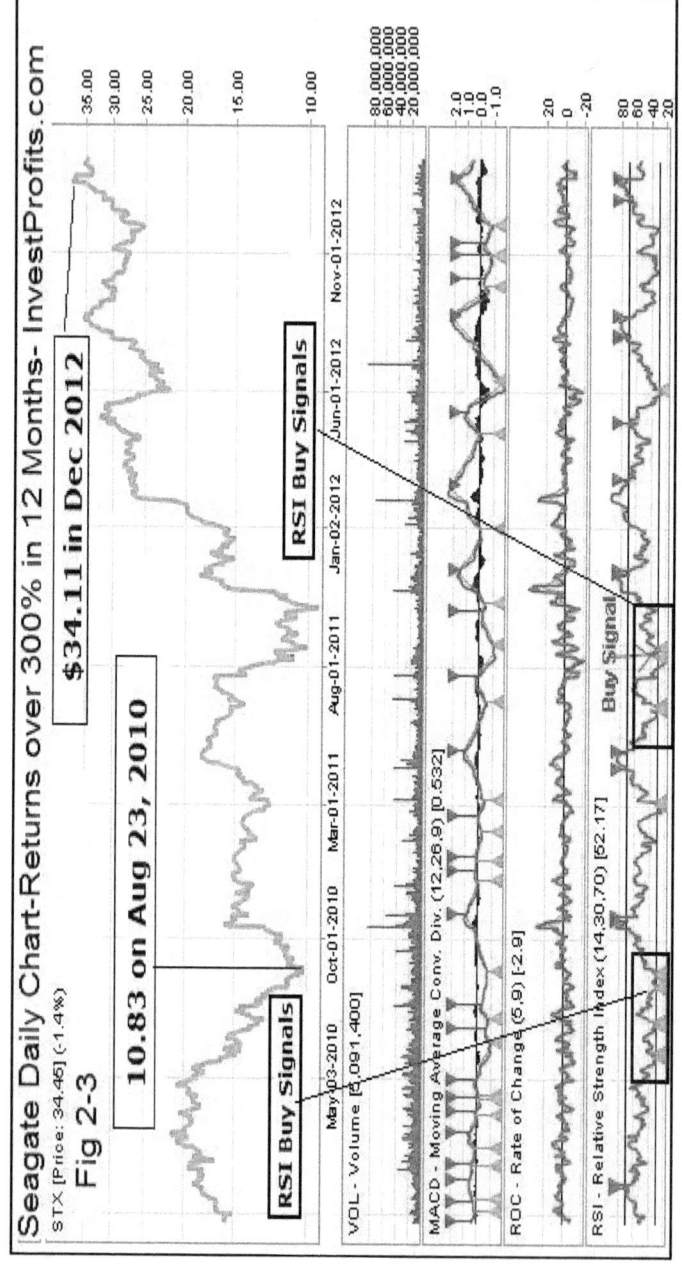

Seagate Stock Returns over 300% in 12 Months-RSI Example #3

Seagate Technologies (STX) (Fig 2-3) shares were trading at $10.08 on August 23, 2011. At the time, the stock had several RSI buy signals very close together, an important indicator of a stock being severely oversold (see upward triangles in Fig 2-3). Then on August 16th, 2012, the shares are trading at $34.11 per share; this resulted in better than in a 300% return. This would have turned a $10,000 investment into $30,000 in one year.

Furthermore, similar buy signals were available back on August 23, 2010 when the stock had several buy signals and the stock traded at $10.83. Either time would have been a great time to buy shares Seagate stock. Conversely, when the stock gets several RSI sell signals occurring close together, the investor should consider selling.

It's important to realize that with more RSI buy signals, the stronger the buying opportunity. Conversely, the less buy signals occurring in close proximity, the weaker the buy signal. However, one does not that you should not buy. It just indicates that the buying opportunity is not as strong as it could be.

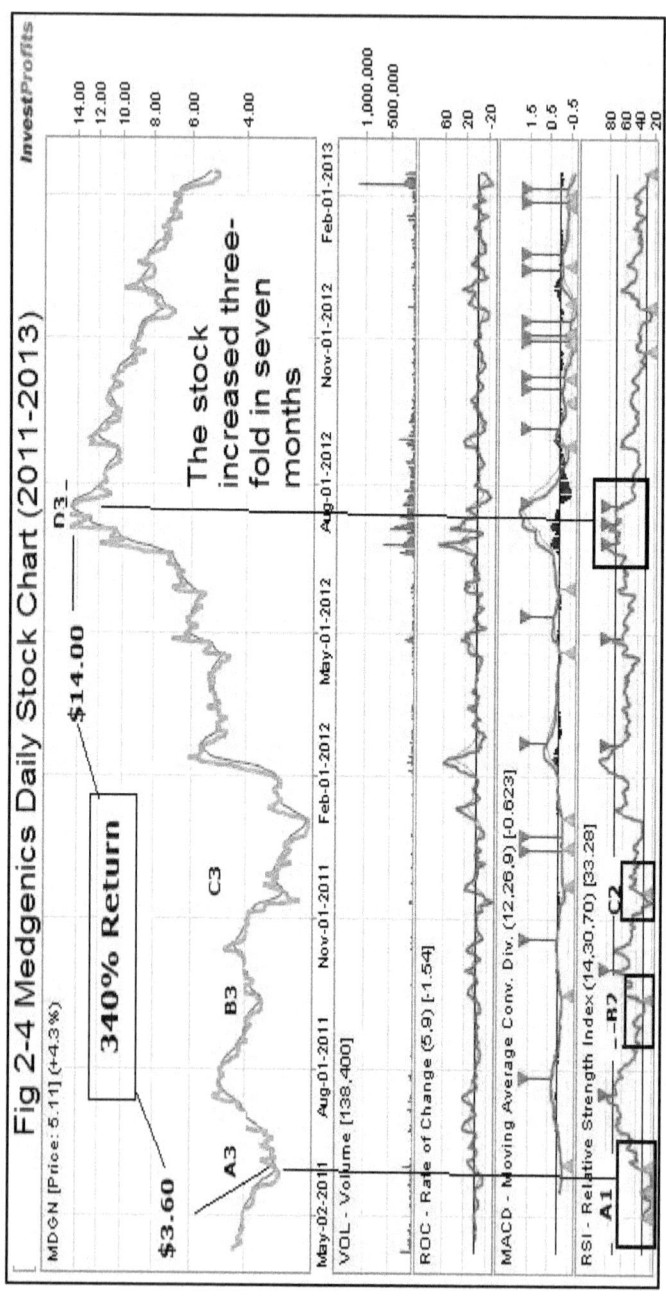

Fig 2-4 Medgenics Daily Stock Chart (2011-2013)

Medgenics Stock Increases Three Fold in Seven Months RSI Example 4:

In June 2011, Medgenics (Fig. 2-4) was trading with 3 RSI indicators close together (see Box A1 at bottom of chart). This would have been a good time to buy Medgenics at $3.60 per share because the stock was severely oversold. There is a direct correlation between RSI signals and buying: the more RSI buy signals there are very close together, the better the buying opportunity is (see A1 in Fig 2-4) for selling indicators. The same principal applies with RSI sell signals: more RSI sell signals indicate a better selling opportunity (see D1 and D3 in chart above).

Select Comfort Rises 670% in 20 Months -RSI Example #5
RSI Example 5: Select Comfort up 670% in less than 2 years (Chart, from InvestProfits.com) Fig 2-5

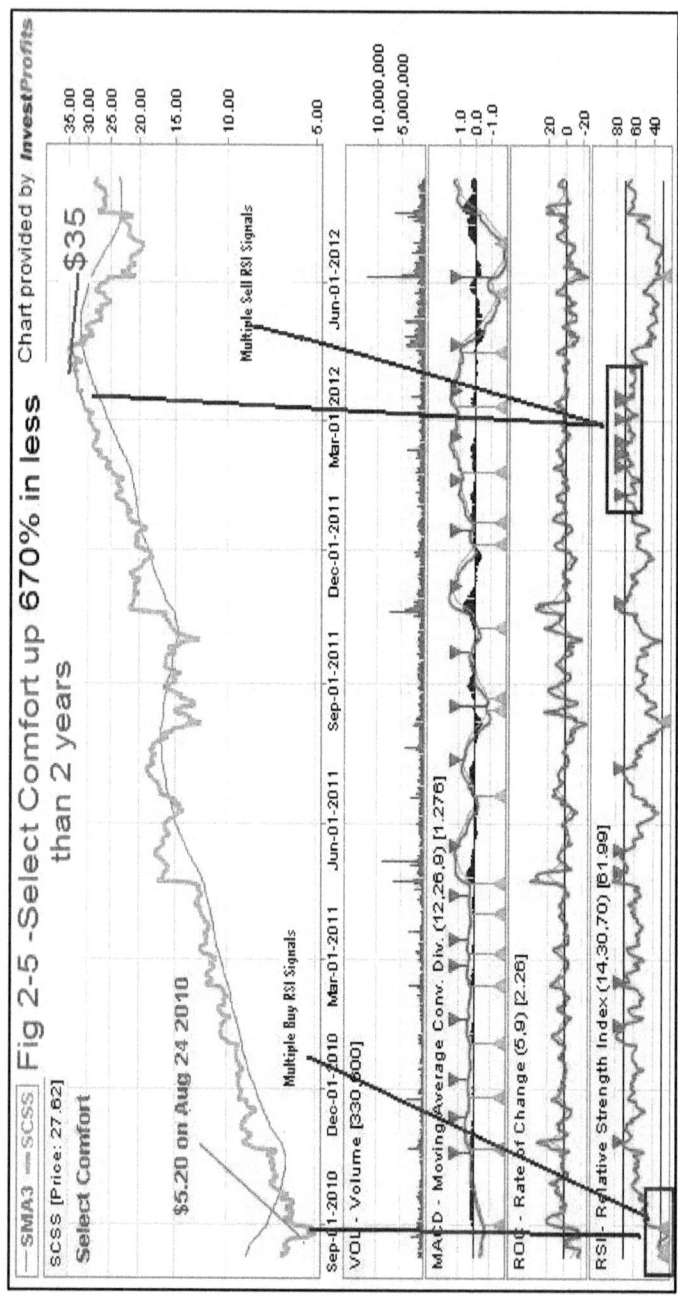

Fig 2-5 -Select Comfort up 670% in less than 2 years

On August 24, 2010, Select Comfort (SCSS) was selling at $5.20 per share. During that time, the stock had several buy signals as seen in the chart (Fig 2-5). The "RSI buy signals" indicated that the stock was severely oversold, making it a good time to buy shares of the stock (see the box in the Select Comfort chart with several upward triangles). Then, in less than two years, the stock reached a price of $35 a share on April 18, 2012. At the time it had many sell signals, as seen in the box on the right. This would have resulted in a 670% return.

Key Points

- RSI Buy Signals are key points for buying, the more the stronger the buy signal
- Several Sell Indicators very close together are a strong sell indicator
- Selling stocks after a sizeable gain can lock in profits

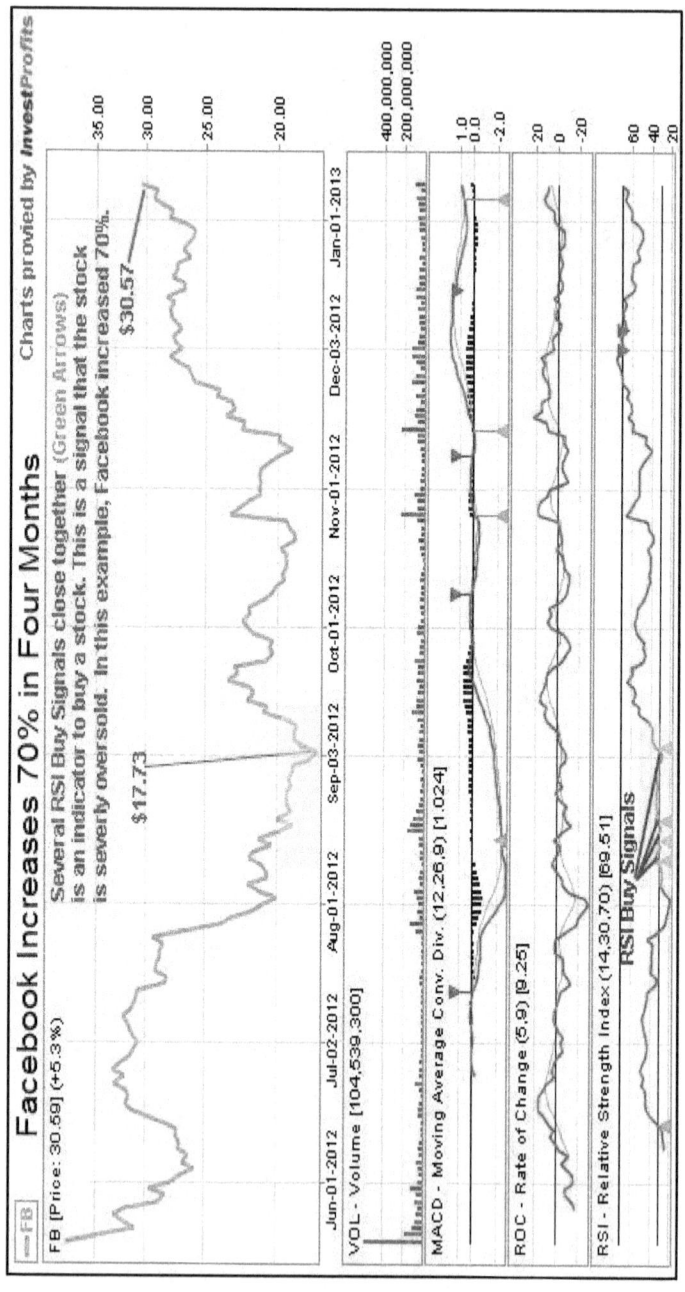

Facebook Increases 70% in Four Months -RSI Example #6

While Facebook's IPO was considered a botched offering my many investors and Wall Street, it did offer a buying opportunity. In the first 12 months after it highly anticipated offering an opportunity arose. As seen in (Fig. 2-6), Facebook shares increased over 70% in four months. Back in September 2012, the Facebook was trading at $17.73 and at the time had four RSI buy signals (noted by upward triangles, bottom left on chart). Then, by January 2013, the stock had increased to over $30 per share, resulting in greater than a 70% increase.

Key Points

- RSI Buy Signals can lead to huge gain in price share as here in Facebook gaining 70% in four months
- Watch sell indicators to prevent loss of recent gains.
- Stocks bought with high P/E's should be watched very carefully as they are more

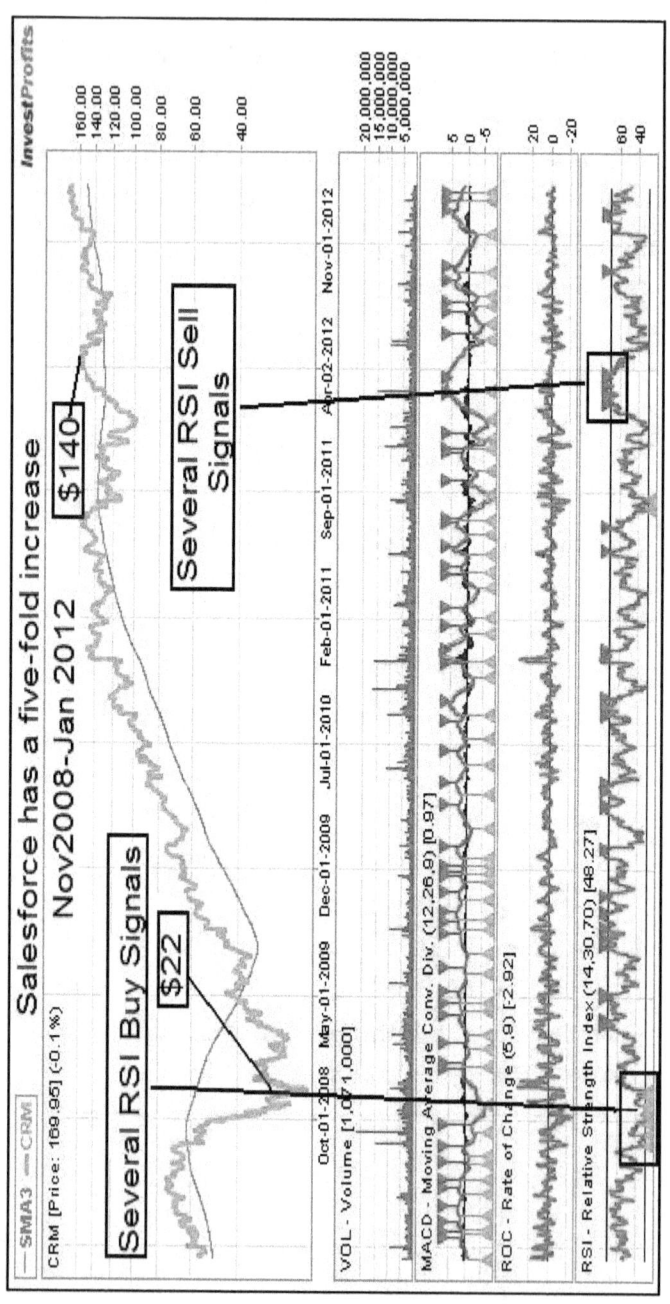

Salesforce.com had Five-Fold Increase RSI Example #7

Salesforce.com (Fig. 2-7) had a big run up going over $100, a five-fold increase. Back in November 2008 it had several RSI buy indicators (as seen in the chart). The company has a good business model, selling customer management services to businesses through its cloud database. The overhead is low. The only question is how long can it continue? I am not sure, but before considering when to sell look at the RSI sell signals and take those into serious consideration...especially if several of them are close together.

Key Points

- Several RSI buy signals can appear many different times offering excelling buying opportunities for stocks that are oversold

- Selling when there are several RSI sell signals (over 80) together should be a time to consider selling, not before

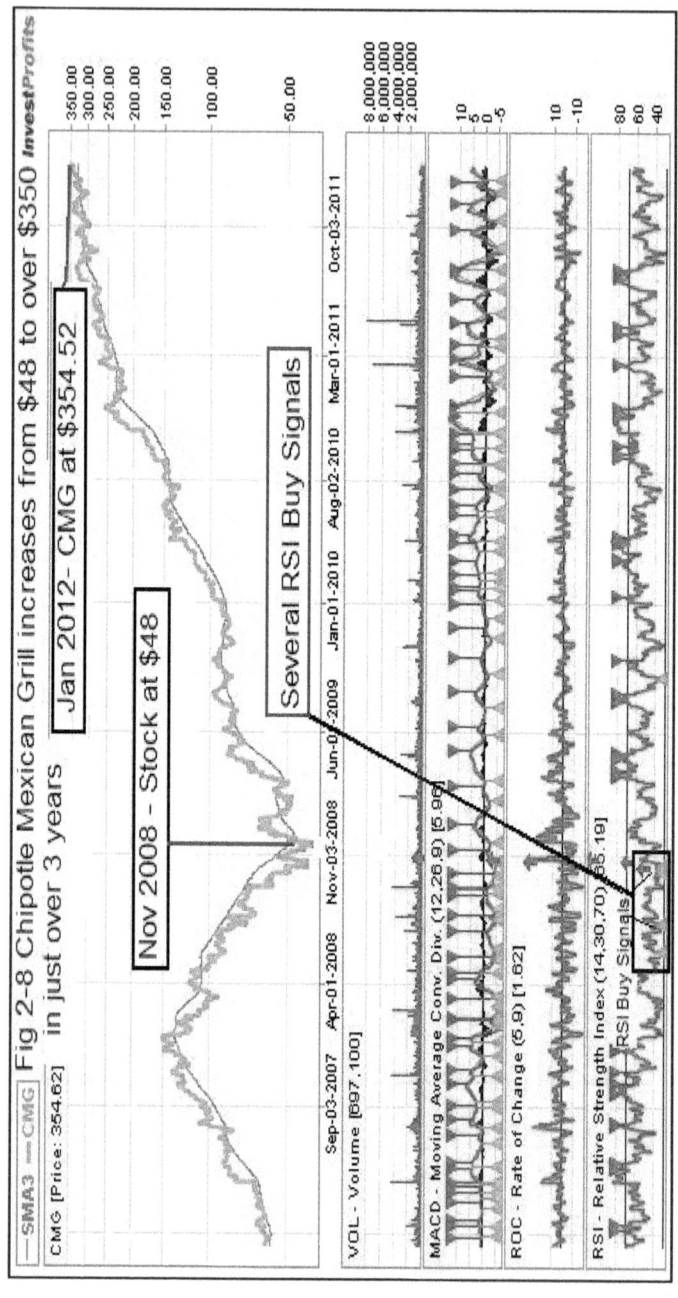

Fig 2-8 Chipotle Mexican Grill increases from $48 to over $350 in just over 3 years

Nov 2008 – Stock at $48

Jan 2012– CMG at $354.52

Several RSI Buy Signals

Chipotle Mexican Grill Increases Seven Fold -RSI Example #8

As promised earlier in this book, Chipotle Mexican Grill (Fig. 2-8) would be discussed and here it is: Chipotle has had a big appreciation since November 2008 when the stock traded at $48 until 2012 when it traded around $364. Additionally, in this chart it did not have enough technical signals indicating a buy.

There were several opportunities to sell as seen in the chart by the areas with several RSI sell indicators. But, patience seems to be a virtue in investing as seen in this example as several sell signals were met with continue stock price increases. Nevertheless, if the stock is selling at a high P/E or has some other negative fundamental, it may well be advisable to heed the sell signals.

Key Points

- Several RSI buy signals can lead to the biggest gains, like with Chipotle Mexican Grill going from $48 to $364 in just over three years

- Hold the best stocks and those with lowest P/E's as they have best chance to continue rising in price.

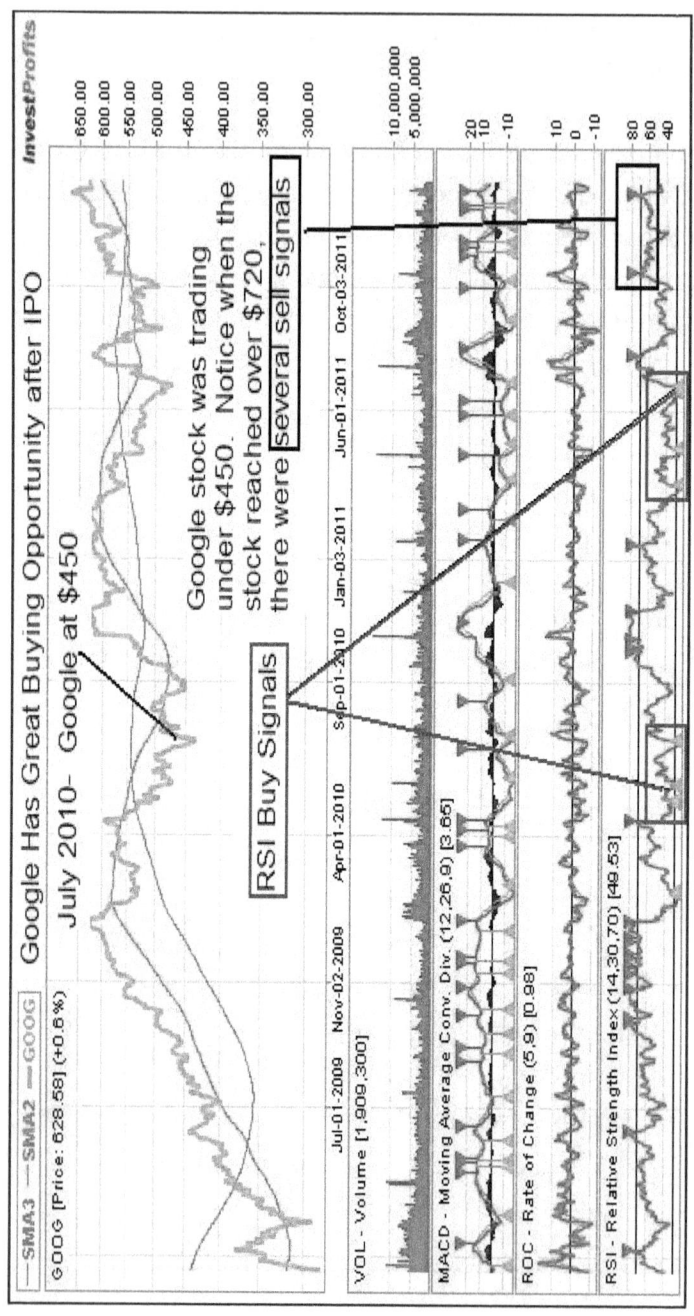

Google Has Great Buying Opportunity after IPO
Google's price has grown significantly since its IPO, but that was not the only time to get in. Back in June 2010, it was a good time to buy. At the time, the stock had several buy signals (as seen in Fig. 2-9) from the many RSI buy indicators. Additionally, (not shown here).

Netflix - 200% Increase with RSI Signals
Netflix was trading at $64 in November 2011 and again in June 2012. At each time there were several RSI buy signals. The closer the signals, the better the confirmation the stock will be as a buy. Any of those times would have been buying opportunities. Then in May 2013, the stock reached $210, a better than 200% price increase. See Fig. 2-10 to see more information on this example.

Key Points

- If you miss the RSI buying opportunities, be patient as many stocks will offer them again, like Google did

- Use other buying indicators like moving averages and MACD indicators

---

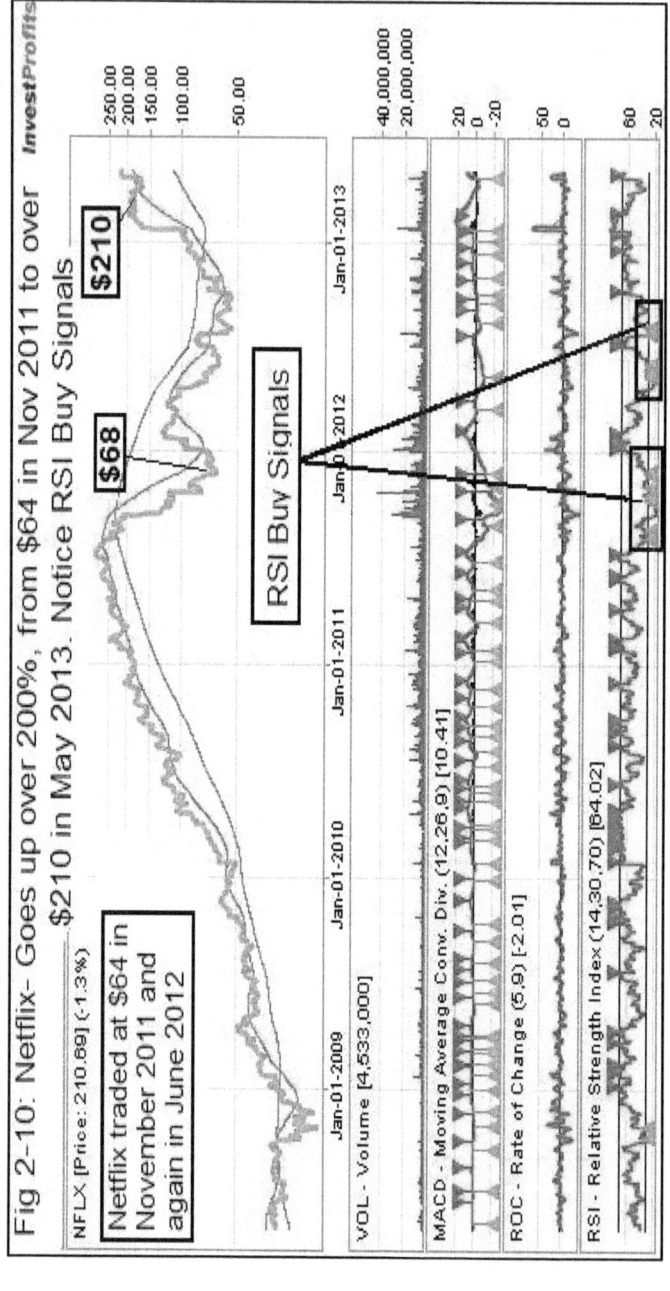

Fig 2-10: Netflix- Goes up over 200%, from $64 in Nov 2011 to over $210 in May 2013. Notice RSI Buy Signals

RSI Summary

RSI, also known as relative strength index, is one of the best technical indicators used. It indicates when a stock is oversold, which is a good time to buy. Conversely, it shows when a stock is overbought, which is a good time to sell. Using both technical analysis and fundamental analysis together works best. This indicator works better when there are many buy signals very close together as the previous nine examples have shown. Likewise, it works best for selling at a time when there are several RSI sell signals together

Bottom line...it should be one of the key technical indicators used when deciding to buy or sell a stock, but it should not be the only one. Another good technical indicator to use with RSI would be a moving average and they come in several types and lengths. The moving averages are available on the stock charts at investprofits.com.

How to Spot Trends!
"The trend can be your friend"

Moving averages can be used in various ways. A simple method is to wait until the market index crosses through the moving average of the same index, either up or down. If up, that is an indication the trend is up and stocks should be purchased; if down, the trend is down and stocks should be sold. They are very good at spotting trends

A simple moving average or SMA is a price line that smoothes out an investment's path to get an indication of the trend. For example, if closing prices over the last five days are $37.00, $36.00, $34.00, $32.00. $31.00 then the SMA would be $34.00 derived from adding all the closing prices then dividing by five. This would create a five-day SMA that could be monitored for trends. The most common moving averages are 20, 50, and 200 days.

50 Day Moving Average
The 50 day moving average is a popular technical indicator which investors use to analyze price trends. Typically, a stock trading above its 50 day moving average can be described as having positive momentum, and possibly a good buy. On the other side, a stock trading below the 50 day moving average is considered to be trending downward and is possibly a sell indication. More can be ascertained by at these examples of LinkedIn in Fig 2-10, and Monster in Fig. 2-11.

50 Day Moving Average of Monster and LinkedIn (as seen in Fig. 2-10b and 2-11) moves above its 50 day moving average and then falls below the average to around $100. It then went sideways in trading after falling below the 50 day moving average and has had trouble finding support resulting in consolidation. Hence, the move above the 50 day moving average (DMA) being an

indication of an uptrend for the stock. Conversely, the fall below the 50 DMA was an indication of a downtrend.

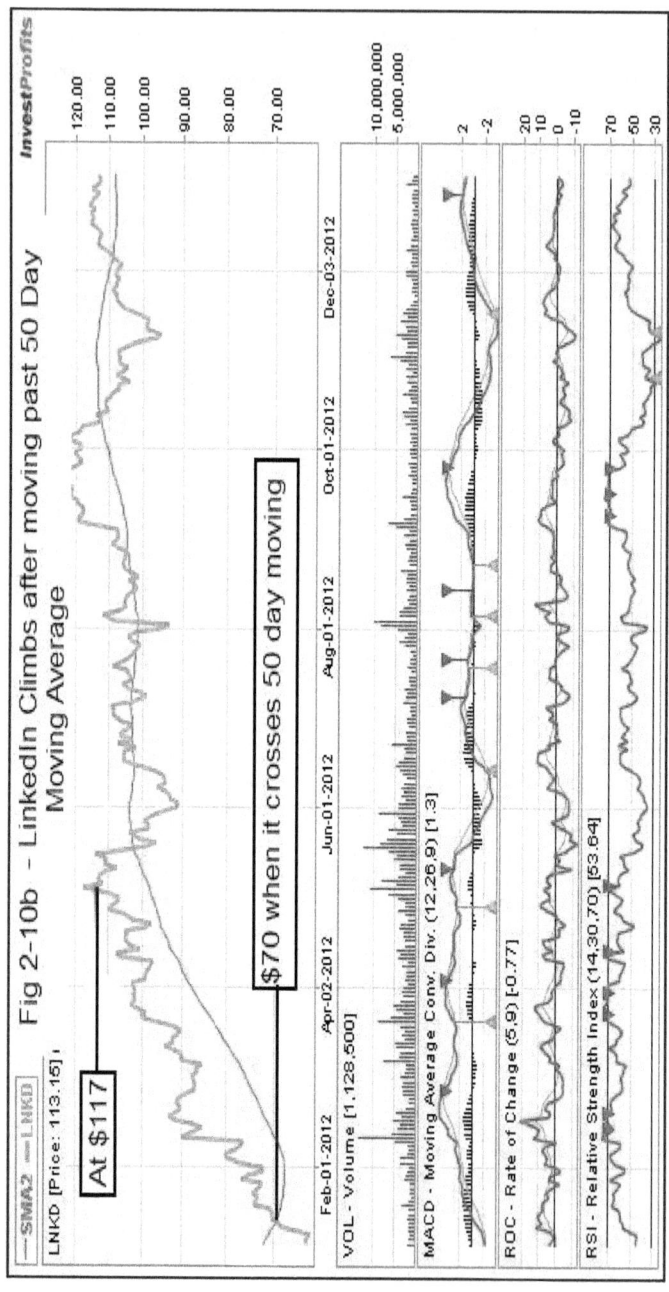

Fig 2-10b - LinkedIn Climbs after moving past 50 Day Moving Average

At $117

$70 when it crosses 50 day moving

Monster Beverage Climbs after crossing 50 Day Moving Average

Monster Beverage Corp. (Fig. 2-11) has been on a nice uptrend going from less than $30 back in July 2009, climbing above $100 in January 2012. Furthermore, it was trading above its 200 day moving average, a good sign showing a trend of upward movement. Both of these moving averages, spotted early and acted on would have resulted in a 333% return.

200 Day Moving Average

The 200-day moving average is very popular, and it is the one---combined with the 50 day moving average—that I use the most. The reason is simple. If both indicators show an uptrend, then the momentum indicated by them indicates more reliability.

Key Points

- 50 Day and 200 Day moving averages are the most common trend indicators
- Buy a stock when it crosses above the 200 day moving average
- 50 Day moving average is a shorter trend indicator

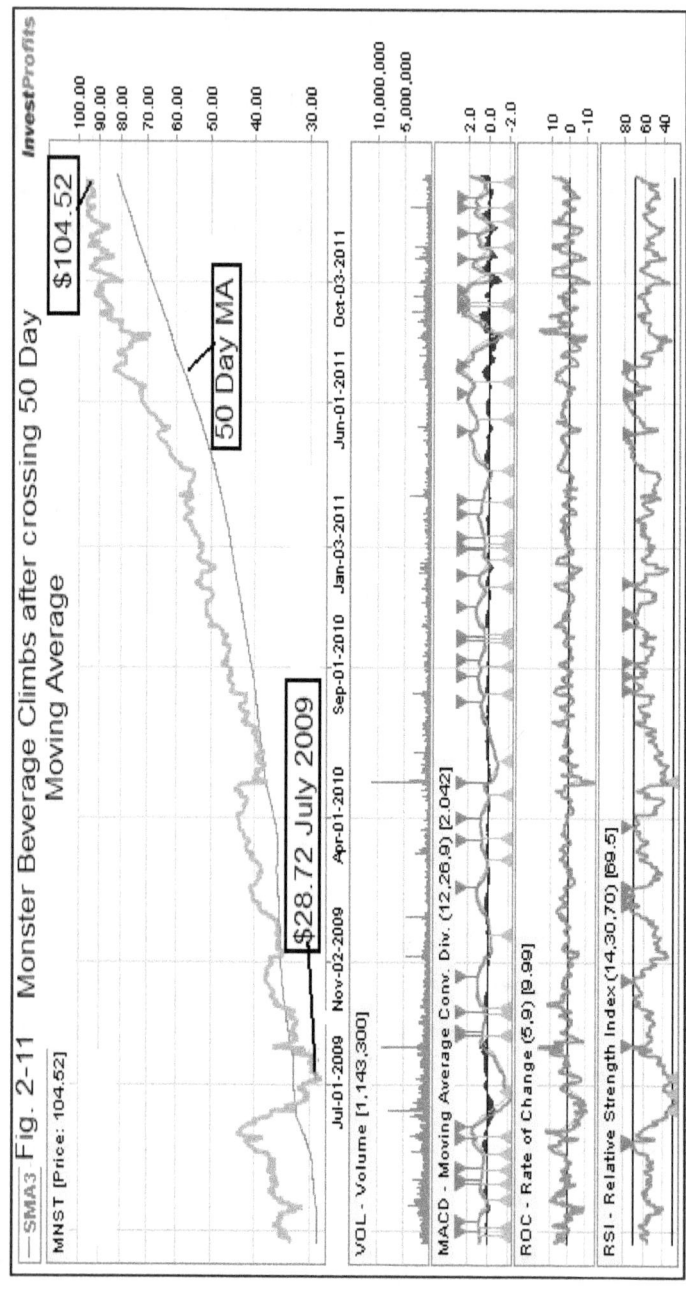

Fig. 2-11   Monster Beverage Climbs after crossing 50 Day Moving Average

200 Day Moving Average Examples:
Buffalo Wild Wings (Fig. 2-12) and Dollar General (Fig. 2-13) reveal stock charts moved above their 50 day and 200 day moving averages. The chart shows the movement of how Dollar General (Fig 2-13) moved above its 200 Day MA and 50 Day MA at the same time. Then, it went from $33 to over $50. Keep in mind that when a stock moves above its moving average, it indicates an uptrend and is bullish for the stock; that is what happened with Dollar General. In the Buffalo Wild Wings Chart (Fig. 2-12), the 200 Day moving average is shown with similar results.

Key Points

- Moving averages are good trend indicators and are used in forecasting of stocks
- Use the 200 Day moving average for longer term investing methodologies
- Use the 50 Day moving average for shorter term investing

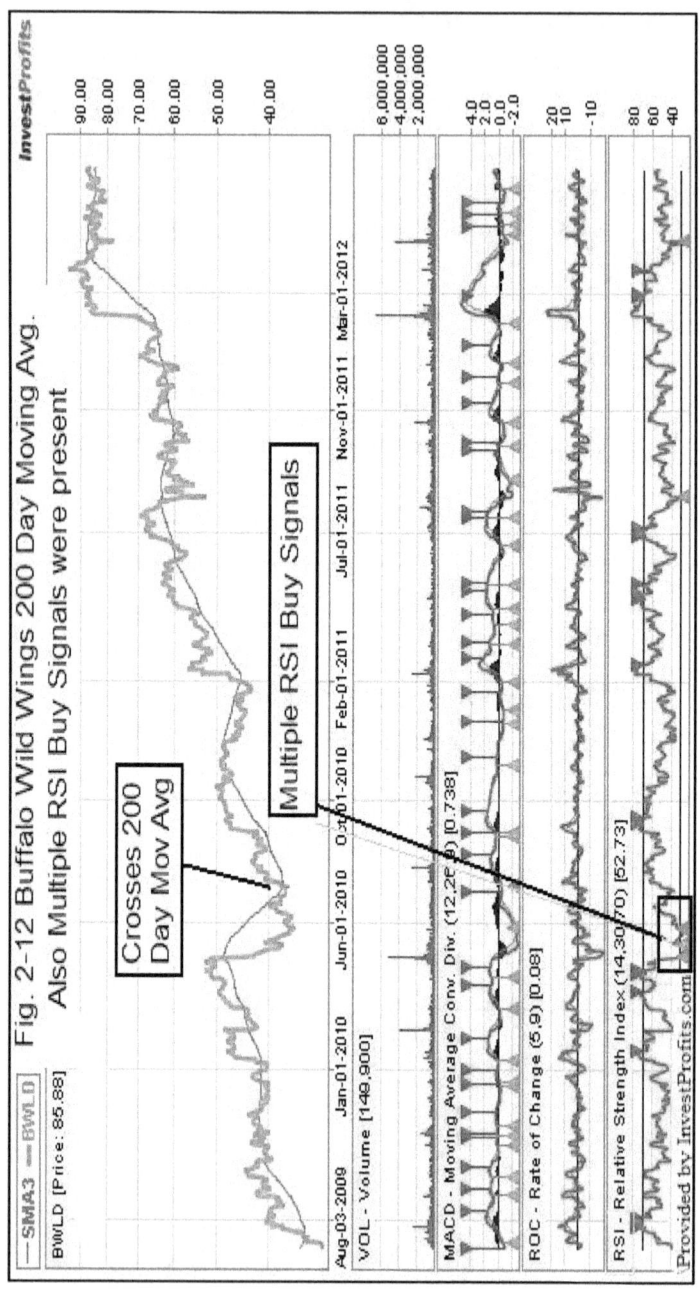

Fig. 2-12 Buffalo Wild Wings 200 Day Moving Avg. Also Multiple RSI Buy Signals were present

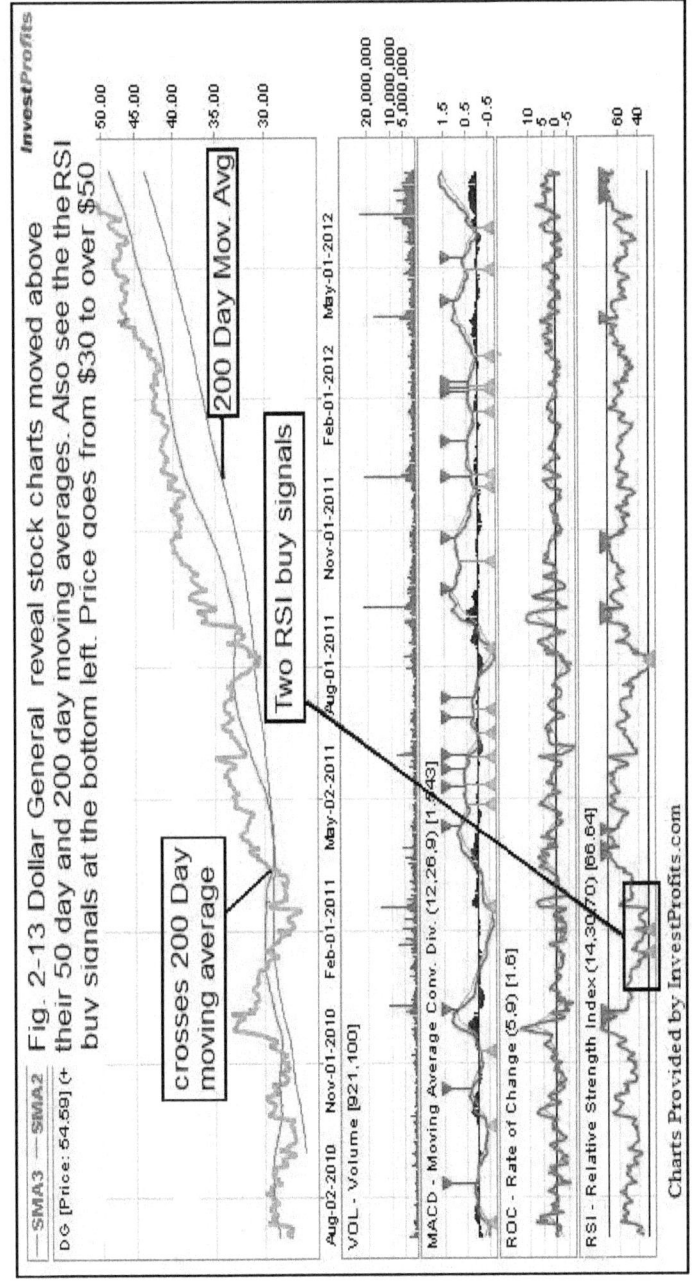

Fig. 2-13 Dollar General reveal stock charts moved above their 50 day and 200 day moving averages. Also see the the RSI buy signals at the bottom left. Price goes from $30 to over $50

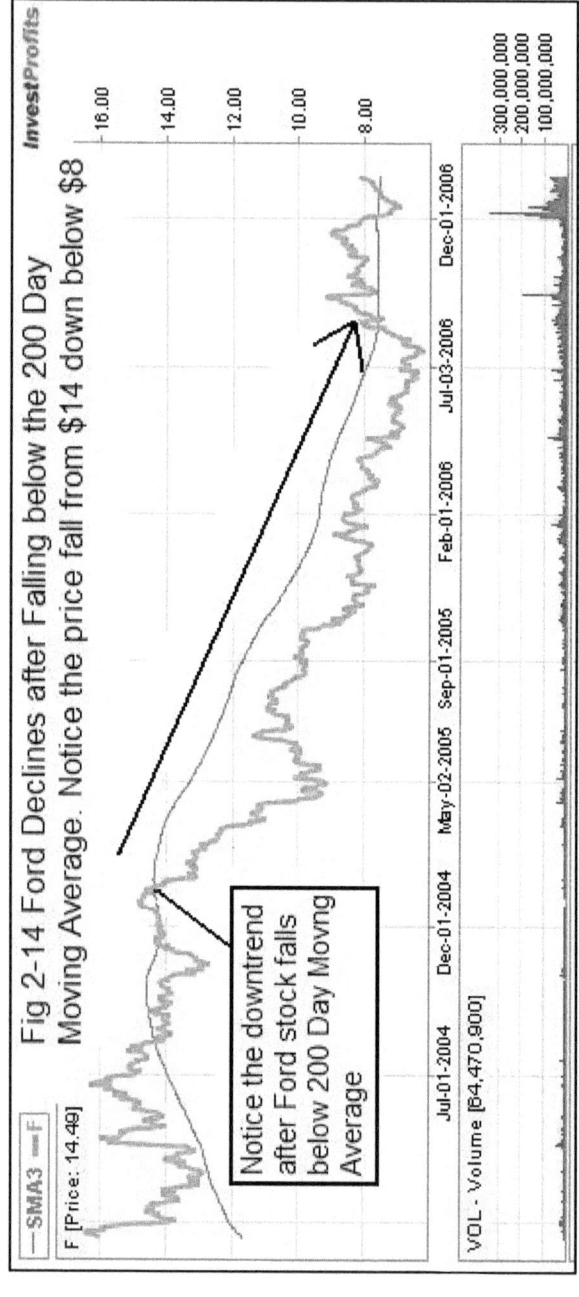

Fig 2-14 Ford Declines after Falling below the 200 Day Moving Average. Notice the price fall from $14 down below $8

Ford Declines after Falling 200 Day Moving Average – 200

If a price is above the SMA, it is indicative of an uptrend and prices usually continue to move up. Conversely, if the stock price moves below the SMA, it is indicative of a downtrend and prices, usually, move downward. In the chart (Fig. 2-14), the 200 day SMA, shows a downtrend around $14.00 when the price of Ford stock falls below the 200 day moving average (SMA). This falling trend is usually an indication to sell a stock before the downtrend continues. This is a sell indicator for sure.

Apple stock has price increase after crossing the 200 Day Moving Average (Chart, Courtesy of InvestProfits.com) Fig 2-15

Key Points

- A stocks downtrend can be a strong sell indication
- A stock that falls below the 50 and 200 day moving average has potential to fall significantly

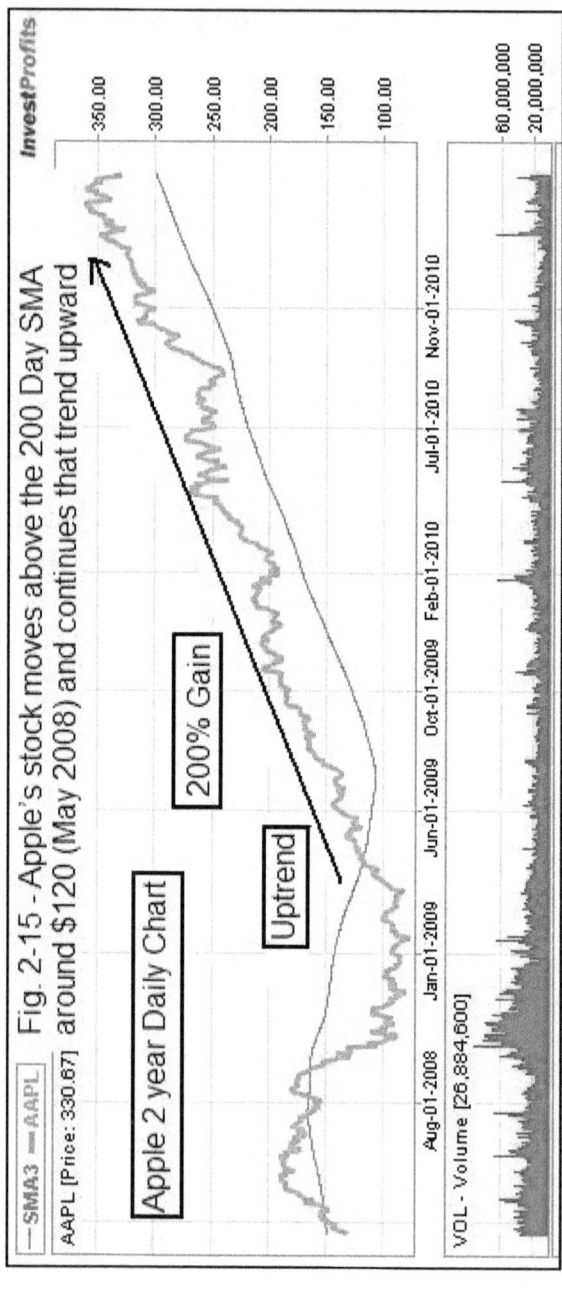

Fig. 2-15 - Apple's stock moves above the 200 Day SMA around $120 (May 2008) and continues that trend upward

Apple Stock Sees Uptrend after crossing 200 Day Moving Average - 200 DMA Example #:

It's true that a stock that moves below the 200 day moving average is a sell indication, and a stock that moves above its 200 day simple moving average, (indicated by the arrow going up) is a buy signal. As a result, it's expected that the upward trend of the stock price will continue. In this example (Fig. 2-15) Apple's stock moves above the 200 Day SMA around $120 (in May 2008) and continues that trend upward.

Key Points

- A trend upward can be found is a stock that moves above the 200 day moving average
- Use stock charts to find uptrend and downtrends of a stock

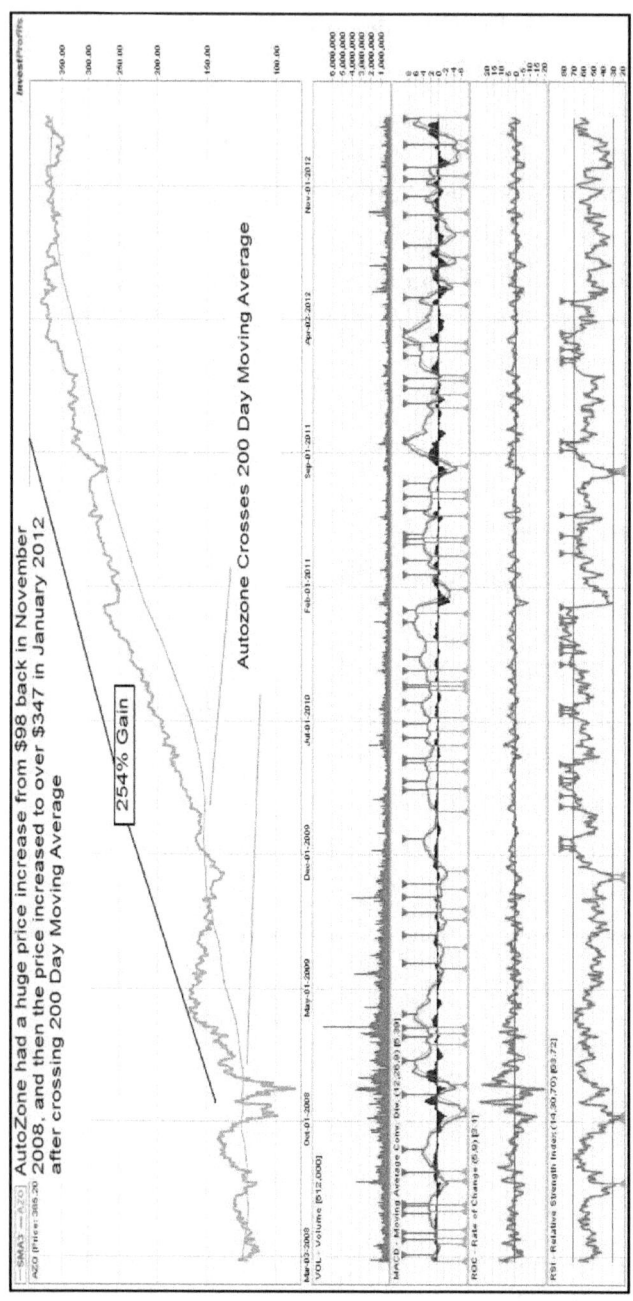

AutoZone Crosses 200 Day Moving Average - 200 DMA Example #4

AutoZone had a huge price increase from $98 back in November 2008, and then the price increased to over $347 in January 2012 after crossing 200 Day Moving Average. In this example seen in (Fig. 2-16), the stock was still trading above its 200 day moving average, a good indicator for the stock trending up. However, it currently has more sell signals (i.e., RSI sell indicators, seen in chart) than buy signals. Potential buyers should do more research before buying in a situation like this due to conflicting signals.

200 DMA: AutoZone Stock Chart (Chart, Courtesy of InvestProfits.com) Fig. 2-16

Key Points

- Significant gains can be spotted when a stock crosses a moving average
- AutoZone crosses 200 day moving average on way to 254% gain

---

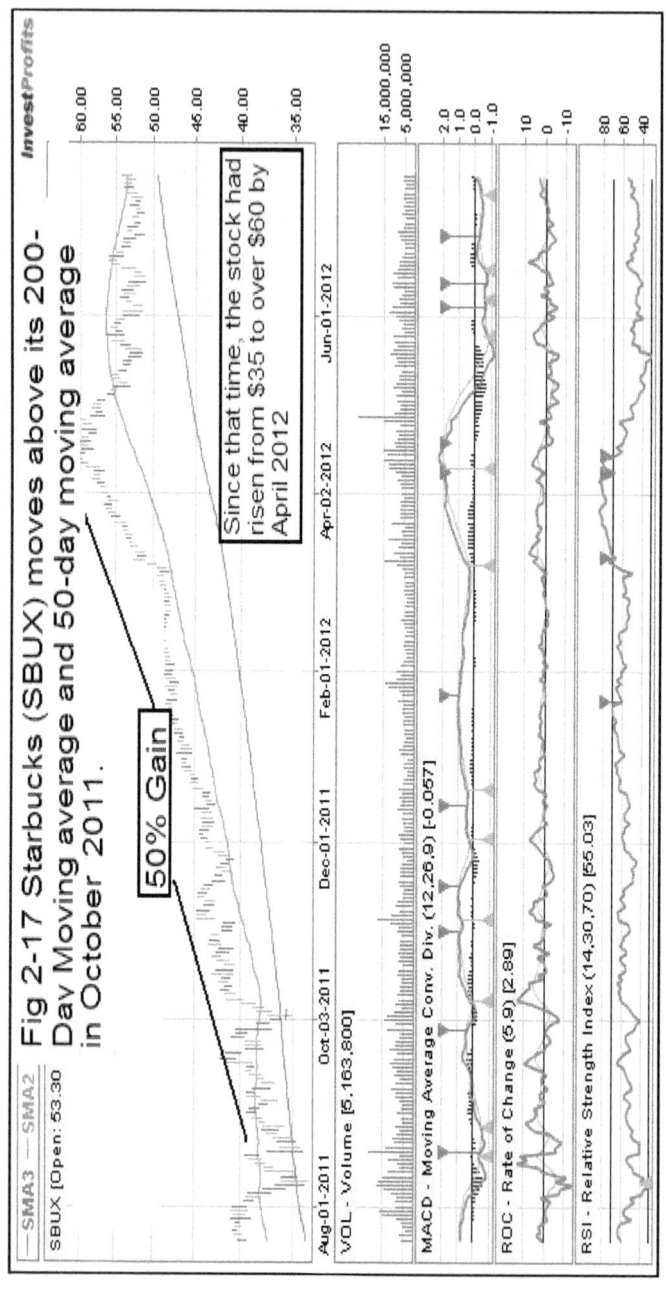

Fig 2-17 Starbucks (SBUX) moves above its 200-Day Moving average and 50-day moving average in October 2011.

50% Gain

Since that time, the stock had risen from $35 to over $60 by April 2012

Starbucks (SBUX) Sees Good Return after Crossing 200-Day Moving Average -200 DMA Example #5

Starbucks (SBUX) moves above its 200-Day Moving average and 50-day moving average on October 3, 2011. Since that time, the stock had risen from $35 to over $60 by April 2012.

In the chart seen in (Fig. 2-17), Starbucks (SBUX) moves above its 200-Day Moving average and 50-day moving average on October 3, 2011. Since that time, the stock had risen from $35 to over $60 by April 2012. It then fell back to $53.30 breaking below its 50-day moving average but finding support above its 200-day moving average. Remember, 200-day moving average is for longer term trends, and therefore is a big picture indicator.

200 DMA Examples: Starbucks Stock Chart (Chart, Courtesy of InvestProfits.com) Fig. 2-17

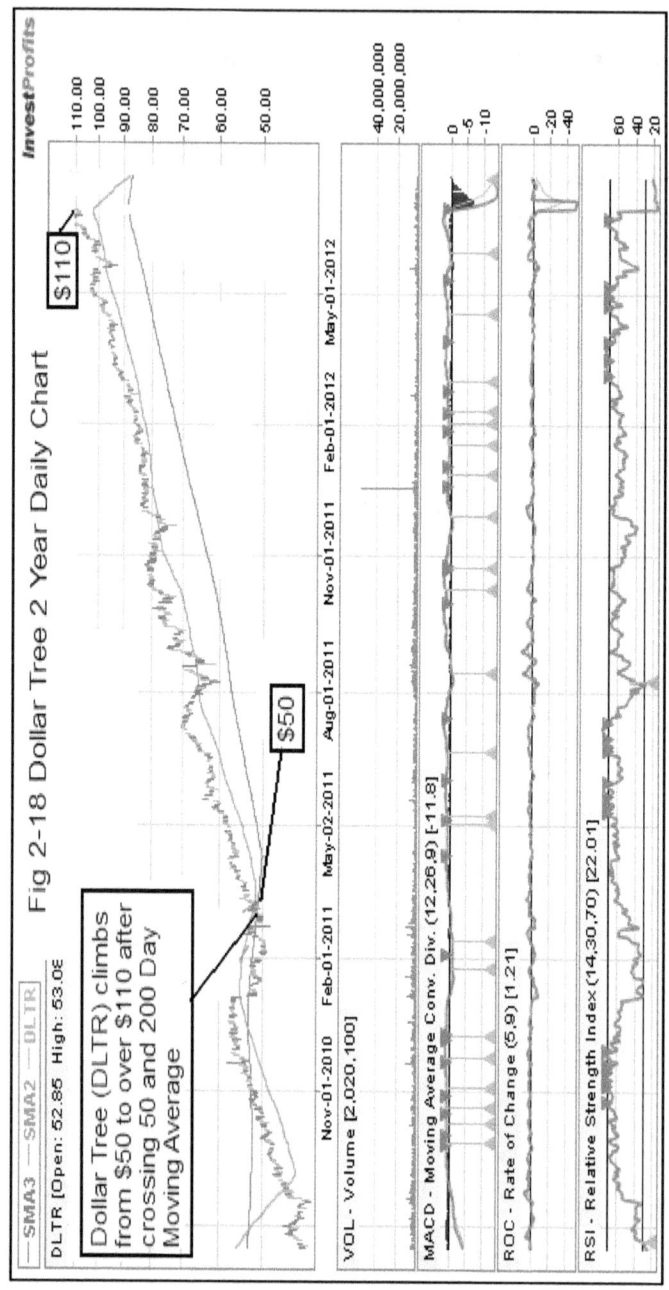

Fig 2-18 Dollar Tree 2 Year Daily Chart

Dollar Tree (DLTR) climbs from $50 to over $110 after crossing 50 and 200 Day Moving Average

88

Dollar Tree: Stock Split after Breaking above 200-Day Moving Average -200 DMA Example #6

Notice how Dollar Tree (in Fig. 2-18) broke above its 200-day moving average back in February 2011 when it traded at $50. Since that time, it has had support by staying above its 200 day moving average increasing to over $110 a share just before a 2 for 1 stock split. See chart for more details.

The 200-day moving average shows a long-term direction for a stock by indicating the trend just like the 50 day moving average. However, it is a more accurate indicator of the direction for a stock than the 50 Day Moving average. Furthermore, it can indicate a down-trend or reversal in a stock. It is used by individual and institutional investors as a market indicator. Bottom line: 200 Day moving average is better at a seeing the bigger picture of the direction of the market. However, there is one indicator that shows you a much bigger picture of a trend...

10 Week Moving Average

The 10 week moving average and the 50 day moving average are very similar (10 weeks X 5 days = 50 days), but with some differences. Many investors will use the 10-week average on weekly charts. It is used to show the big picture of a stock's trend either upward or downward. Many times I use the weekly chart for the 10 week moving average. Then, the 50 day and 200 day moving average are used on daily charts. See this example of Priceline and see how this trend can be applied.

Priceline (PCLN) had a Big Uptrend after January 2012 - 10 WMA Example #1

10 WMA Example 1: Priceline Weekly Stock Chart, (Courtesy of InvestProfits.com) Fig 2-19

Back in January 29, 2012, Priceline (PCLN) had 4 weeks of an uptrend and was trading above its 10 week moving average (see chart Fig 2-19). At the time, there was a bullish indicator to buy based on the fact that it was trending up and had strong earnings. Back then, Priceline was trading at $659.36 and then it went above $750 before falling below its 10 week moving average; that was a good time to sell and take some profits off the table. Notice in the chart, the stock is finding support at its 10 week moving average after falling below it on May 7, 2012.

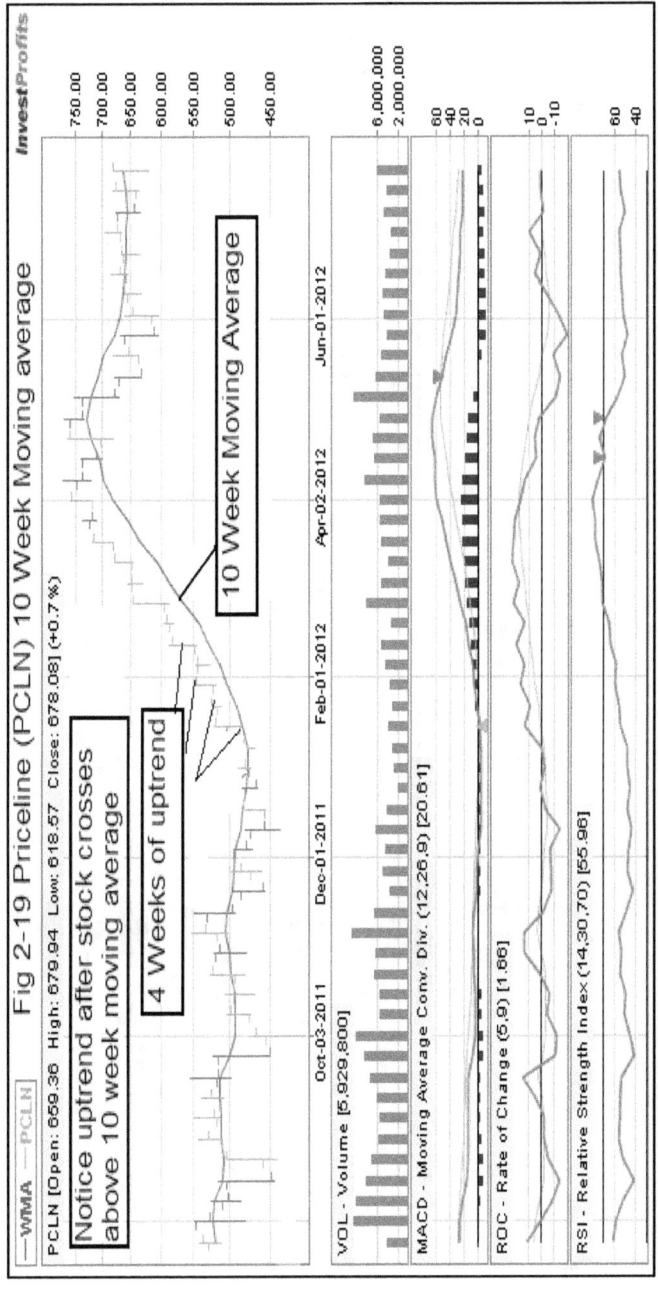

Fig 2-19 Priceline (PCLN) 10 Week Moving average

PCLN [Open: 659.36 High: 679.94 Low: 618.57 Close: 678.08] (+0.7%)

Notice uptrend after stock crosses above 10 week moving average

4 Weeks of uptrend

10 Week Moving Average

VOL - Volume [5,929,800]

MACD - Moving Average Conv. Div. (12,26,9) [20.61]

ROC - Rate of Change (5,9) [1.66]

RSI - Relative Strength Index (14,30,70) [55.96]

91

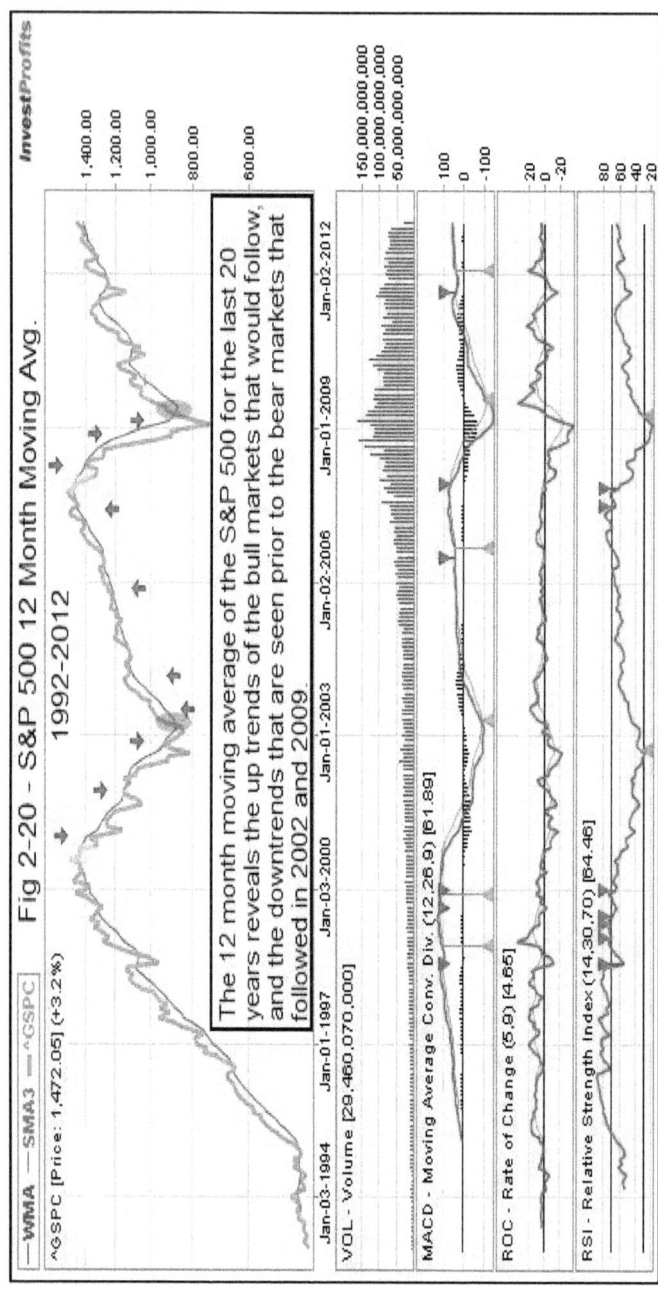

Fig 2-20 - S&P 500 12 Month Moving Avg. 1992-2012

The 12 month moving average of the S&P 500 for the last 20 years reveals the up trends of the bull markets that would follow, and the downtrends that are seen prior to the bear markets that followed in 2002 and 2009.

Fig. 2-20 S&P 500 12 Month Moving Average Chart, Courtesy of InvestProfits.com

12 Month Moving Average:

With a longer moving average, it can be easier to get a big picture of the uptrend or downtrend. The 12 month moving average of the S&P 500 for the last 20 years reveals the up trends of the bull markets that would follow. Conversely, there were downtrends that are seen prior to the bear markets that followed in 2002 and 2009 (see Fig. 2-20). In the S&P 500 chart, the yellow ovals indicate the start of the bear markets that began in February 2001 and February 2008. At those times the SP 500 crossed below the 12 month moving average (yellow oval). Then the S&P 500 crosses the 12 month moving average (blue oval) in April 2003 and April 2009. Both times would have been good opportunities to get back into the stock market.

Candle Stick Charts-

The advantage of candlestick charts is the ability to highlight trending weakness and reversal signals that may not be apparent on a normal bar chart.

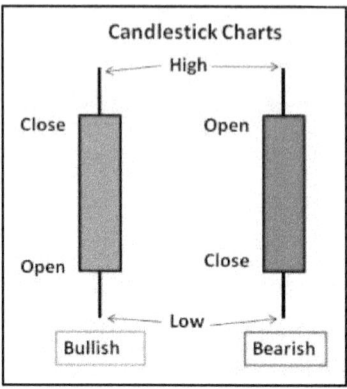

Fig 2-21

When a stock closes higher for the day than where it started, it will be green or black, (the candle on the left in Fig 2-21), and is bullish. If a stock closes lower than the price it opened, it is bearish and red (on the right side of Fig 2-21).

Key Points

- A Candlestick chart that closes higher than it opened, will be green
- A Candlestick chart closes lower than it opened, will be red

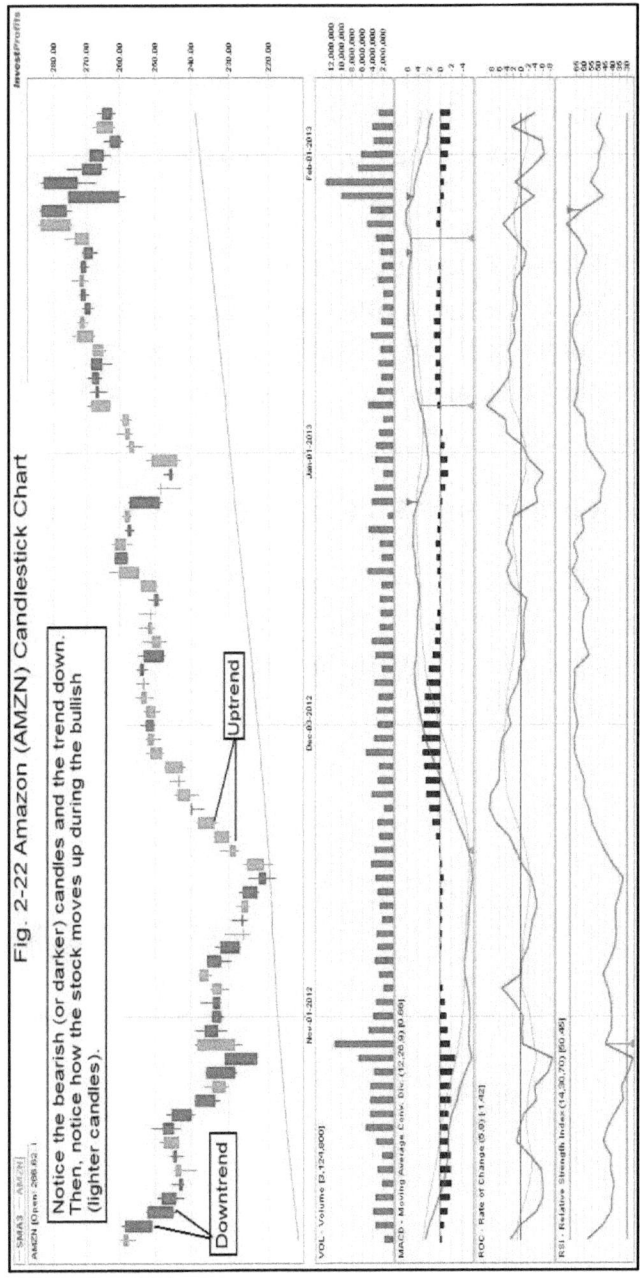

Fig. 2-22 Amazon (AMZN) Candlestick Chart

Notice the bearish (or darker) candles and the trend down. Then, notice how the stock moves up during the bullish (lighter candles).

The wick is the end of the candlestick that occurs at both ends. This shows the stocks high for the day and the wick on the lower end shows the low for the day of that particular stock.

Candlestick Chart Example: Amazon
In (*Fig. 2-22*) the Amazon.com candlestick chart, notice the bearish (or darker) candles and the trend down. Then, notice how the stock moves up during the bullish (lighter candles).

AutoZone was trading at $320 and increased to over $370
In January 2012, AutoZone was trading at $320 and increased to over $370 on February 2012 (as seen in *Fig 2-23*). AutoZone's stock chart had a buy signal as seen in the weekly candlestick chart.

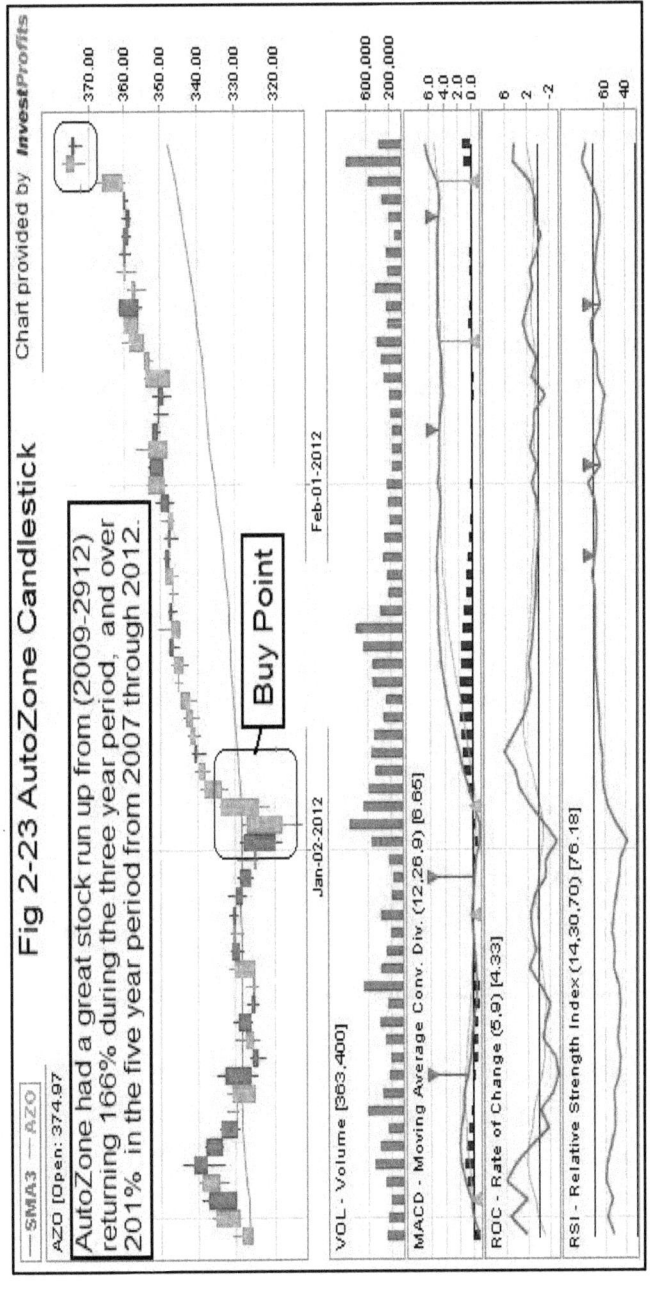

Fig 2-23 AutoZone Candlestick

AutoZone had a great stock run up from (2009-2912) returning 166% during the three year period, and over 201% in the five year period from 2007 through 2012.

Buy Point

The Investing Guide: Using Technical and Fundamental Analysis

Based on the chart in February, it was at a hold, as Fig 2-23 AutoZone Candlestick, (provided by Investprofits.com) indicated by the chart in Fig 2-23. Therefore, an investor should wait for a buy point. AutoZone had a great stock run up from (2009-2912) returning 166% during the three year period, and over 201% in the five year period from 2007 through 2012. AutoZone has been a great buy over the last several years, especially during the recovery of the Great Recession. Many of their customers who were already cash strapped become more cost-conscious during the recession.

Key Points

- MACD shows the measurement of an investment by revealing the difference between fast and slow exponential moving averages
- Combine MACD with other indicators like RSI and Moving Averages

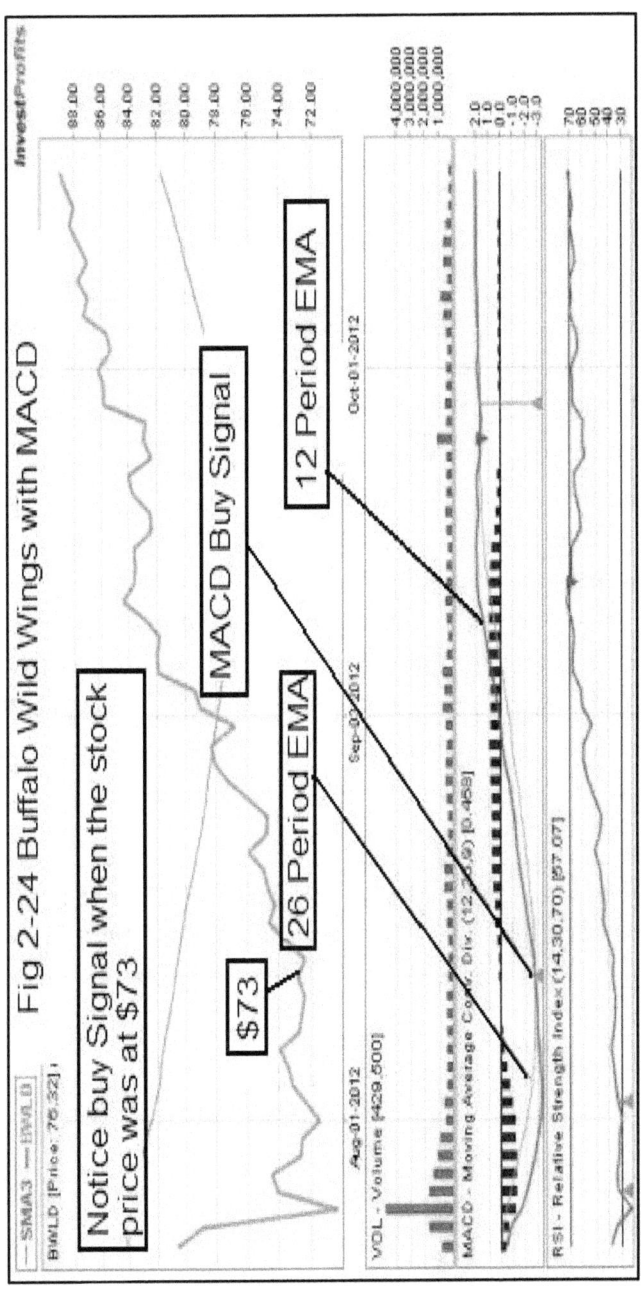

Fig 2-24 Buffalo Wild Wings with MACD

MACD (Moving Average Convergence/Divergence)
The moving average/convergence divergence (MACD) shows the measurement of an investment by revealing the difference between fast and slow exponential moving averages, known as EMA's. A buy signal happens when the 12 period EMA crosses over the slower moving 26 period EMA. A sell signal happens when the fast moving 12 period EMA crosses below the slow moving 26 period EMA. (See Fig 2-24) Charts with buy and sell signals are available at www.investprofits.com.

A crossover involving a stock's moving average when the short-term moving average (such as 50-day moving average) moves above its long-term moving average such as 200-day moving average, will produce a golden cross. It works for both individual stocks and indexes (e.g. S&P 500). However, it is particularly beneficial, and highly relevant, to find the direction of the overall market.

This golden cross usually results in better returns over the next 12 months for the S&P 500. Notice the Golden Cross in this chart that occurred on February 1, 2012.

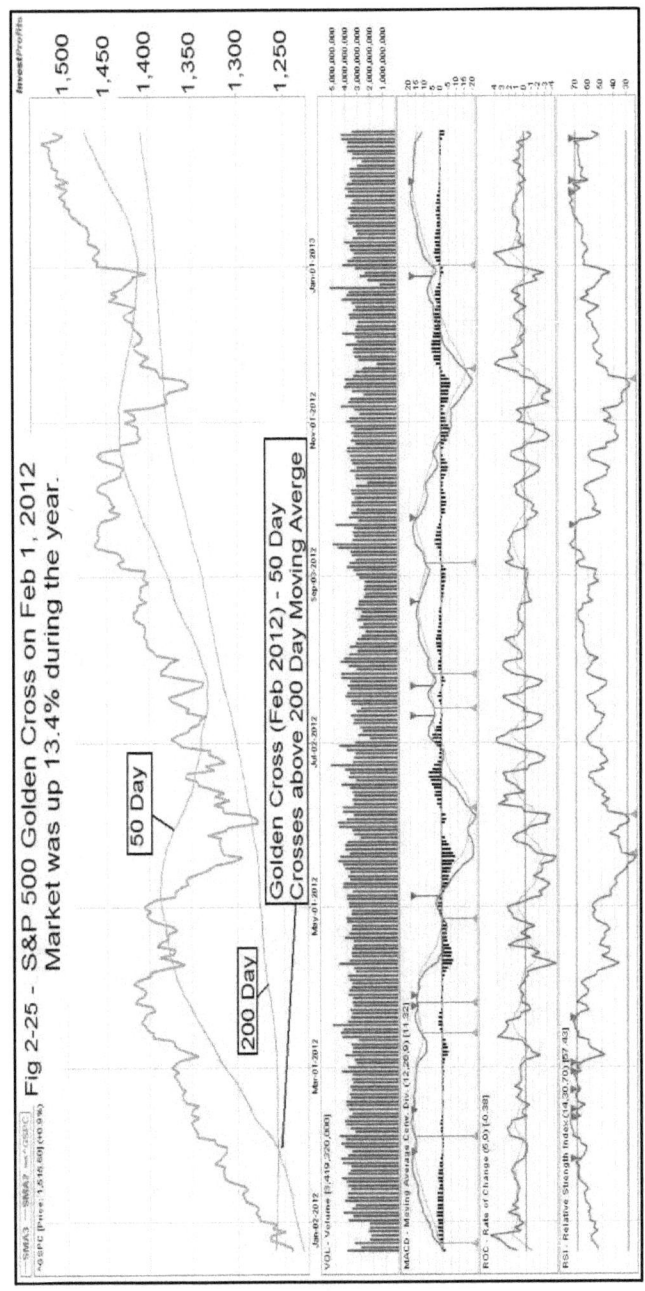

Fig 2-25 - S&P 500 Golden Cross on Feb 1, 2012
Market was up 13.4% during the year.

Golden Cross (Feb 2012) - 50 Day Crosses above 200 Day Moving Averge

50 Day

200 Day

Fig 2-25 S&P 500 Golden Cross Feb 2012 – Resulted in a 13.4% return for the S&P 500 Index for 2012.

Golden Cross

A golden cross happens after the 50 day moving average crosses above the 200 day moving average. Anytime the S&P 500 has a golden cross it indicates a very good year ahead for the stock market. This golden cross usually results in better returns over the next 12 months for the S&P 500. Notice the Golden Cross in this chart that occurred on February 1, 2012.

The S&P 500 Returns 13.4% after February Golden Cross

A Golden Cross occurred back in February 2012 for the S&P 500 as seen in the chart (in Fig 2-25). It was indicative of a bull market and the result of this indicator was positive. In 2012, the S&P 500 returned 13.4% for the year, 16% with dividends included.

In another example, notice the golden cross in the salesforce.com chart in Figure 2-26. The cross occurred in May 2009 when the stock was trading at $40. Then, the stock price climbed to $140 before hitting a death cross, which is the opposite of a death cross. Furthermore, there was a death cross in October 2008 as the stock price fell from $55 down to a closing price of $21.96 on November 19, 2008.

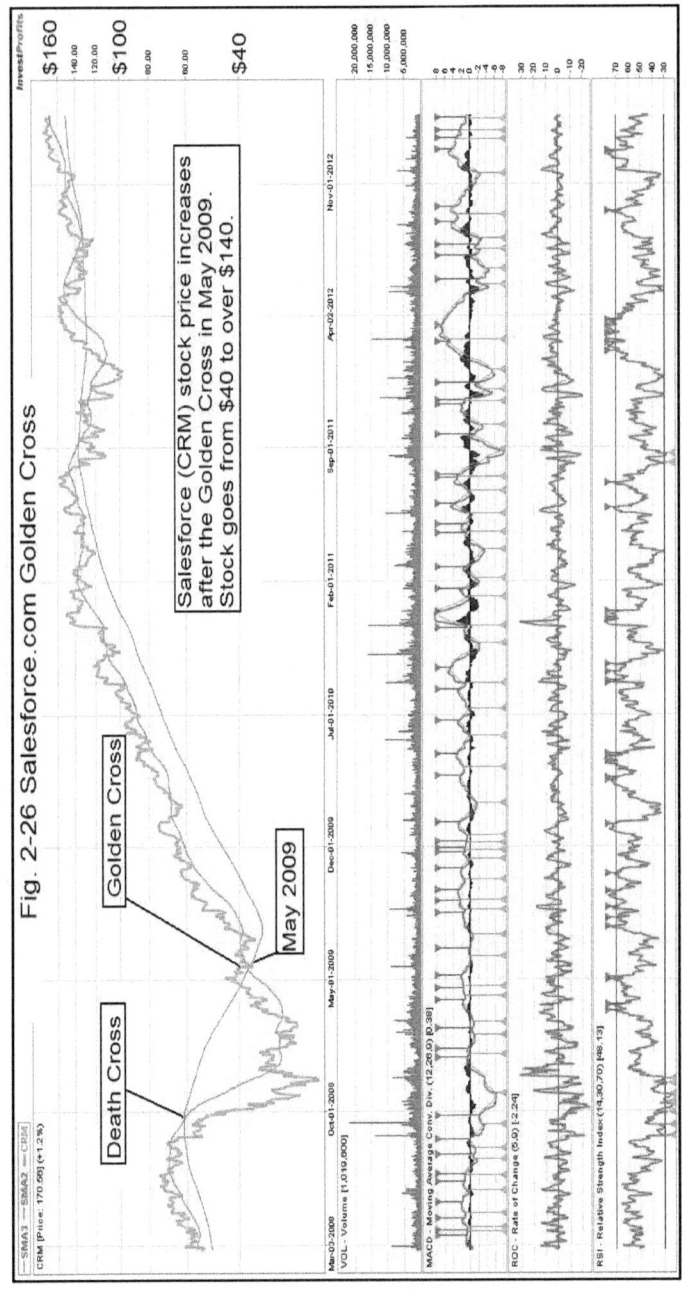

Fig. 2-26 Salesforce.com Golden Cross

Death Cross

Golden Cross

May 2009

Salesforce (CRM) stock price increases after the Golden Cross in May 2009. Stock goes from $40 to over $140.

Fig. 2-26 Salesforce.com Golden Cross - Notice the how stock price increases after the Golden Cross in May 2009. Stock goes from $40 to over $140.

Death Cross

A death cross is the opposite of a golden cross. It occurs when the 50 day moving average moves below the 200 day moving average. Notice the many death crosses that occurred in the chart in Fig 2-27. They were followed by declines in the market as noted by the chart of the FTSE (Fig. 2-12) (Chart provided by InvestProfits.com) index (See Fig 2-27).

Key Points

- A Death Cross is a strong indicator of a stock or index, like the S&P 500
- A Death Cross is a sell indicator
- The Death Cross works best on Indexes (like S&P 500) than on individual stocks

---

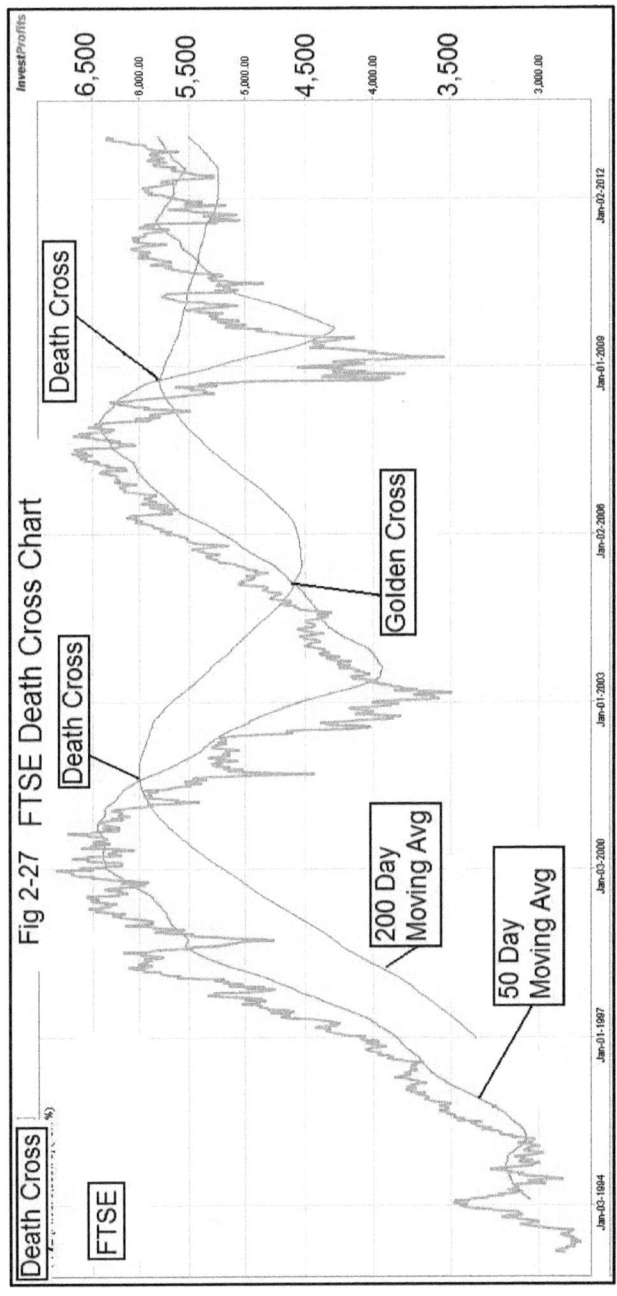

Fig 2-27 FTSE Death Cross Chart

What is notable is how accurate the 'golden cross' was as a buy signal (marked by the arrows pointing up) has proved to be. Further anecdotal evidence can be seen as the S&P 500 had a golden cross in February 2012 and returned 13.4% for the year.

Past Performance

Being careful about when to sell a stock can depend on many factors and can influence the amount of profit realized. In Fig 2-28, the 6 month chart of Amazon and Apple reveal a return of 16% for Amazon while Apple was down at a -25%. During the period from July 30, 2012 through Jan 29, 2013 there was a difference of 41 percentage points between Amazon and Apple stock.

Fig 2-28 – Six month chart: (Amazon vs. Apple) Notice how Amazon performs better than Apple in the period from July 30, 2012 through Jan 29, 2013, a difference of 41 percentage points.

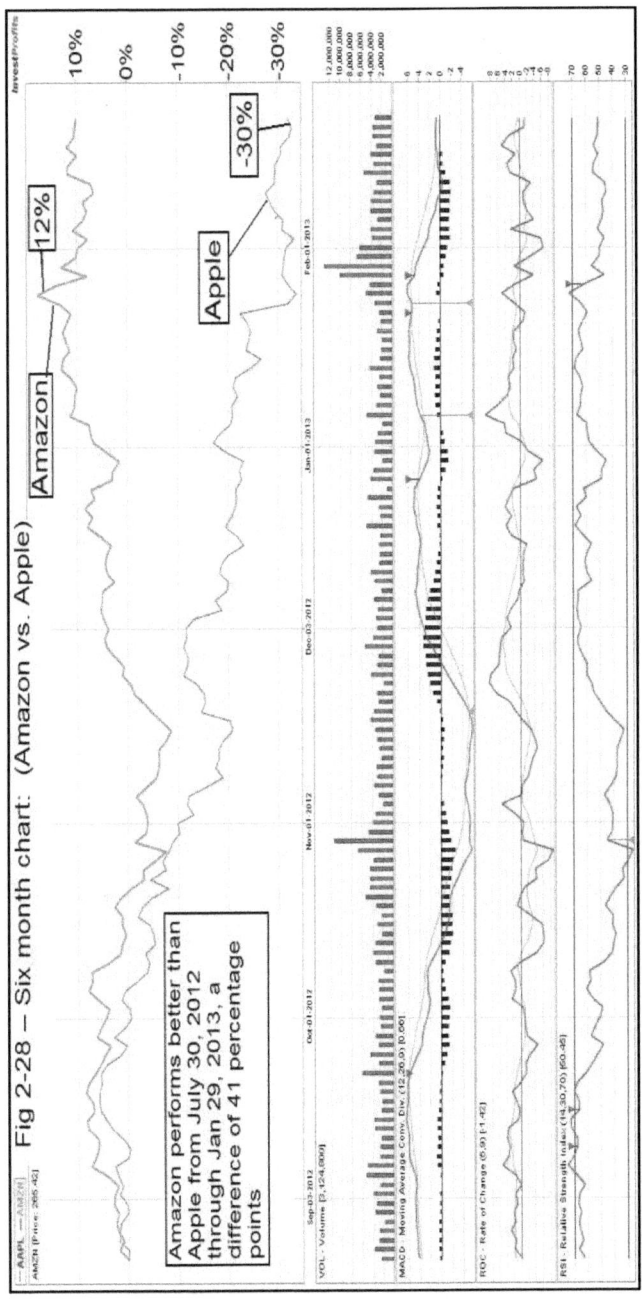

Fig 2-28 – Six month chart: (Amazon vs. Apple)

Amazon performs better than Apple from July 30, 2012 through Jan 29, 2013, a difference of 41 percentage points

The investing mantra, "past performance is no guarantee of future results" is never more evident than here. Take for example the six month period from September 23, 2011 through March 21, 2012: just the opposite result happened during that time. Apple had a positive return of over 50% while Amazon was down a -15% (Fig 2-29).

Fig 2-29 – Six month chart: (Apple vs. Amazon)
Apple had a positive return of over 50% while Amazon was down a -15%. See how different the results were in Fig 2-28.

Key Points

- Past Performance is no guarantee of future results
- A stock that outperforms another in its industry can lose that advantage very quickly

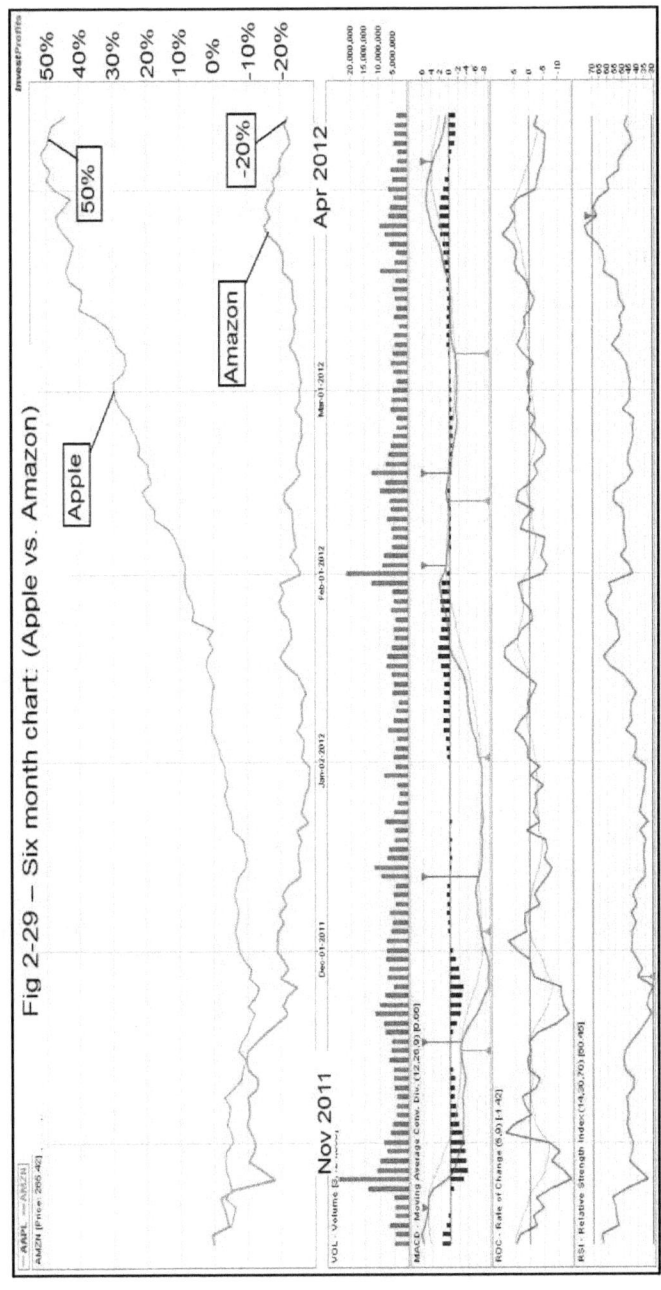

Fig 2-29 – Six month chart: (Apple vs. Amazon)

Summary of Technical Analysis:

In closing out this chapter on Technical Analysis, it is important to remember that not all indicators are equal. Also, sometimes an indicator can be wrong. However, more times than not, the moving average and relative strength index (RSI) are two of the better technical indicators. They can be very useful in spotting trends and stocks that are oversold and overbought. After investing with only mild results using only fundamental analysis, I began using charts and technical analysis to find and analyze stocks. Did it work? Yes, it resulted in better investment returns.

Chapter 3:
Long Term Investing

L ong term investing should always include Fundamental Analysis as it is used many times by long term investors. This can help an investor find both growth stocks and value stock and build wealth over time. If used correctly, it can be very beneficial in finding undervalued stocks. This is the method Warren Buffett implements with great success. Some of the key concepts of fundamental analysis will be covered here. However, this chapter will focus on several other long-term concepts used by investors such as finding growth stocks. This can be done with great success by using the concepts in this chapter along with those in chapter 2 (Technical Analysis). .

111

P/E Ratio

The price to earnings ratio, or P/E ratio, of a stock is the price of a stock divided by its earnings per share. Typically the lower the P/E, the better the value and lower the risk of the security. This indicator is very valuable when combined with technical analysis indicators. In the past, several stocks have sold for very low P/E and have increased in value over time; this is one of the financial tenets used by Warren Buffett in his value investing method of picking stocks. Other investors have bought stocks with very high P/Es and done very well...while others have done poorly with high P/E stocks. Investors who buy a stock without regards to how high the P/E may be, are usually considered growth investors, or a speculative investor. A growth investor may buy a stock even if it has a P/E above 100.

Jeremy Seigel authhor of Stocks for the Long Run found work by Sanjoy Sasu that found that, "stocks with low price-to-earnings ratios have significantly higher returns than stocks with high price-to-earnings ratios, even after accounting for risk." Additionally further studies have been done that seem to bear this out: Warren Buffett has used this in his investing techniques as did his mentor, Benjamin Graham. See the P/E chart in Fig. 3-1 for more on what different P/E ranges and what they indicate:

P/E Ratio (Range)	What it Means:
0-10	The stock is very low and is expected to have low growth in the future
11-20	This is the normal range for most stocks. Many of the S&P 500 stocks are in this range.
21-30	Many stocks in this range can be considered to be on the verge of getting expensive
31-50	Stocks with a P/E in this range are very expensive and should be bought only with extreme caution
above 51	Stocks in this range are very risky. They are typically stocks that have been hyped up or have high growth expectations

Fig. 3-1

Growth Stock and P/E Ratios

While a low P/E is a good way to value a stock, sometimes a high P/E can have positive returns as well. For example, in 2012, 3D systems had a high P/E yet the stock returned 223% in one year. Take a look at Fig. 3-2 for more examples of stocks with high P/E's that had big gains in stock price.

Stocks with High P/E's and High Percentage Returns

Company name	Symbol	Market cap	P/E ratio	52w price change (%)
3D Systems Corporation	DDD	3.45B	90	223
Pulte Group, Inc.	PHM	8.13B	50	177
Lumber Liquidators Holdings Inc	LL	1.62B	40	170
Ocwen Financial Corporation	OCN	5.09B	41	164
AMN Healthcare Services, Inc.	AHS	531.75 M	51	161
M/I Homes Inc	MHO	594.04 M	108	153
Carriage Services, Inc.	CSV	250.83 M	34	150
The Ryland Group, Inc.	RYL	1.82B	50	126
Eagle Materials, Inc.	EXP	3.13B	66	126
Standard Pacific Corp.	SPF	1.79B	51	123
Marriott Vacations Worldwide Corp	VAC	1.53B	51	115
Bonanza Creek Energy Inc	BCEI	1.28B	45	97
Alon USA Energy, Inc.	ALJ	1.16B	33	96
Western Refining, Inc.	WNR	2.86B	39	95
Michael Kors Holdings Ltd	KORS	11.25B	45	93
Texas Industries, Inc.	TXI	1.60B	87	85
Spartech Corporation	SEH	297.87 M	112	84
Brown Shoe Company, Inc.	BWS	718.88 M	44	82
Qihoo 360 Technology Co Ltd	QIHU	7.17B	78	78
Tenet Healthcare Corporation	THC	4.11B	44	77

Fig. 3-2 *Stock with High P/E and High Percentage Returns (Highest to Lowest % chg.)*

114

Company name	Sym- bol	Market cap	P/E ratio	52w price chang e (%)
Rack space Hosting, Inc.	RAX	10.18B	104	76
Spectrum Brands Holdings, Inc.	SPB	2.62B	55	76
Macquarie Infrastructure Company LLC	MIC	2.19B	61	73
Solar Winds Inc	SWI	4.03B	54	72
Harbinger Group Inc	HRG	1.15B	56	71
Coca-Cola FEMSA, S.A.B. de C.V. (ADR)	KOF	31.62B	33	65
Team Health Holdings LLC	TMH	2.26B	36	64
Huaneng Power International, Inc. (ADR)	HNP	14.04B	40	63
Bank of America Corp	BAC	122.66B	46	63
Cabot Oil & Gas Corporation	COG	11.04B	95	63
Midas, Inc.	MDS	165.70M	40	58
Visa Inc	V	103.11B	83	57
Extra Space Storage, Inc.	EXR	4.13B	41	54
Nomura Holdings, Inc. (ADR)	NMR	20.91B	43	53
EPL Oil & Gas Inc	EPL	953.00M	35	53
Tyler Technologies, Inc.	TYL	1.65B	54	53
Covance Inc.	CVD	3.64B	40	53
Briggs & Stratton Corporation	BGG	1.11B	95	52
Koninklijke Philips Electronics NV (ADR)	PHG	28.50B	85	51
Weyerhaeuser Company	WY	16.21B	42	51

Fig 3-3 Stock with High P/E and High Percentage Returns (Highest to Lowest % chg.)

Stock with Low Price to Book Ratio

While a high P/E stock can have positive returns, low P/E stocks tend to outperform those with a high P/E. However, combining low P/E and low Price to book (P/B) is better.

Buying stocks with low Price to book (P/B) ratio can be profitable. Warren Buffett and his value style of investing results in generous gains and can prove beneficial for any long term investor. See fig. 3-4 for examples of stocks that had high returns in 2012 and had low P/B ratios.

Stocks with Low P/B Ratio (Highest-Lowest) Fig 3-4

Company name	Symbol	Market cap	52w price chang	Price to book
Pulte Group, Inc.	PHM	8.13B	177	4.2
Ocwen Financial Corporation	OCN	5.09B	164	3.7
AMN Healthcare Services, Inc.	AHS	531.75 M	161	3.7
M/I Homes Inc	MHO	594.04 M	153	3.0
Carriage Services, Inc.	CSV	250.83 M	150	2.0
The Ryland Group, Inc.	RYL	1.82B	126	3.7
Standard Pacific Corp.	SPF	1.79B	123	2.7
Marriott Vacations Worldwide Corp	VAC	1.53B	115	1.3

116

Bonanza Creek Energy Inc	BCEI	1.28B	97	2.4
Alon USA Energy, Inc.	ALJ	1.16B	96	3.0
Western Refining, Inc.	WNR	2.86B	95	3.5
Texas Industries, Inc.	TXI	1.60B	5	2.4
Spartech Corporation	SEH	297.87 M	4	1.7
Brown Shoe Company, Inc.	BWS	718.88 M	2	1.8
Tenet Healthcare Corporation	THC	4.11B	7	3.6
Spectrum Brands Holdings, Inc.	SPB	2.62B	6	2.7
Macquarie Infrastructure Company LLC	MIC	2.19B	3	3.2
Harbinger Group Inc	HRG	1.15B	1	1.0

Return on Equity (ROE)

One of the most important profitability parameters is the ROE, and the one I like to use most often combined with a low P/E ratio. This is a very good indicator of potential growth for the company. If ROE has been rising in past quarters, it indicates a very good stock to buy because it's indicative of a company that's growing its earnings. Conversely, if the Return on Equity is falling in the last several quarters, it would be wise to sell. While individual stock picking can be very prosperous, it is wise for the investor to also use long-term investing via dollar

117

cost averaging as a part of their investing portfolio. Of course, individual stocks should be added to the mix. Since individual stocks can reap the most profits in the shortest amount of time, they are more risky. They should be bought with a limited portion of your total funds. Conversely, a larger portion should go to dollar cost averaging.

Dollar Cost Averaging For Steady Growth

The history of the stock market has resulted in a long term return between 9-12% per year. Using the Rule of 72 to divide 12 % into 72 would give 6 years.

Rule of 72 is important to remember because it will indicate how long it will take to double an investment. This philosophy can be

Rule of 72

$$\frac{72}{6} = 12 \text{ Years}$$

applied to consumer purchases. For example, when a new gadget you want to buy costs $100, ask yourself if the item is really worth $400 12 years from now by applying the rule of 72. (72/12 = 6) means that $100 will double to $200 in 6 years, then the $200 will double again in 6 more years for a total of $400. A 12% return was used in this example because that's an approximate rate of return in an index fund. If the answer is yes to that question, then you should purchase the gadget.

To further exemplify the rule of 72: if investing $3,000 dollars at 12%, you would double your investment to $6,000 in 6 years. In 30 years, it would have doubled 5 times and turned your initial investment of $3,000 into $96,000.

In another rule of 72 scenario, had an investor invested $3,000 initially and added $500 every month, after 25 years, their investment you have grown to over $851,000 (see *Figure 3-1* for other rates of return and how an investment can grow).

How to Dollar Cost Average (DCA)

Dollar cost averaging is a technique designed to reduce market risk through the systematic purchase of securities at predetermined intervals and set amounts. Many successful investors already practice DCA without realizing it. Many others could save themselves a lot of time, effort, and money by beginning a plan. In this section, you will learn the steps to beginning a dollar cost averaging plan by looking at concrete examples of how it can lower your cost basis. Also, you can discover how it reduces risk.

Example of a Dollar Cost Averaging Plan

An investment of $3,000, with monthly contributions of $500, will turn into $851,003 assuming a 12% annual return (the stock market's historical average based on the S&P 500). The chart in Fig 3-5 covers more possible returns based on different amounts invested and various rates of return.

Investing at Different Rates of Returns (Useful for DCA)
In Figure 3-5, notice how an investment of $3,000, with monthly contributions of $500, will turn into $114,000 in

	Monthly → $500			Sart → $3000			
Year	1	2	5	10	15	20	25
You Invested→	$9,000	$15,000	$33,000	$63,000	$93,000	$123,000	$153,000
Rate→	Can Become→	Can Become→	Can Become→	Can Become→	Can Become→	Can Become→	Can Become→
1%	$9,030	$15,120	$33,759	$66,087	$100,064	$135,775	$173,306
2%	$9,060	$15,241	$34,536	$69,355	$107,798	$150,242	$197,104
3%	$9,090	$15,363	$35,333	$72,815	$116,267	$166,641	$225,037
4%	$9,120	$15,485	$36,148	$76,477	$125,544	$185,242	$257,873
5%	$9,150	$15,608	$36,983	$80,354	$135,708	$206,356	$296,522
6%	$9,180	$15,731	$37,837	$84,457	$146,845	$230,335	$342,063
7%	$9,210	$15,855	$38,712	$88,800	$159,051	$257,582	$395,777
8%	$9,240	$15,979	$39,608	$93,396	$172,429	$288,555	$459,181
9%	$9,270	$16,104	$40,524	$98,260	$187,093	$323,774	$534,075
10%	$9,300	$16,230	$41,462	$103,406	$203,167	$363,832	$622,586
11%	$9,330	$16,356	$42,422	$108,850	$220,786	$409,404	$727,236
12%	$9,360	$16,483	$43,404	$114,610	$240,099	$461,254	$851,003
13%	$9,390	$16,611	$44,409	$120,702	$261,268	$520,250	$997,409
14%	$9,420	$16,739	$45,437	$127,145	$284,468	$587,380	$1,170,611
15%	$9,450	$16,868	$46,488	$133,959	$309,894	$663,761	$1,375,515
16%	$9,480	$16,997	$47,564	$141,163	$337,754	$750,661	$1,617,907
17%	$9,510	$17,127	$48,664	$148,779	$368,277	$849,514	$1,904,603
18%	$9,540	$17,257	$49,789	$156,829	$401,713	$961,947	$2,243,627
19%	$9,570	$17,388	$50,939	$165,337	$438,333	$1,089,796	$2,644,419
20%	$9,600	$17,520	$52,115	$174,327	$478,432	$1,235,141	$3,118,075
21%	$9,630	$17,652	$53,317	$183,825	$522,331	$1,400,328	$3,677,625
22%	$9,660	$17,785	$54,546	$193,858	$570,380	$1,588,009	$4,338,361
23%	$9,690	$17,919	$55,802	$204,455	$622,958	$1,801,174	$5,118,210
24%	$9,720	$18,053	$57,086	$215,644	$680,478	$2,043,196	$6,038,176
25%	$9,750	$18,188	$58,397	$227,457	$743,386	$2,317,877	$7,122,840
26%	$9,780	$18,323	$59,738	$239,927	$812,169	$2,629,495	$8,400,954
27%	$9,810	$18,459	$61,108	$253,087	$887,354	$2,982,870	$9,906,112
28%	$9,840	$18,595	$62,507	$266,973	$969,512	$3,383,417	$11,677,533
29%	$9,870	$18,732	$63,937	$281,623	$1,059,262	$3,837,228	$13,760,969
30%	$9,900	$18,870	$65,397	$297,075	$1,157,276	$4,351,142	$16,209,743

10 years assuming a 12% annual return (the stock markets historical average based on the S&P 500). For more examples on the power of compounding on different amounts go to Appendix A in back of the book.

Mutual Funds

For investors who are interested in buy and hold, it gets very difficult to beat mutual funds. For example, an S&P 500 mutual fund from either Vanguard or Fidelity will match the performance of the S&P 500. Based on the history of this index, it has returned around 10-12% annually since 1926. Therefore, many mutual funds are measured against the S&P 500.

However, many managed mutual funds under perform this index year after year. Most years active mutual fund managers will not beat the index. Usually only about 20% of actively managed funds will perform better than an S&P 500 index fund. That doesn't mean that an investor should rule out actively managed funds, just be diligent and knowledgeable when picking one over an index fund.

While small cap stocks have the potential for a significant growth potential, they are far more risky. In fact, small cap stocks have outperformed large cap stocks at times...and if you are looking to buy single stocks, then some small caps can be very profitable. But if you are looking to buy mutual funds...and you should for your long-term investments....investing in large cap stocks in the form of the S&P 500 Index mutual fund is a good investment. This way you have some long term financial security if some of your individual stock purchases perform poorly. Whether they are small cap or large cap, this contingency plan will allow you to become wealthy over the long term. Remember, investing is very unpredictable and getting it right every time is difficult. Even with the charting methods used in this book, investing returns can be unpredictable and sometimes negative. Therefore, you want a contingency in case you buy one stock...or two...or three ...and they don't go as planned. The likelihood of all stocks going down instead of up is highly unlikely...it's just that you don't want to *not* have a backup plan. Backup investing plans are always good to have. Even if you have great returns investing in individual stocks it is always a good idea to have mutual funds for the long term. The mutual funds that should be highly considered are large cap funds. They should be the ones you have in your portfolio.

Top Performing Mutual Funds Fig 3-6

Mutual Fund Top Performers - 1 Year		
Fund Name	Symbol	Ann. Ret.
Federated MDT Tax Aware/All Cap Core I	QITAX	50.24%
Morgan Stanley Equally-Wtd S&P 500 W	VADWX	49.77%
Federated MDT Tax Aware/All Cap Core A	QATAX	49.75%
ING Strat Allocation Growth Port Adv	IAGRX	48.96%
Nuveen Symphony All-Cap Core I	NSAIX	48.74%
Federated MDT Tax Aware/All Cap Core C	QCTAX	48.70%
Nuveen Symphony All-Cap Core A	NACAX	48.38%
Nuveen Symphony All-Cap Core R3	NCCRX	47.98%
ING Pioneer S2		47.47%
Nuveen Symphony All-Cap Core C	NACCX	47.20%
Fig 3-6 -Top Performing Mutual Funds (as of Dec 2012)		

Mutual Fund Top Performers - 3 Year Period		
Fund Name	Symbol	Ann. Ret.
PIMCO Stocks PLUS Long Duration Instl	PSLDX	25.29%
UBS US Large Cap Equity B	BNQBX	24.81%
Dreyfus Tax-Managed Growth B	DPTMX	24.08%
JHVIT Large Cap Trust Ser NAV		23.84%
JHVIT Large Cap Trust Ser I		23.79%
JHVIT Large Cap Trust Ser II		23.53%
Dreyfus Core Equity B	DPEBX	23.52%
JHFunds2 Index 500 NAV	JIFNX	22.83%
Wells Fargo Advantage Social Sust Adm	WSRAX	21.65%
Wells Fargo Advantage Social Sust A	WSSAX	21.33%

Mutual Fund Top Performers - 5 Year Period		
Fund Name	Symbol	Ann. Ret.
PIMCO Stocks PLUS Long Duration Instl	PSLDX	10.83%
Yacktman Focused Institutional	YAFIX	10.61%
Yacktman Focused Svc	YAFFX	10.59%
Yacktman Svc	YACKX	9.68%
PIMCO Fundamental Index PLUS TR Inst	PXTIX	9.07%
PIMCO Fundamental Index PLUS TR P	PIXPX	8.92%
PIMCO Fundamental Index PLUS TR Admin	PXTAX	8.77%
PIMCO Fundamental Index PLUS TR D	PIXDX	8.62%
PIMCO Fundamental Index PLUS TR A	PIXAX	8.62%
PIMCO Fundamental Index PLUS TR C	PIXCX	7.81%

Fig 3-6

Be Careful of High Turnover

When a mutual fund has a high turnover ratio, it can diminish returns. An 100% turnover would indicate that the fund manager is selling the entire portfolio and buying new stocks once per year. Turnover is costly. It involves transaction fees, spreads, increased management costs, and higher tax costs for the investors. While this may seem like a small concern, it can adds up quickly compared to funds with low turnover ratios. Take for instance a fund with a 20% turnover would indicate that the fund manager buys and sells every stock in the portfolio every 5 years; this is a low turnover ratio and therefore desirable.

Conversely, some funds have a turnover ratio over 300%; this would mean that the fund manager buys new stocks and sells existing ones in the fund every 4 months, or 3 times per year. It is in situations like this that the expenses can become costly and eat into the fund's real returns. It is important to consider the expense ratio along with the average returns for the fund you are considering before buying the fund.

Why Large Caps can perform better than Small Caps

First let me begin by pointing out that I am not against small cap stocks. Sometimes they are the better choice in an investment. However, for a long term investment, Large Caps are preferred. With this disclosure, I bring to you the following question:

Where do you invest your money when you are looking for a long term investment the stock market? My advice is to use a mutual fund or exchange traded fund. Here I will discuss some exchange traded funds (ETF). They are a good way to get into the stock market and gain a good

124

return of 8-12% or more annually by letting a professional manage your money. However, what method should one use to decide on a mutual fund? There are several criteria that should be looked at. I will discuss them as I evaluate three funds: DJ Total Market Fund (IYY), S&P 600 Small Cap Fund (IJR), and the Russell 1000 Fund (IWF).

Let's begin with the DJ Total Market Fund (IYY). It represents the Dow Jones Total Market Index. It has many things to offer. For instance, it is a balanced portfolio of stocks in one fund. It has a very low expense ratio of .20%. This is one of the lowest fees in the stock market at the time of this writing. Therefore, it will take five years to equal 1% fees; this equates to $10 out of every $1,000 invested for a 5 year period. It offers continuous pricing updates throughout the day, unlike mutual funds which are priced at the end of the business day. Of course this benefit holds true of all ETF funds including the ones discussed here. It invests in about 95% of the overall U.S stock market; as a result, it should mirror the historical returns of the S&P 500. Based on several years of studying the market, it should be noted that the historical average of the stock market since the mid 1920's is around 12%, even after adding in the great depression and the bear market of 2000-2002. However, that number is beginning to decrease due to the Great Recession. Consequently, the historical return has been lowered to around 10% per year.

Nevertheless, one will not beat the market by much or lose to the market by much due to the fact this fund closely mimics the S&P 500 index. So beating or losing in the market is very minimal with this ETF and very small when it does happen. This can be both a good and bad thing, at least on the upside when beating the market. Low risk can be seen when a funds beta is low. This ETF has a beta of 1.01. As for the returns of the past 1, 3, 5 year it has returned: 16.11%, 11.01% and 2.12% respectively. Note that the five year return is low, mostly due to the Great Recession. These bad years bring down the annualized gains for the 5 year period. So, I expect better returns from this fund, something more in the range of 10-12 % long term. That's something that can happen since this ETF closely matches the S&P 500. Also, this fund falls in the large cap category of stocks since it is made up of mostly large cap companies like those in the S&P 500. As a result, this looks like a good fund in which to invest and possibly the best of the three. But, there are others to look at before the final decision is made.

The next closed end fund to consider is the iShares S&P 600 Small Cap fund (IJR). While I tend to like actively managed small cap funds with good track records, I typically am not fond of index funds based on small caps over an index of large caps.

Furthermore, based on the title of this fund, you would think that it is a Small Cap fund and therefore should be measured against the S&P Small Cap 400 Index. While it is a small cap fund, it is not measured against the Small Cap S&P 400 index. This is a Small Cap fund but, it is measured against the S&P 500, as are all three funds discussed in this section. This fund tracks the S&P Small Cap 600 Index, and due to the great returns of small caps the last few years, this fund has had the best 3 year annualized gains of all the funds evaluated here: 13.96%. Like the IYY fund, this fund offers a low expense ratio of .16% which is below the average for most mutual funds. Anything below .80% is considered good in my opinion.

Also, it offers the growth opportunities of several growing companies. This leads to great profit potential for any long term investor. However, many financial experts expect large cap companies to out-perform small caps. Also, small caps have much higher volatility than large caps. Consequently, there is more risk with small caps. Additionally, this fund has a higher turnover ratio than the IYY fund, at 14%; the IYY fund has a very low ratio of 6%.

The last fund, the iShares Russell 1000 fund (IWF) is a fund that makes up about 50% of the Russell 1000 Index. Like the others, it offers a diversified portfolio in one easy transaction. It too has a low expense ratio of .20%. This fund's 1, 3 and 5 year returns are 15.03%, 11.14%, and 2.95% respectively.

While I know that past performance is not an indicator of future success, the 5 year return for the IWF fund does not bode well compared to the Large Cap IYY fund at 2.12% and Small Cap IJR at 11.34%. I say this with the notion that more emphasis should be placed on the 5 year returns than the 1 and 3 year returns. And while Small Cap IJR has the best 5 year gain, I like the one that comes in second place during the 5 year period: the Large Cap IYY at 2.12% annualized gain. This is based on the fact that while IJR did have the best 5 year period, I expect that in the long term IJR being a small cap fund will not beat the large cap fund of IYY for a long term period of 10 years or more. Also, with a beta that is almost identical to the S&P 500 (at 1.01), the IYY is less risky than the IJR small cap, which has a beta of 1.6.

Real Estate Investment Trusts
Some Real Estate investments have done very well the past: Real Estate Investment Trusts (REIT). REITs are a good investment due to the fact that many pay dividends and had a good appreciation due to the recovery from the housing bubble. However, with the bursting of the housing bubble, many REITs declined in value during the recession. Prior to the bursting of the housing bubble, some experts were saying that it was a bad time to buy homes and to not buy any REIT. This was a good call. While the residential market has boomed since the recovery of the housing market, the commercial market has seen only moderate growth. And since most REIT's are focused in the commercial market, it only seems

logical that buying a REIT today is still a good buy as the housing recovery will lift commercial real estate. Furthermore, a large portion of their rental income is paid out to shareholders in the form of dividends making them a good form of fixed income.

Due to the huge run-up of homes, around 15% nationally during the housing bubble, the housing market was in for a huge correction. Think about it: at 15% growth home values would double in less than 5 years, (72/15 = 4.8 years). That's exactly what happened. The price of homes had grown so fast nationally that it had outpaced wages and therefore was unsustainable. This made for a recipe where potential homeowners could not afford to become homeowners. In July 2006, there were already signs of a slowing housing market, and the only way to make homes affordable again was to have a lowering of home prices. Home prices in Florida and California were beginning to slow. There are some things an investor can do to make informed choices about real property.

Also, an investor can take it slow by buying one property at a time and wait to see how the housing market moves. An especially good technique for a real property investor would be to keep his/her full time job. This will lower the chances of failure as it takes time for real estate to pay off. Additionally, most investors should avoid being overleveraged: being too far in debt on real property can lead to tragic results. This can happen due to having too much debt, the same thing most public companies try to avoid in order prevent going bankrupt. Last but not least, the investor looking to buy real property should avoid hot areas as they are the most overpriced.

In the end, it looks like ETF funds can be a good investment, and the one most likely to prosper in my opinion is the IYY Dow Jones Total Market Fund. While it has been beaten by the small cap fund, IJR, over its 5 year period, the IYY is invested mostly in large cap stocks and should outperform the small caps in the long term. IYY at 2.12% for its 5 year annualized gain may not be so great now but give it time and it will bounce back. Additionally, buying into real estate may be good if one chooses REIT's but not so good if one decides to buy residential properties for investment purposes when the area is over heated...like those seen during the housing bubble. So, for investors looking to add assets to their portfolio, it may be that large caps fit better than small caps.

How to Choose a Good Mutual Fund: They Call Him Bruce

His name is Robert B. Bruce and he has an excellent track record, but more about him later. With over 8000 mutual funds out there, it can be difficult to find a true winner. Having spent large amount of money investing thus far, I decided to spend $20,000 on a mutual fund that had low turnover. Since a high turnover can cut into profits by forcing capital gains taxes, I chose a fund that has a turnover ratio below 33 percent. Also, after using the rule of 72 to determine how long it takes to double my money, I decided that wanted a fund that has a good long term track record that at least matches or beats the S&P 500. The S&P 500 average the last 10 years (Jan 2000-2013) has been 6.2%. In looking for a fund that beats that number, I finally came up with one. Additionally, I was not looking for a fund with a manager who is lucky (or good) at timing the market. Rather, I was looking for a manger with a good long term track record thereby reducing luck from the equation. I want a fund with a low expense ratio, lower than 1.2%. With all this in mind, I am set to choose a mutual fund (and manager) that will get my $20,000 investment.

The fund I chose was the Bruce Fund. Its investment style is best characterized as small-cap growth. It has a very low turnover, at 10.4%. That means that it takes 9 years for the manager to change all the holdings in the portfolio. Mutual funds usually have an indirect correlation between turnover and performance: as turnover went up performance went down. Furthermore, it's possible to get lower fees just by picking the Bruce Fund which has a low turnover of just 10.4%. Additionally, it has been said that funds with high turnover have a higher expense ratios (typically around 1.31) than those that trade less. This means that managers who trade less are more concerned with the long term interests of the investor and less concerned with filling his own pockets. While turnover is important, there are other attributes I look at, like beating the S&P 500.

Therefore, it is impressive that this fund has had great long term returns. With an annualized return of 15.86% the last ten years, this fund would double the $20,000 every 4.5 years. This would mean that $20,000 would turn into $160,000 in 13.6 years, a net gain before taxes of $140,000. Next, let's take a look at the background of the fund's manager.

Robert B. Bruce has been the fund manager since the fund's inception in 1983. Mr. Bruce has worked as an independent investment manager since 1974. He also holds the Chartered Financial Analyst designation. And with a 10 year return of 15.86% annually, he has beaten the S&P 500 by 7.4 percentage points per year during the period. Therefore, the fund's performance was not accomplished by a new manager with no proven track record and no experience. It was accomplished by a manager with tenure. For an investor investing for the long term, this fund is exceptional. Additionally, due to its low turnover, 10%, it is much lower than the limit I set for my fund picking limit, which happens to be 33% or less. This low turnover leads to less capital gains taxes and less transaction fees. Also, one should consider the fund's fees before buying. These fees are known as the expense ratio.

To pay for ads, pay the fund manager, and to make money fund companies have an issue they must address. That issue is called the expense ratio. While I will not buy a fund with a load, it is necessary to pay the expense ratio fee. Therefore, I like to keep this as low as possible. I like a fund with a low expense ratio, lower than 1.2%. The Bruce Fund has a 1.03% fee annually; this would cut $10.30 from every $1,000 invested every year. While this can add up over time, it is still lower than the parameter I set for choosing a mutual fund: less than 1.2%. That's much lower than the industry average for actively managed funds. However, this is a no-load fund therefore a transaction cost for purchasing this fund does not exist. You should never buy a mutual fund with a load attached to it. In most cases they are a waste of money, and nothing more than a sales fee.

The Bruce Fund has returned

Trailing Returns	As of 12.31.2012
Year to date	7.9%
1 Year	7.9%
3 Years (Annualized)	12.8%
5 Years (Annualized)	6.6%
10 Years (Annualized)	15.8%

Bottom line: mutual funds are a good investment for diversification. To have good returns they should have low expenses, a good manager, a high return that can beat the market, have a low turnover, and have no load attached to them. This can lead to a profitable investment for anyone, even a man named Bruce.

Global Investing

The most difficult and complicated foreign equity to buy is one that takes place in a country where the firm is located because it must be carried out in foreign currency. With this you add the risk of foreign currency fluctuations. As a result, buying foreign equities can take on added risk. But with the large U.S. trade deficit and the amount of outsourcing to other countries, it would seem wise for an investor to buy foreign assets. For example, in many ways these products offer the first low-cost way for U.S.-based investors to gain access to significant portions of the global economy. One way to do this would be to purchase an ETF fund that specializes in foreign companies.

ETF funds can be a great way for an investor to buy a fund like the iShares MSCI (EWT) for a price lower than its NAV. This is similar to the way Warren Buffet invests: buying assets for pennies on the dollar. For Buffett, this results in a "margin of safety" as Buffet and his mentor Benjamin Graham always proclaim. This may be possible if an investor buys a EWT fund that is trading for a 15% discount to its NAV. For example, it's like buying 85 cents on the dollar. But, there are other variables to consider when looking at this investment, like the total return and the EWT fund has not been impressive.

The Taiwan Index Fund (EWT) returned 1.61% in the last five years; the fund's inception date is 6/20/2000. In

2012, it was up 18.65%. However, this may be a sign of a fund that is in need of intensive care. Although it has a short life (12 years), it has been through the horrific bear market of 2000-2002 and the Great Recession. Consequently, during its lifetime it has returned a measly -0.68%. It does have some good news. From 2003 through 2006, it returned 16.99%. This could be a reason to like this fund...but not for the most diligent investor. Conversely there are other specialty funds that are better. They would be Sector funds, those funds that specialize in one specific industry.

Sector Funds
Sector funds are an investment fund that makes investments solely in businesses that operate in a particular industry or sector of the economy. Because the holdings of this type of fund are in the same industry, there is a lack of diversification by sector associated with these funds. Nevertheless, they can be a great way to invest. The one I like best would have to be one that is involved with the care and treatment of the aging population in the U.S. That would be a sector fund that is involved with healthcare. The one I like best is the Vanguard Healthcare Fund (VGHCX).

This Healthcare fund has had a phenomenal record and has room to grow in the coming decades. In 2005-2006, it has returned 17.37% while the S&P Health Sector Index returned only 9.28%. Additionally, it has outperformed this index during the 3, 5, and 10 year periods by returning 10.85%, 6.08% and 9.54% during those time periods respectively. All of this was done while the Spliced Health Sector Index returned 10.58%, 4.55% and 6.01% respectively. Since its inception, it has returned 16.25%, dating back to 5/23/1984. This would make a huge investment gain during the last 28 years. For example, $10,000 invested in this fund during that time period would have turned into $650,000 before fees and taxes. But, the sceptical investor is always quick to point out that, "Past performance is no guarantee of future returns." Are they right? Sure they are. So would it be a good investment? Yes I think so...it has maintained a great record for so long. But be careful as this funds manage has been there only 4 years, so he is not fully proven himself yet.

However, due to the fact the nation is getting older, there will be greater profits to be had in the healthcare industry. With 50.5% of its holdings in pharmaceuticals, 14.9% in healthcare equipment and 11.8% in managed healthcare, it seems poised to have future returns that are equally impressive. Additionally, it has a low turnover rate of only 7.7%. This is important as it lowers the capital gains taxes and historically results in better returns than funds with higher turnover ratios. The fund was closed to new investors in March 2004, but has since been opened to new investors. However, there is one downside: as stated earlier, the fund's manager has only been there 4 years. This should lead you to consider another healthcare fund as an alternative: the Vanguard Health Care Viper (VHT).

The VHT has a low expense ratio of .26%, which is very characteristic of Vanguard funds. Their funds are usually lower than the industry average. This fund also has a very low turnover rate of 9%. Two of its largest five holdings are Pfizer and Merck, both of which have been beaten down by recent litigation making them prone to future gains in the near future. There are additional advantages: tax efficiency and asset stability.

All index funds allow greater tax efficiency due to their low turnover, and their buy and hold strategy. Vipers have an additional advantage: cash flows. Conventional mutual funds have to buy at the NAV which is constructed at the end of the trading day. Conversely, Vipers enable the manager to purchase stocks at current prices. Then when the manager needs to sell, he can sell the securities to meet redemptions while allowing the cash lots to be sold at highest cost to realize a tax loss. This is something that cannot be done with regular mutual funds. Additionally, these tax losses can be used to offset capital gains for years to come.

Asset stability is another benefit of Vipers over conventional mutual funds. Vanguard Vipers are the only ETF's to track indexes created by MSCI, a provider of investment decision tools to investment institutions. The MSCI has an investment style that is objective, not subjective for index construction. Additionally the MSCI benchmarks include segmentation, style, and construction methods that Vanguard seeks in market benchmarks.

Bottom line: While the Taiwan Index Fund (EWT) has a poor return during its lifespan, it may have some future for an investor looking to diversify their portfolio. This can be especially due to the huge trade deficit and corporate outsourcing. However, sector funds may have more lifeblood and investment potential. For example, the Vanguard Healthcare fund has produced stellar returns the last 28 years but has seen a change in the fund's management in recent years. Conversely, Vanguard, has a new Viper Health Care Fund (VHT) that has been open since January 2004 and has returned 19.08%, 11.68% and 5.42% over the 1, 3 , and 5 year periods respectively. This ETF could have the same good returns that will keep it out of poor performance territory and could place it in a marathon much like its predecessor, the VGHCX.

Paid Investment Newsletters
Many times investing newsletters will dupe their prospects into subscribing. The way they do this is that many times they will inflate the investment returns of their recommendations to impressive numbers. However, they usually just make up these returns to sound impressive. As a result, they are able to fool their prospects into buying a subscription of their lengthy (years usually) and very expensive newsletters. This is done many times in order to get new subscribers to believe in the "hyped up numbers" even though the recommendations in the newsletters don't come

138

anywhere close to providing the kind of returns that they claim.

Many times investors who subscribe to these investing newsletters expecting great returns will only to be disappointed at the poor returns. Most of the time, they are better off buying no newsletter subscription whatsoever and merely investing in S&P 500 Index fund. Or better yet, they should buy individual stocks after careful research.

I have subscribed to a reputable, well-known investing newsletter only to be disappointed. After a one-year subscription in which my returns were abysmal, I cancelled the subscription and was happier and more successful picking my own stocks. In other words, the low returns of the recommendations for almost every stock that was selected by the newsletter did not do very well as a whole or even individually. Therefore, my recommendation to you is to forgo the investing newsletter because most likely the person making money on the newsletter is not the subscribers, but rather the person running the newsletter. You, as a newsletter subscriber, will not.

Think about it! A newsletter can get the owner of the newsletter very high returns for each member who subscribes for and pays a fee. If their recommendations were as profitable as they proclaim, they would not give away all his investing secrets in a subscription newsletter.

Rather they would keep the tips for themselves and make the money in the market. The real way they make money in the stock market it so fill their subscriptions up with subscribers to their newsletters. Conversely, some investing newsletters can be very educational and therefore can be a solid educational tool for investors.

Key Differences about Percentages

There are big differences between percentage points and percentages. Since the differences are quite significant, investors should be aware of them. For example, if 10% increased to 12% it would be a difference of two percentage points, (12%-10%=2%). However, the percentage difference is more significant: it is actually a 20% difference (10% X 20% = 2%, then added to 10% = 12%). In other words, 20% of 10% is two percentage points. Therefore when add the two percentage points are added together with the 10% and you get 12%. Thus, the difference between 12% and 10% is both 20% and 2 percentage points. It is important to understand these differences when reading financial literature. The reasons should be obvious.

Therefore don't be misled by magazines or media that say that an investing newsletter or stock has outperformed S&P 500 by 200%. While it sounds impressive, it may not be. The 200% outperformance may be not as significant as you would otherwise think. For example, a newsletter claims that their newsletter beat the S&P 500 by 200%. Then you find that the S&P 500 was up by only 4% last year, and the investing newsletter was up 8% for the year.

140

It clearly could have beaten the S&P 500 by 200% because the percentage difference may between 4% and 8% is 200% but it is only a 4 percentage point difference (8% - 4%).

Rebalancing a Portfolio

The rebalancing a portfolio is important because it keeps the investor in his set risk and reward balance. This helps the investor to have the best opportunity to buy low and sell high. For example, if the investor rebalances his portfolio every year (or sooner) he is able to sell his stock after reaching optimal highs. Conversely, those that hold certain assets too long (i.e., poor performing stocks, mutual funds) may diminish their returns and end up with mediocre returns. Rebalancing is a way to reassess your investments and move money around as needed at regular intervals.

Chapter 4:
Income Investing

Investing In Bonds

Bonds are one of the best ways to add income to an investment portfolio. They are also used by conservative investors due to their ability to produce income and low risk. Bonds should be at least a small part of investor's portfolio.

Municipal Bonds

Since municipal bonds are generally exempt from federal income tax (and usually from state and local taxes), they are most beneficial to someone in a high tax bracket. For example, an investor would have to get 6% from a non-tax exempt bond –or bond fund– to equal that of a municipal bond paying 3.6% because of the tax benefits. That is provided that the investor falls in the 40% tax bracket. If the investor is in the 35% tax bracket, a 3.9% municipal bond would equal a 6% non tax-exempt bond. For example, an investor with 10 million to invest (yes, it is a large amount, but I am using it to illustrate a point) in a tax exempt bond municipal bond could make $390,000 in income in one year at 3.9%. Conversely, if the investor invested in a non-tax exempt bond or bond fund at 6%, his income would be $600,000. But if his tax bracket was 40%, he would end up paying $210,000 in taxes and net him $390,000 (exactly the same as the exempt bond would net at 3.9%) (See figure 5.1 for more on the real returns of municipal bonds).

If a Bond Returns	& Income Tax Bracket	Real Return after Tax =
6.0%	40%	3.6%
6.0%	35%	3.9%
5.5%	40%	3.3%
5.5%	35%	3.6%
4.8%	40%	2.9%
4.8%	35%	3.1%
3.8%	40%	2.3%
3.8%	35%	2.5%

Figure 5.1

Investing for Income

Investing for income can be a very good way to get a stream of income on a regular basis. But, bonds are

144

usually bad investment for the long term when compared with stocks. Nevertheless, they should be used for investors looking for a safe haven and those looking for a stream of income. After a portfolio has individual stocks and mutual funds, investing in bonds can be wise choice. Therefore, when you get closer to retirement, your portfolio should contain a larger portion of bonds. However, it is best to keep some of your portfolio in stocks even as you get near retirement.

Additionally, investors already in retirement should have some stocks, albeit a small portion of their portfolio. Before critiquing this strategy, think about it. A retiree could live another 30 or 40 years in retirement, and what better way to grow a nest egg than to have some of your money in equities. Of course this recommendation to retirees is only recommended if they have enough to live in retirement from all income they currently receive. As this chapter is focused on bonds, it is critical to point out the disadvantages of bonds. They do have their downside.

Bonds have an inverse relationship with interest rates. When rates go down, bond prices go up. And the opposite is true: when interest rates go up, bond prices go down. As the price of a bond goes down, the lower the overall return for bond investor. With interest rates so low in 2012 and 2013,it is likely that bonds in the future years will have very low returns. When you add the real rate of return...that is, the return after inflation...bonds may have a negative return for investors. There are ways to avoid this bond trap and that would be to buy intermediate or short term bond funds. These funds can have good returns as they mature at different intervals. Why is that important? Because when the bond matures, the fund manager will replace it with another bond.

If the new bond added to the fund was bought when interest rates are higher, the result is a fund that will average up leading to better investment returns for the entire fund. Several mutual fund companies have some good bond funds to consider. Vanguard and Fidelity are some of the more reputable ones, but there are others so don't limit your options. However, if you want to buy an individual bond, consider a municipal bond before making a decision to buy a taxable bond.

Dividend Stocks

Another way to get income from investing is to buy dividend paying stocks. In 2012, the payout ratio (cash on hand that is paid out to shareholders) of companies in the S&P 500 was 34%. This is well below the historical average of 54%. This indicates that much of the cash on hand could be paid out to shareholders in the form of dividends, and is a likely outcome in the future.

More on Rising Interest Rates

What impact do interest rates have on our daily lives? Is it better for rates to go up or go down? Well that depends on who you ask. It can be good when interest rates are moving up...well sort of. Let me explain the pros and cons of rising interest rates. The pros of rising interest rates are: an increase in the stock market and it can control inflation.

However, the negative side of rising interest rates are costly. They result in higher borrowing costs for consumers to buy a home or auto. Also, it leads to higher costs for businesses to operate as they must borrow at higher rates when they want to expand. As already discussed, bond prices go down which results in lower returns for bond investors.

Benefits of Higher Interest Rates
However, when interest rates go up, not all of the outcomes are negative. It allows those invested in equities to earn more. This can happen as businesses begin to see a rise in demand for their products as consumers have more money to borrow and spend. Furthermore, investors will shy away from bonds and move to stocks which in turn will raise stock prices. However, when the Fed raises interest rates in a weak economy, it will usually slow the economy and lower stock prices.

It should be noted, however, that rising interest rates could have a negative impact on companies as businesses are forced to borrow at higher rates, thus reducing their earnings. Nevertheless, generally the rise in interest rates causes an increase in prices (at the wholesale and retail level) resulting in more profits for companies. But, high

interest rate environment is not the situation we see in
2012-2013 as interest rates are low even from a historical
perspective.

THE BOND KING: Maybe the Best Bond Manager

Investing in a world of bulls and bears, it can seem logical
to pick a bond fund over a stock mutual fund. But, where
does one go to get the best value and return while
reducing risk. That answer can be found in the PIMCO
Total Return Admin (PTRAX) managed since May 10,
1987 by Bill Gross. He has been labeled the Bond King
by the media. Typically, I like index funds for their low
expense ratios and consistency. However, it's wise to
give Bill Gross a try. After all, he has had a phenomenal
record during his tenure as the manager of the PIMCO
Total Return Admin.

With a return of 7.41% since the fund's inception, an
investor could double their money every 9.7 years. This
means that an investment of $250,000 would double to
$500,000 in less than 10 years. While this is lower than
the higher returns seen in many stock mutual funds, it is
very good for an investment since bonds are more secure
and less volatile than stocks. His PIMCO fund invests
mostly in investment-grade corporate bonds and Treasury
bonds. And with an expense ratio of .68% it is below the
average bond fund expense ratio of .71%. Furthermore, it
is eligible for dollar cost averaging, a steady way to make
an ongoing investment. The fund could be purchased at
PIMCO's website at no fee. Additionally, the low risk

148

of their principal. Of course this assumes a steady rate of 7%, and does not account for inflation.

Whether it's from their jobs or from portfolio income, people like to keep the money they earn. Why work so hard to give your money to Uncle Sam or to an investment firm? This is a key concept for most investors. Therefore, one key ingredient for investing should always be keeping as much money for you as possible. That's why low operating fees are very important. The operating fees for index funds have always been lower than those of actively managed funds. The reason: index funds will not need a manager to pick bonds. The index fund just matches the bonds found in the Lehman Brothers Aggregate Bond Index. Therefore, the expense ratio, which consists of the fund managers fees, is lower. For example, the expense ratio of the Vanguard Total Bond Market Index is a low .18%, compared with 1.1% average for actively managed bond funds. This results in an additional $65,500 after 20 years on a $100,000 initial investment assuming an annualized 7% return. Of course there are other reasons to like index funds.

One of the best ways to reduce risk when investing is to have diversification. Much can be said for diversification. It is one of the reasons why mutual funds (both of bonds and stocks) are so successful. It is one of the keys to keeping your money safe in the event of a bankruptcy, or sector that goes bad, like the tech sector of the late

1990's. It does this by allowing one to invest their money in several bonds, thus reducing the risk and this can be done with smaller amounts of money. The Vanguard Total Bond Market Index is an index fund that tracks the entire bond market. Therefore, this fund is more diversified than almost all actively managed bond funds. As a result, the amount of risk is reduced. For example, if the fund has 50 companies, and 1 goes bankrupt, there could potentially be a 2% loss. But, if there are 100 companies involve the loss would be only 1%. Therefore, many times the more companies involved, the lower the amount of risk. However, index bond funds have their disadvantages.

The fact that some very talented bond fund managers may be left out of one's investment portfolio has its drawbacks. Bill Gross of PIMCO has more than three decades of experience managing money in the bond market. This type of experience may not be enough in and of itself, but Mr. Gross does have a stellar record: 9% in the last decade. Additionally, his PIMCO fund has a low expense ratio of .43%. Therefore, the return on $100,000 in his fund would return an additional $110,071 (based on past performance) over the index fund like the Vanguard Total Bond Market Index during a 20 year period. Therefore, ignoring actively managed funds can have its disadvantages. There may be other reasons investors chose actively-managed funds.

I believe that many people still invest in actively-managed funds due to many reasons. One reason may be that some investors are not aware of them. Also, sometimes investors chase risk and since some actively-managed funds outperform index funds, these investors are trying to beat these bond indexes. To their credit, sometimes they are right but most of the times they are not.

As discussed earlier, it can be seen that index funds are passively managed and therefore they have lower expense ratios and a lower turnover ratio. They also have more diversification due to the fact they include all the bonds of the Lehman Brothers Aggregate Bond Index which thereby decreases risk as the greater the amount of companies involved, the lower the percentage of loss if one should go bankrupt and not be able to pay its creditors. Additionally, they are consistently returning 7.05% over a ten year period making them a good investment. However, passively investing can have its drawbacks when compared to actively managed funds. For example, the stellar returns of the PIMCO fund by Bill Gross makes actively managed funds look like a good buy. Additionally, some investors still invest in actively-managed funds even though they usually don't beat index funds. This may be due to lack of knowledge of index funds. But, overall I like the passively managed bond funds like the Vanguard Total Bond Market Index Fund due to their consistency, low expenses, and diversification. That is why boring can be fun...and profitable.

153

Chapter 5: Economics, Business Cycles, and Investing

Stock Market Overview

The stock market is one is one of the best ways for companies to raise money for their capital ventures. They will offer IPO's, and sell bonds to raise cash for their operations and to grow.

Additionally, exchanges also act as the clearinghouse for each transaction, and guarantee payment. This lowers the risk to the investor that the counterparty could default on the transaction. The smooth operations of all these activities promotes economic growth and lowers costs and risks while promoting the production of goods and

155

services and employment for the workforce. In this way the financial system contributes to increased prosperity.

Societies increased interest in investing in the stock market, either buying individual stocks or through the purchase of mutual funds. The major part of this adjustment in financial portfolios has gone directly to shares, but a good deal now takes the form of various kinds of institutional investment for groups of individuals such as pension funds, mutual funds, and hedge funds. The trend towards forms of saving with a higher risk has been accentuated by new rules for most funds and insurance, allowing a higher share to bonds. The New York Stock Exchange has an admission about the severe impact of tighter and more costly regulations that were introduced in the wake of the Enron scandal on the number of international companies coming to Wall Street.

Stock in a Non-U.S. Company

An American Depositary Receipt (ADR) is the method that some of the foreign companies trade in stock markets. Instead of buying shares of foreign-based companies in overseas markets, Americans can purchase shares in the form of ADRs. These so called ADRs, which are issued in cooperation with the foreign company whose equity shares will underlie the related American Depositary Shares (ADS), are eligible for listing on a major U.S. Exchange and get the benefits and rights, and the right to receive reports. Un-sponsored ADRs, issued without the involvement of the underlying foreign company, may not

156

get those same rights and the shares generally trade over-the-counter.

In summation, it can be seen that it can be difficult for U.S. companies to raise money in the U.S. than in the rest of the world. However, it is not generally worthwhile for a non-U.S. company to get lost on a U.S exchange due to things like inflation, interest rates, GDP growth rates, and political and economic risks. Furthermore it can be said that these variables happen for U.S. corporations listed on a foreign exchange as well.

How Inflation Effects Investing

Inflation can be harmful at times. With some investors tying their money up in real estate, it would seem that inflation could be a good thing. Conversely, for an investor who has most of his assets in the stock market, and none invested in real estate, inflation would have a harmful impact on some investor's finances: both their pay check and investments. I will further discuss the impact inflation would have on some investor's finances and how it may be a good thing for others.

First of all, inflation has a way of lowering the purchasing power of one's income. A worker's pay check would dwindle if there was a large increase in inflation. Currently most workers pay raises are usually between 2-4% per year. If the rate of inflation was substantially higher than this, it would be appropriate for the Federal Reserve Chairman to lower the interest rates...provided that inflation is occurring. This would lower the rate of inflation. Therefore, the purchasing power of a worker's income would not suffer. If there was rampant inflation, many consumers would not be interested in buying a car or home. Furthermore, many consumers would be interested in saving more money in money market accounts as the interest rates paid would rise due to a rise in the Fed funds rate. This would happen due to the fact that the Fed reserve would be trying to curtail inflation. Thus, with the rise its interest rates would spill over into banks giving higher returns for deposit accounts. As for investing, it can be difficult to make wise decisions during inflationary periods. Nonetheless, a good choice in an inflationary period would be a real estate investment trusts (REITs).

Real Estate Investment Trusts

When investing during high inflationary time, an investor would be wise to chose real estate investment trusts (REITs). This decision comes from the fact that some investments in the stock market could be reduced. For example, if an investor in an S&P 500 were to get 12% annually per year for 10 years, and the rate of inflation during this time was 8%, the real return would be a mere 4% per annum. This would be very low considering the amount of risk placed in such an investment when the historical real rate of return over the last 70 years in the S&P 500 has been around 8-9% after accounting for inflation. REITs would be a wise investment choice in a high inflationary period. This would occur due to the amount of rents going up on the commercial and

158

residential properties owned by REITs. Additionally, REIT owners would gain wealth by the appreciation of the properties owned in these funds. Therefore, inflation would be beneficial for REIT investors. There are other ways to make money during high inflation. One of those ways would be to investing real estate.

Due to an increase in prices and the decrease in purchasing power of the dollar by inflation, one of the best hedges against inflation is to own real estate. After all, it is going to cost more money to reproduce a piece of property due to higher costs of materials and higher costs for labor. This would result in rapid appreciation of most real estate in most parts of the country. Therefore, just like owners of REITs, those that own real estate, inflation can become tolerable and maybe enjoyable due to potential prosperity. This hedge against inflation should be considered by investors concerned about an overheated economy.

It can be said that inflation can have a negative influence in most people's lives as it lowers the purchasing power of one's income. Furthermore, investments can decrease as the real rate of return is lowered by the amount of inflation encountered, something known as inflation risk. But, if someone invests in REITs or buys real estate, the negative impact from inflation can seem tame and maybe even welcome to some investors.

Raising the Fed funds rate controls inflation

When the money supply is abundant due to low interest rates, many businesses are inclined to raise prices thereby causing inflation. Therefore, when in 2000 Federal Reserve Chairman, Alan Greenspan, began to raise rates it was due to a fear of that ugly situation: inflation. Of course part of the rationale for this action had to do with the housing bubble that we were experiencing. Now for another positive and negative outcome of rising interest rates: bond prices go down. That is good for the buyer of a bond, but bad for the existing holder of that bond.

As noted earlier, bond prices tend to go down when interest rates go up. Therefore, if an investor wants to invest in corporate debt during rising interest rates, he would expect to pay less for the bond, thus yielding higher interest rates on his investment. This is one of the cons of rising interest rates as it allows investors another place to park their money, especially those investors looking for a fixed income stream. However, the existing holder of the bond will lose out to the bond's price decline.

Another disadvantage of higher interest rates: higher borrowing costs for a home. For example, the average rate on a 30 year fixed mortgage was around 3.5% in 2012. With rates low, it would seem wise to get a mortgage before interest rates climb significantly higher.

The Banking Act of 1933 and Investing

The Glass-Steagall Act was enacted during the Great Depression to protect banks and safeguard consumers and the financial systems. Since its enactment, the Glass-Steagall Act has restricted the securities activities and affiliations of banks, separating commercial banking from investment banking. This was done due to several reasons such as the conflicts of interest for depositors and the banks; the decreased trust in the banking systems; and the possibility of further banking failures, just to name a few problems that this act supposedly corrected. However, there were some reasons for repeal. I will cover the effects of this repeal on banks, bank customers, and for investors.

First, to look at the effects of the Glass-Steagall repeal on banks, it is wise to consider why the repeal happened in 1999. To begin, it was started to lower the likelihood of a conflict of interest with commercial banks and their customers in 1933, just after the Great Depression. However, several studies were conducted and found that commercial banks had little responsibility for the occurrence of the 1929 Great Depression. A second action that helped to repeal the Glass-Steagall Act was that regulators allowed U.S. Banks to undertake limited securities and insurance practices in recent years. This, along with the fact that new technology at the time allowed for cost reduction of cross selling financial products, resulted in the repeal. Legislators claim that the repeal of Glass-Steagall will save consumers of financial services some 15 billion a year.

Looking at the benefits to investors of the Glass-Steagall, it is apparent that there can be some negative implications from this repeal. Some proponents of the Glass-Steagall Act consider it useful. For example, a serious conflict of interest exists when a bank underwrites securities issued by a corporation that has loans outstanding. In effect, control of the underwriting process may enable the bank to shift potential loan losses to public investors.

Further conflicts of interest can be daunting for investors: A practical example concerns the securities underwriting business, which pits the interests of the issuer of the securities against those of the acquirers of the securities in the sense that a good price for one is less good for the other. Although conflicts of interest are inherent in many financial institutions, it appears that this repeal may have increased that inherent risk. Nonetheless, I feel that it has some benefits for investors.

Ethics and regulations in brokerage services and the insurance industry is the responsibility of the government and business leaders. For example Sarbanes-Oxley Act is one of the investor protection acts implemented by the Securities and Exchange Commission (SEC). This act is in place to require enhanced accounting standards by public companies. Further responsibility belongs to the CEO and Board of Directors of these companies. Of course these laws and ethics must be implemented and followed. As a result, the benefits (for investors) of the repeal of the Glass-Steagall Act can be seen in improved services and lower costs for investment services.

For example, Bank of America offers online trading accounts for as low as $10 per trade for checking account customers, while non account customers are charged $14 per trade. This $4 savings can add up over time for active traders. The focus here is banks. It is duly noted that brokerage firms can offer much lower trading fees...and therefore should be a first consideration.

Bottom Line: Banks and their customers seem to be winners in the repeal of the Glass-Steagall Act. Investors, according to many experts, seem to be potential losers in this change due to the possibility of conflicts of interest. Nonetheless, investors too can benefit from lower brokerage and insurance costs from the banks, and ultimately the conflicts of interest can be curtailed by CEO's and Board of Directors doing their part by abiding by securities laws and upholding business ethics.

Capital Asset Pricing Model (CAPM)

In looking at the different types of asset pricing models such as CAPM and APT, I find that there are advantages and disadvantages to both. First, I will look at the advantages and disadvantages of Capital Asset Pricing Model (CAPM). Then, I will look at the advantages and disadvantages of Arbitrage Pricing Theory (APT).

In the end, I find that even though both have advantages and disadvantages, APT seems to be the best approach for financial professionals to use.

Basically CAPM says that the expected return on an asset is equal to the risk free rate (like a T-Bill) plus a premium based on the asset's beta, and the expected risk on the market portfolio. Therefore, if a stock has a beta of 0, then the formula of CAPM will nullify the expected return to be any higher than the risk free rate. Therefore, if the risk free rate is 5% (for example, like a T-Bill), and then the expected return on a stock with a beta of zero will be 5%. Likewise, a stock with a beta of one and a market portfolio of 13%, will result in an expected return of 13%, which is equal to the stock market, due to the beta of 1, E(R) =5% + 1(13%-5%) = 13%. Likewise a stock with a beta with a beta of 2 will be expected to have an expected return of 21% (all other variables being equal), E(R) =5% + 2(13%-5%) = 21%. One would expect double beta rate of 2 to produce an expected return of double 13%, resulting in an expected return of 26%, but this is not the case. This is one of the strengths of CAPM, as it gives investors a higher expected return for investments that have higher risk. Also, because investors can diversify, they can have portfolios that maximize expected return for any level of risk. This can be seen in the linear relationship that CAPM has with expected return and risk: the higher the expected return, the higher the beta, moving in a linear relationship. However, there are some disadvantages to CAPM: false assumption of a constant risk-free rate and the fact that no investment is risk-free; and a constant, non-changing beta. These are shortcomings for CAPM.

First, CAPM assumes a risk-free rate that will stay the same all the time. This is not the case. Changes in interest rates, inflation, and other economic factors can have an influence of the risk-free rate (like that of T-Bills). This can lead to Treasury securities that can fluctuate over time. Also, no investment is truly risk free, even treasury securities, like T-bills are backed by full faith in the U.S. government. As a result, these are disadvantages in CAPM.

These shortcomings in CAPM come from using Beta. Betas can change from time to time, and not stay constant as CAPM assumes. This can lead to an ineffective expected return for an asset priced using CAPM. Also, since CAPM measures securities differently based only on their differences in beta, this makes it an asset pricing model that has one variable. This makes it one-dimensional and less effective than other asset pricing models. Now, let's look at Arbitrage Pricing Theory (APT).

APT is considered an alternative to CAPM. It is seen as one that assumes that investors know returns on assets to follow a relationship of risk being equal to the sum of many risk factors such as interest rates, inflation, exchange rates, oil prices and economic growth. These are

165

systemic risks and cannot be overlooked. Systemic factors are the major sources of risk in portfolio returns (Roll, 1995). Actual portfolio returns can vary as they are sensitive to each risk factor in different ways. Because of these systemic risk factors, they signify the expected return and risks involved in a portfolio. Consequently, stocks with the same risk factors should offer the same expected return. Unlike the CAPM asset pricing model, which is a single-factor driven model, the APT pricing model is determined by a group of several factors. Therefore, each risk factor has its own set of risk factors. This places a more comprehensive asset pricing model for APT than CAPM. Even though APT is more thorough and therefore accurate than CAPM, it does have its shortcomings.

Due to the fact that asset returns are also affected by influences that are not systematic to the economy, it can place certain influences on a particular industry. This can lead to a shortfall in the accuracy of APT. Furthermore, APT offers no guidance on which factors should be the most important or how many factors to include. This leaves much to interpretation, making APT somewhat subjective.

Bottom line, it seems that CAPM is a single beta factor used in asset pricing; it is easy to use and has been in use by professionals for many years. However, CAPM has many disadvantages, one of them being beta fluctuations. In looking at APT, we can see that it seems to be a more thorough asset pricing model in that is uses more betas to assess the expected return of an asset. In looking at both, I feel that APT is the best approach for financial professionals to use.

CAPM: Case Study

In this scenario, John uses a beta of .811 for ConocoPhillips (COP), which is lower than the S&P 500, but higher than the risk free rate of zero. Therefore, looking at COP in a portfolio of companies, it would seem that John is taking more risk than in buying a T-bill, and likewise would expect a greater return for the higher risk. The hypothetical analysis would go as follows:

Since the securities markets give no reward for bearing unsystematic risk and only a reward for systematic risk, John is looking for companies to complement COP. Therefore, in terms of choosing COP, he is dealing with a company with a beta that has lower risk than the overall market. In using CAPM to calculate the expected rate of return, John finds the following: the expected rate of return for COP with its beta of .811 and using a risk free rate of 5% and an expected market rate of 12% would result in an expected return of, $E(R) = 5\% + .811(12\% - 5\%) = 10.68\%$. Because the stock has a relatively low beta, the expected return is below that of the overall market expected rate of return. Next, John adds to this portfolio a stock with a high beta and comes up with a higher expected rate of return.

167

In this Yahoo scenario, he uses a beta of 2.922 for Yahoo. Using the CAPM model, he comes up with the following: E (R) = 5% + 2.922(12% - 5%) = 27.45%. In finding such a high-expected rate of return for a higher risk, he would be tempted to place a mix of 60% in COP stock and 40% in Yahoo stock if there were only two assets in the portfolio. However, the second company he adds in this portfolio is Pfizer (PFE).

In this Pfizer scenario, John uses a very low beta of 0.413. With such a low beta, the expected rate of return will no doubt be lower than the overall market of 12%, as computed below:

E (R) = 5% + .413(12% - 5%) = 7.89 %. Because of the low expected rate of return, especially if the risk free rate is 5%, John would make the mix of portfolio as follows: 40% Yahoo, 30% COP, and 30% Pfizer. We can see how the numbers compute below: 27.45% (.40) + 10.68 % (.30) + 7.89% (.30) = 16.55 %.

With this mix of assets being diversified and having a good rate of return at 16.55%, John would feel good about this portfolio of assets. With this mix of Yahoo with a high beta, 2.922, and Pfizer and COP with their low betas of .413 and .811 respectively, John's portfolio is diversified overall with a good expected rate of return, 16.55%.

FIAT and the Money System

In the history of money, many things are involved which include, the Royal monopoly of Minting, paper money, bills of exchange, Virginian Tobacco, and the Gold Standard, just to name a few. With most of these standards of money one of the most important is "the gold standard". It would seem that we have evolved into a better money system by moving to the Fiat system. Therefore it seems that there are many reasons to both like and dislike the gold standard. I will discuss the pros of the gold standard such as how it prevents inflation and sets a fixed pattern of exchange rates (which has both pros and cons).

As I will discuss, it seems that the best method may be to stay with the Fiat system and oppose Jack Kemps' point of view on the gold standard due to three key factors of the Fiat system: less likely to experience depressions; potential for higher unemployment with the gold standard; and the gold standard sets a fixed pattern of exchange rates, which can lead to a shock in one country affecting another.

First, let's discuss the benefits of the Gold Standard as it is so favored by Jack Kemp. While the gold standard prevents a country from printing too much money, it controls the amount of money printed by preventing too much paper money. Additionally, since too much paper money in circulation causes inflation, the gold standard helps to control inflation. As a result, paper money has its

169

ups and downs since its value changes so much with economic conditions. When there is a large amount of money in circulation, prices go up and paper money buys less. This is inflation is its purest form and inflation is a killer to the real returns of bond holders.

Since most buyers of 10 year bonds are buying on the hopes that there will be little inflation during the 10 year period of their purchase, it would be a loss of their money if inflation was 6 % and their bond was paying only 5%. This type of situation makes inflation seem detrimental to bond investors. Therefore, many bond investors are obsessed with inflation. It is well documented that inflation in the 1970's and early 80's was out of control. Coincidently, the inflation occurred after President Nixon signed into effect the Fiat monetary system effectively stopping the gold standard. Consequently, inflation soared above historical averages when the gold standard was removed and replaced with the Fiat system. Additionally, with the Fiat system during the time period of 1971 to 1990, the inflation average was 4.2 percent. Conversely, there are pros to the gold standard as evident of fixed exchange rates.

The gold standard sets a fixed pattern of exchange rates which cause the price levels around the world to move together. This happens by growth in one country enhancing another. The end result would be a balance of prices among countries. When prices have a degree of uncertainty such as the case with the Fiat system, it tends

170

to make economic analysis difficult for countries to make trades. This can have an economic impact on all countries that trade internationally. However, having a fixed exchange rate can have a negative effect as well.

It is less likely that we will experience a depression as seen during the Great Depression; not even the Great Recession of 2007 was as severe. With the use of the Fiat system the Federal Reserve was semmingly able to stop one potential great depression. During the 1987 stock market crash, in which the loss was greater than the crash of 1929, the Federal Reserve was able to respond with an expansion of the money supply. This led to a continued growth of the 80's and 90's leading to one of the greatest economic booms of all time in American History. This would not have been possible with the gold standard in place. Therefore, it seems that the gold standard has major flaws, to include higher unemployment and less stable control of the economy.

Problem with Gold Standard

The gold standard has a potential for higher unemployment. Since the gold standard gives government little authority to control the use of monetary policy, economies are less able avoid monetary shocks. As a result, unemployment was higher during the gold standard. It averaged 6.8 percent in the United States between 1879 and 1913 versus 5.6 percent between 1946 and 1990.

This in itself bodes well for the Fiat system and discourages the gold standard as a monetary system. Additionally, another disadvantage of the gold standard is fixed exchange rates.

The gold standard sets a fixed pattern of exchange rates which can lead to a shock in one country affecting another. If a country had a monetary disaster, other countries could not protect themselves from the mishap. For example, when the Great Depression struck the U.S, it quickly affected markets overseas. So many people were left holding banknotes that were reduced by about one third. This reduction would not have happened worldwide with a Fiat system. However, with the gold standard it did and as a result many countries severed ties with it. Britain left the gold standard behind in 1931.

Bottom line: While it seems that the gold standard had its place in our monetary system, it seems that the Fiat system may be a better money system. It is less likely to lead to depressions, lead to lower unemployment, and reduce the risk of monetary shock in one country affecting another. Nonetheless the gold standard did have its advantages which included the fact that it prevents inflation. It could further be seen that the gold standard had benefits from the fixed exchange rate which seemed to be a double edged sword: it can be positive (it can make trade and planning easier and more economical) and negative (by making countries volatile to each other). In the end, I do not agree with Jack Kemp about a return to the gold standard. I like the Fiat system best for all its advantages discussed earlier. After all, it is more than a car.

Investor Confidence and Scandals

Is more desirable or less desirable to be to a CFO in today's scandal ridden corporate world? CEO's and CFO's have a strong influence on a corporation, like deciding when a company will pay or increase a dividend, or what a company's needs are and how it will finance them. It seems that there is more here than meets the eye and that many factors would lead me to believe that it is less desirable to be a CFO. The fact is that many of today's CFOs face more stress due to a very volatile economy, increased rigid accounting guidelines that prevent fraud, and the recovery from the Great Recession.

Due to the very nature of the fact that Wall Street expects good earnings reports for companies, it can lead to many executives in an organization competing to meet these expectations to satisfy Wall Street. The result can lead to abuse via scandals, like the one that brought down Enron in 2001. This can be further compounded by the fact that the economy is still recovering from the recession. This leads to investors not having confidence in the market. To rebuild the image of Wall Street and the market, many executives will fabricate the numbers. This in turn will increase shareholder value but at a cost. The perceived increase in stock value can have a domino effect. This in turn can lead to other executive at competing companies doing the same thing to boost their earnings so not to look bad in the face of the competition. As a result, it is very stressful for the CFO.

Add to this the Sarbanes-Oxley act, and the overall responsibility of the financial condition of the company, and you have a very demanding situation for an executive. This can be controlled in an environment that has a strong business, very little competition, and good financials. But how long can a situation like this last? Well, to be certain the job of CFO is very stressful at best.

The job of the CFO is further compounded by the Securities and Exchange Commission (SEC), who is there to protect the shareholder's interest. While the SEC is needed to prevent fraud, deceit, and misrepresentation by corporations, it can lead to companies not meeting earnings report deadlines and the need to re-state earnings. This all leads to investor mistrust. Who wants to invest in company who has to re-state earnings? I would not choose a company that has any indication of possible accounting irregularities as an investment. The very nature of corporations today is to meet expectations and beat competitors in their industry. This problem can be further increased by the fact that many investors have lost confidence in the stock market after the technology bust. So what happens to investor's money today?

Housing Boom and Bust

From 2001-2007 many people became interested in the housing boom and the quick rise in home prices. This euphoria for homes led to more money going into real estate instead of the stock market. This resulted in less demand for stocks and lower stock prices. With so much money in real assets and less in equities, it can lead to a more demanding job for executives, especially the CFO. Furthermore, when economists and financial analysts predict a slow recovery, it becomes a self fulfilling prophecy as it lowers investor confidence. This further perpetuates distrust in the market. After all the bear market that ran from 2000-2002 led many investors to believe the stock market to be a big gambling machine. The same thing is happening during the recovery from the Great Recession. Therefore, retail investors had to ask themselves: why should they put their money in the stock market when they can buy a tangible asset like real estate?

Furthermore, the combined results of the volatile stock market decreased investor confidence. Combine this with a shift in investor money to real estate and the job of the CFO becomes more complex. Therefore, the position of CFO seems to be less desirable position than in the past, especially in the times before the Enron scandal.

Using Currency Hedging

Currency hedging is used both by financial investors to lower the risks they encounter when investing overseas, as well as by non-financial actors in the global economy for whom multi-currency activities are used.

In weighing the costs/benefits of hedging by multinational firms, it can be said that there are some advantages and disadvantages. However, in weighing the costs and benefits, I feel that it is beneficial for firms to use it at times.

The cost of labor variables dictate that much of the commodities created in the global economy today goes on in China and Asia. The cost benefit of moving manufacturing to outsource providers outweighs the uncertainties of never having done business in foreign countries. Many businesses are jumping into the fray and becoming part of the globalization trend of moving manufacturing operations overseas. The benefits of doing this, however, come with numerous risks that were never a problem when manufacturing was done at home. One of these risks is currency risk.

Currency Risk

Currency risk is the cost of manufacturing goods in another country's currency other than the one in which you sell the finished goods. As a result, there is the risk that the foreign country's currency may be extremely volatile and therefore it may destroy the margin between what a company pays to produce its product, and what it can collect when they sell it. The fact that a company may be selling its product in a foreign country, it must

176

hedge against the currency risk. Therefore when a company converts all costs on the production side, and all sales receipts from the retail side back into its home currency, the company may be alarmed to find that its profits have diminished somewhat, or possibly disappeared completely. The currency risk that multinational companies must deal with when they have many product sales in foreign countries is paramount to doing business globally. Therefore, currency hedging is the life insurance a company can purchase to limit the impact of doing business in a foreign country. This unpredictable risk impacts a business, the same way not having home insurance on a home to protect it from unexpected events beyond your control. However, it can be difficult to implement.

Sometimes currency hedging is not always available, but is readily found at least in the major currencies of the world economy to include Europe, Japan. Currency hedging, like many other forms of financial hedging, can be done in two primary ways: with standardized contracts, or with customized contracts.

It may be that a hedge fund based in United States finds a great company to invest in, but doesn't want to necessarily be investing in the currency of the country this company resides in, like a company that is based in Brazil. Therefore, the hedge fund can separate out the credit risk from the currency risk by hedging out the currency risk. In effect, this means that the investment the hedge fund makes into the company is effectively a USD investment in Brazil. Hedging their product allows the investor to transfer the currency risk to someone else who does want to take a position in the currency. The U.S. based hedge fund has to pay this other investor to take on the currency exposure, the same way you pay any insurance company to provide insurance against an unknown outcome. The gamble the insurance provider takes is that the ultimate outcome during the period insured will not exceed the amount the buyer paid. However, the insurance provider may be hedging their own risk on a similar transaction.

In this way, the global economy becomes more efficient, because two investors are able to take positions they both want. Let's take a look at what would happen if the hedging product weren't available: the hedge fund in the U.S. isn't able to strip out the currency risk from the credit risk it wants to take. Therefore, it decides not to make the investment in the Brazilian company because it is too risky for its risk tolerance. The Brazilian company runs out of operating capital because it can't get credit locally, and therefore the company has to shut down or cut back. Brazil loses both jobs, as well as economic output. Additionally, the investment returns of the hedge fund may suffer as well.

Among the risks companies can address with credit derivatives are investment portfolio exposures, loan portfolio or line-of-credit exposures, counterparty credit risks, or credit risks associated with supply contracts.

The most common credit derivatives are credit default swaps, in which the buyer of protection transfers credit risk to a second party for a price, often expressed in basis points on a notional amount. In return, the seller agrees to make a certain payment to the buyer of the protection should there be a credit event such as bankruptcy or failure to pay on the part of the reference entity underlying the transaction.

Another type of hedge tool that a company or investor can use is options. Options come in two forms: put and calls. Put buyers are bearish and therefore purchase a put with the hope that the underlying stock will go down. Conversely, a call option buyer is bullish on the underlying stock. Therefore, they purchase a call option with hope that the option contract on the underlying stock goes up. Since a call option uses leverage, the investor can get a higher rate of return with a small amount of invested dollars. Nonetheless, there are ways to use options as a hedge: married puts.

Options can't be exercised unless they hit the strike price. For this reason, options selling out of the money (i.e., haven't hit the strike price) are usually less expensive than one selling in the money, all other variables being equal.

An option is considered to be out of the money when the underlying stock price is lower than the strike price of the option.

Bottom line, it can be seen that companies that trade globally can reduce risk in many ways by hedging their risks in these foreign countries by using currency hedging and other forms of hedging to reduce the currency exchange risks. Therefore, it seems worthwhile for companies to incur these risks to offset the currency fluctuations from other countries currencies.

Chapter 6:
When to Buy and When to Sell

Investors use several different methods for deciding when to sell a stock. Some of the more important ones are listed in this chapter. Both technical and fundamental indicators should be applied and used when deciding to buy or sell a stock.

When to Buy a Stock

Low Price/Earnings Ratio (P/E) -- This is a fundamental indicator that show the value of a stock based on its earnings in relation to its current stock price. The lower the P/E ratio, the cheaper the stock is considered to be. Therefore, a low P/E ratio is usually a good time to buy, usually below 15. However, this number is relative. For example, if Company A has a P/E

181

of 20 and the industry average for other companies in the same industry is 40, and then Company A with a P/E of 20 would be considered low.

Stock is above 50 Day Moving Average-- When a stock moves above its 50 day moving average it is indicating an uptrend for the stock and is usually a good time to buy a stock. This is especially true if other buy indicators exist like a stock that is above the 200 day moving average.

Stock is above 200 Day Moving Average-- This is indicative of a longer uptrend than the 50 day moving average. Therefore it is widely used by investors and traders looking for a stock that is trending up.

Relative Strength Index (RSI) –
This is the technical indicator that I like the best. If the RSI has been below 30 for an extended period of time it is a good time to buy. Or, if the RSI has moved below 30 several times recently that would be another good buy indication. Use stock charts such as those at InvestProfits.com or Yahoo Finance to get a good indication of the RSI indicator on an individual stock you want to buy.

Fundamentals

P/E Ratio is below 15-- One of the best times to buy is when the P/E ratio is below 15; or the P/E for a stock is lower than others in their industry. For example, if Apple has a P/E of 12, and all other companies in their industry are higher than 12, Apple could be considered a good buy and a low risk.

The Stock Price is below its Growth Rate, (Low PEG Ratio)—if a stock is selling at a P/E that is lower than its projected growth rate, it is considered a good buy. A low PEG ratio (one below 1) is a very good indication that a stock is a valuable buy. For example, if Google has a P/E of 17 and a growth rate of 20%, it will have a PEG of .85

When to Sell a Stock

Technicals

200 Day Moving Average-- When it is selling 70% above its 200 Day Moving Average it is likely to have possibility to fall due to its high run up above the 200 day moving average. If you bought, the stock and it never goes above 70% above its 200 day moving average, you should when falls below its 200 day moving average. This is indicative of a stock that is trending down

50 Day Moving Average - If the sock is below its 50 day moving average and the 200 day moving average, you should consider selling.

Relative Strength Index (RSI) --When the RSI is above 80 and has moved above that mark more than once in recent days, weeks, then it is a good time to consider selling as this is an indication of a stock that is oversold. Online websites have good charts that will show you this

signal. InvestProfits.con has indicators that will give you
sell and buy signals. I like this technical indicator best.

Fundamentals to use when choosing to sell a Stock

A Change in a Company's Fundamentals—Lower
earnings or a decrease in ROE is a good time to consider
selling

Cash Flow Problems—be wary of companies with cash
flow problems...they can lead to insolvency for the
company. Usually you want to see growing cash flow on
balance sheets

The stocks too hot-- You should compare a stock's P/E
with that of the overall market, the average P/E of its
industry, or against the company's past P/Es. If the
company's ratio is unusually high, it could have a hard
time sustaining that price.

Don't put much emphasis in any one fundamental or
technical indicator. Sometimes investors use technical
analysis to gauge when to buy and sell shares. There is no
proof these signals are 100% accurate every time, but they
should be correct more times than not. From my
experience, it is best to use a minimum of two signal
technical indicators and two fundamental indicators. I like

the Relative Strength Index (RSI) and moving averages for the technical indicators combined with the P/E ratio and Return on Equity (ROE) on the fundamental side.

Don't Hold a Stock too Long

Back in July 2005, I looked at the future financial prospects of the different companies on Yahoo's Finance page, and I found a company with a good chance of a successful future growth and profit. That company would be ConocoPhillips (COP). Below is an analysis from July 2005 as seen in Figure 6-1.

> "*The company has had strong media attention due to its good stock returns due partially to the high demand for oil. In looking at COP using the balance sheet and income statements, I find the following ration analysis:*"

				July 2005 Results
			In Thousands	
Current Ratio=	Current Assets=	$13,475,200	=	
	Current Liabilities	$11,744,100		1.15
Debt Ratio	Total Liabilities=	$25,284,600	=	
	Total Assets	$42,572,800		59.39%
P/E Ratio	Price=	$61.25	=	9.16

	Earnings Per Share	$6.69		
Net Profit Margin	Earnings For common Stockholders=	$5,813,400	=	
	Sales	$22,938,600		**25.3 4%**

Fig. 6-1: All data retrieved from Yahoo's Finance Site (2005) and compiled in Excel.

From July 2005 Analysis: In looking at the table above, it is apparent of some very positive financial date: good liquidity; a moderate amount of leverage; a low P/E ratio; and a good net profit margin. For example the current ratio for COP is 1.15 meaning the company has good liquidity allowing it to meet obligations for the coming year.

As for the debt ratio, it is moderate at 59.39%, but this can be good as it allows the use of leverage allowing better returns on capital. The best reason I like COP is the low P/E ratio. With the S&P 500 averaging a P/E ratio of 16-17 today, COP has a very

186

low P/E of 9.16 as noted the in table above. Also, COP's profits look good. With a net profit margin of 25.34, COP looks very good. Also, the high demand for oil has spiked oil prices making COP look like a very good buy.

Looking at COP with a discount rate of 15%, a current price of 63.75, and a projected growth rate of 6.90%, I come up with the following facts and results:

This is a one year growth of 6.90% leading to a price of $69.39 a difference of $5.64 ($69.39-$63.75) $5.64 appreciation plus a dividend of $1.24 for a total gain of $6.88 resulting in a future price of $70.63.

Then I took the projected 1 year growth price of $70.63 and discount it 15%. To come up with a price of $67.40, I used a Texas Instrument BA-35 calculator to compute the following: $70.63 (FV,) 15% (interest), 1 (number years), and then computed the PV to be $67.40. Therefore, I would pay $6,740 for 100 shares of COP (100 x $67.40).

As I have discussed, the discount rate for a company like COP should be around 15% due to various factors: the boom of the energy industry and oil prices that may cool; the risk of investing in one stock; the low beta; and the comparison of CD investing. All these factors lead me to believe that investing in COP should be with a discount rate of 15%."

I bought Conoco Phillips back in July 2005 and held it until March 2012 when it dropped back to $62...virtually breaking even. It turns out the optimal time to sell was after reaching a high of $93.10 in June 2008, but this purchase happened before I started using technical analysis to buy and sell stocks.

Bottom line: don't hold a stock too long, and use technical analysis to find the best opportunities, especially Relative strength index as an indicator. Another example of holding too long can be seen in Apple stock.

The Investing Guide: Using Technical and Fundamental Analysis

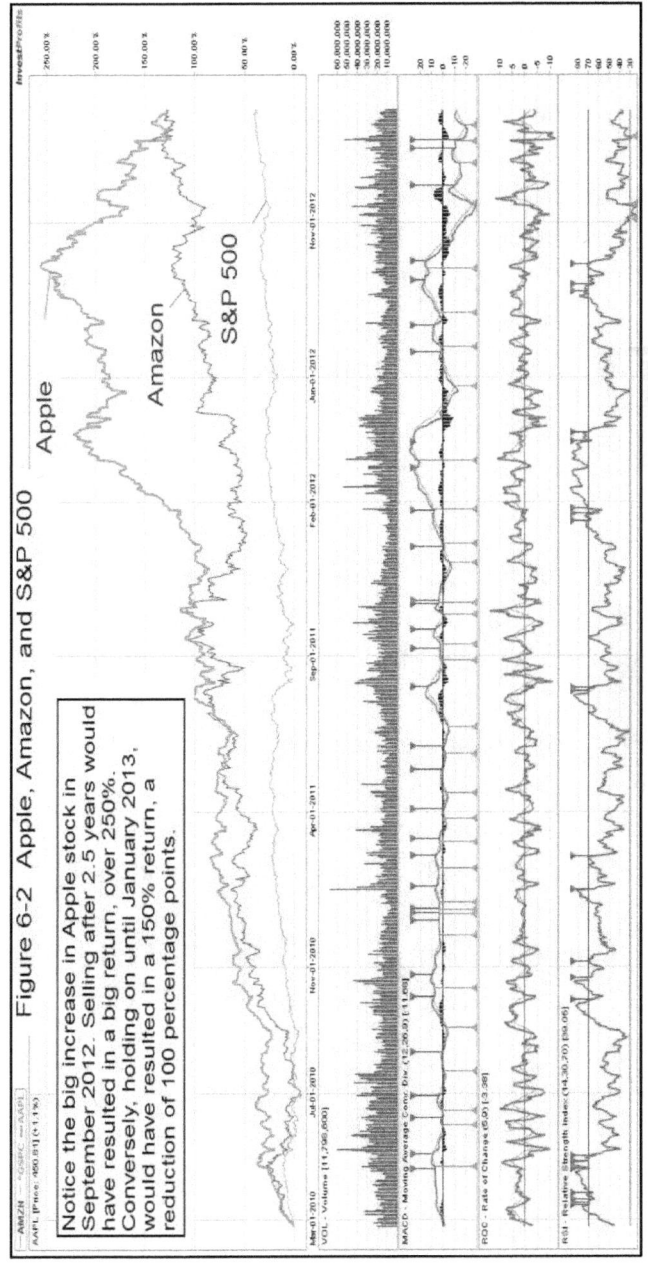

Figure 6-2 Apple, Amazon, and S&P 500

Notice the big increase in Apple stock in September 2012. Selling after 2.5 years would have resulted in a big return, over 250%. Conversely, holding on until January 2013, would have resulted in a 150% return, a reduction of 100 percentage points.

189

The returns for the SP 500 over the 3 year period from 2009-2012, has been small compared to those of technology companies, such as Apple and Amazon (see Figure 6.2). But getting too confident and holding a stock too long can prove a losing cause. Look at the returns for Apple 3 year period from 2009-2012 and you will see that holding on until January 2013 would have resulted in a significant decrease in profits. Conversely, had an investor sold it earlier, the returns would have been significant.

Look at Fig. 6-2, and notice the big increase in Apple stock in September 2012. Selling after 2.5 years would have resulted in a big return, over 250%. Conversely, holding on until January 2013, would have resulted in a 150% return, a reduction of 100 percentage points. Bottom line, some stocks should not be held too long, unless they are in a retirement account or other long-term portfolio. Furthermore, if a company is innovating and has good fundamentals, holding long-term is advisable.

Investing in mutual funds can be beneficial over the long term. However, investing can be more profitable by investing in individual stocks along with mutual funds.

190

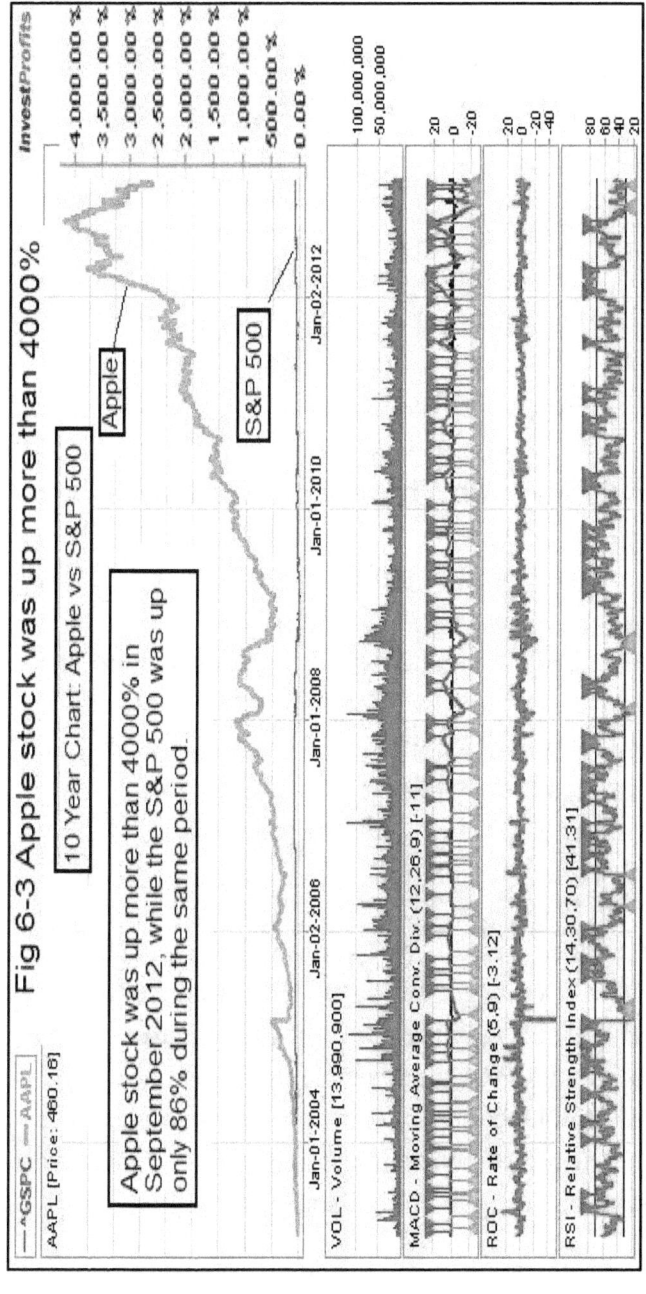

Fig 6-3 Apple stock was up more than 4000%

10 Year Chart: Apple vs S&P 500

Apple stock was up more than 4000% in September 2012, while the S&P 500 was up only 86% during the same period.

191

Take this example seen in Fig 6-3: the 10 year stock return for Apple going from February 2003 to February 2013 was up more than 4000% in September 2012, while the S&P 500 was up only 86% during the same period. Therefore, $10,000 invested in Apple stock during the period would have turned into over $400,000. Conversely, the same $10,000 invested in an S&P 500 mutual fund would turn into only $18,600, a difference of $381,400. More details can be seen in Fig. 6-3.

Word of Caution on Short-Term Trading: 7 Days or less

While I am not against high frequency trading, I do have some reservations.

I have never been someone who day trades due the very nature the fact it produces three things and they are all negative: 1.) taxes on capital gains; 2.) high transaction costs; 3.) and anxiety (from knowing when to sell). A scenario about caution can be seen when I bought the following stocks in 2005.

The companies I bought were Bank of America (BAC), Amgen (AMGN), Qualcomm (QCOM), and Conoco Phillips (COP). I bought each for various reasons and in various amounts. First the reasons, then the amount purchased, and last, the amount of loss/gain on each company. However, a little disclosure: these stocks were chosen without using technical analysis. So RSI and moving averages were not used to analyze these stocks. In fact, I didn't use any charts at that time.

As you can see from the chart in *Fig 6-4*, I bought these four companies: Bank of America, Amgen, ConocoPhillips, and Qualcomm.

Reasons I like these stocks in the short term.				
Com-pany	1 Week return	5-Yr Rtn	P/E Ratio	Reason to buy
Bank of America (BAC)	- 6.63%	+14.65%	10	Good return last 5 years. Mortgages are good
Amgen (AMGN)	- 5.38%	+0.70%	22	It is the world's largest Biotech stock; threat of avian flu
Conoco Phillips (COP).	+7.43%	+20.12%	7	Very Low P/E; Energy stocks I expect to continue to rise.
Qualcomm (QCOM)	+6.96%	+11.27%	32	Has a patented chip format used in cell phones

Fig 6-4

As seen in the chart in Fig 6-5, I bought BAC due to its good return in the last five years (2000-2005) at 14.65% average annual return. Also, with a P/E of 10, it is 33 percent below that of the S&P 500; thus, I expected the financials market to rise in the short term. But with a return of -6.63%, the company actually lost money. With a purchase amount of $100,000 my return on this stock would have been $93,370, almost a $7,000 dollar loss.

Next, my purchase of Amgen at $25,000 worth of stock was due the threat of Avian Flu (at the time) and the fact that it is the world's largest independent biotech firm making it look like a potential short term gainer. But, after a negative 5.38% loss on $25,000, the loss would have been $1,345. Thus, the net loss on these two companies totals a negative $7,975. Now for some winners, as you can see from the chart in Fig 6-5, there were some gains.

Company	Amount purchased	Loss/Gain
Bank of America (BAC)	$100,000	$93,370
Amgen (AMGN),	$25,000	$23,655
Conoco Phillips (COP).	$100,000	$107,430
Qualcomm (QCOM),	$25,000	$26,740
Sub-Total	$250,000	$251,195
Less Transaction costs (at $4/transaction at sharebuilder.com)	8 total transaction (4 stocks bought and sold	-32
Total		$251,163
Less Capital used		-$250,000
Net Gain		$1,163

Fig. 6-5

Conoco Phillips returned a positive 7.43% on my investment of $100,000. Such a large amount was placed on this company due to the winter months in the northeast possibly leading to high heating costs. Thus, this would lead to profits for an oil company that has a very low P/E compared with the broad market. With so much invested and a good return, the gain on COP was $7,430, as can be seen in the chart in Fig 6-5. Therefore with 2 losers and 1 gainer, I am currently at a negative $545. However, further gains were seen in a telecom maker with a patent.

Qualcomm, the maker of patented chip for cell phones, has become the standard in the U.S. With so many people choosing to upgrade their phones, the potential for growth was great for this company. As a result of buying $25,000 worth of this stock, and a positive return of 9.96%, the initial investment grew to $26,740, a gain of $1,740.

Overall, the gain on $250,000 invested turned into $251,195, a gain of $1,195 before transaction costs. Using Sharebuilder.com, at $4 per trade the total transaction costs came to $32 reducing the overall gain to $1,163 on $250,000 invested. This does not include capital gains taxes that must be paid on the profits. Basically, it seems that short term investing is very difficult and left to someone who has more belief in this type of investing. I believe in investing for the long term: 5 years or more using value investing, or 6 months or more using technical analysis like those discussed in chapter 2. Finally, making money in 7 days or less is not always as easy as it seems...my suggestion...invest carefully. Remember this was 2005 and I had not yet used any stock charts in analyzing stocks, that about 3 years later in 2009.

In summary, investing can be both profitable and risky. The more astute an investor is and the more prepared, the better his returns can be. This involves both using technical and fundamental analysis as well as due diligence in assessing one's risk tolerance. It is imperative to find your investing strategy and stay with it, while avoiding the desire to blend various methodologies. Additionally, the desire to follow the herd can be detrimental to one's financial health as it usually will result in diminished returns; many investors will buy when the stocks are flying high, and sell when the market is falling. The result: "buying high and selling low". It happens very frequently in the market and history has a way of repeating itself. It's imperative to use astute and disciplined techniques of technical and fundamental analysis discussed earlier and include both long-term and short-term strategies in your portfolio.

APPENDIX A

Investing at Different Rates of Return

In this Appendix, you will find that Long-Term investing can be a significant wealth builder. Look at different investment amounts, along with monthly additions, to see how an investment can grow over time. See how various rates of returns can have an impact on your investment.

To use these charts, look at a specific dollar amount and use the corresponding years to see how many years it takes to reach your retirement goal. This chart can be very useful in estimating how a long-term investment plan, like investing in mutual funds, can result in future wealth.

Appendix A (Returns at various rates of return)

	Initial Investment	$1,000				
Years ->	1	5	10	15	20	21
Percent						
1%	$1,010	$1,051	$1,105	$1,161	$1,220	$1,232
5%	$1,050	$1,276	$1,629	$2,079	$2,653	$2,786
10%	$1,100	$1,611	$2,594	$4,177	$6,727	$7,400
15%	$1,150	$2,011	$4,046	$8,137	$16,367	$18,822
20%	$1,200	$2,488	$6,192	$15,407	$38,338	$46,005
25%	$1,250	$3,052	$9,313	$28,422	$86,736	$108,420
30%	$1,300	$3,713	$13,786	$51,186	$190,050	$247,065
35%	$1,350	$4,484	$20,107	$90,158	$404,274	$545,769

	Initial Investment	$2,000				
Years ->	1	5	10	15	20	21
Percent						
1%	$2,020	$2,102	$2,209	$2,322	$2,440	$2,465
5%	$2,100	$2,553	$3,258	$4,158	$5,307	$5,572
10%	$2,200	$3,221	$5,187	$8,354	$13,455	$14,800
15%	$2,300	$4,023	$8,091	$16,274	$32,733	$37,643
20%	$2,400	$4,977	$12,383	$30,814	$76,675	$92,010
25%	$2,500	$6,104	$18,626	$56,843	$173,472	$216,840
30%	$2,600	$7,426	$27,572	$102,372	$380,099	$494,129
35%	$2,700	$8,968	$40,213	$180,317	$808,547	$1,091,539

	Initial Investment	$3,000				
Years ->	1	5	10	15	20	21
Percent						
1%	$3,030	$3,153	$3,314	$3,483	$3,661	$3,697
5%	$3,150	$3,829	$4,887	$6,237	$7,960	$8,358
10%	$3,300	$4,832	$7,781	$12,532	$20,182	$22,201
15%	$3,450	$6,034	$12,137	$24,411	$49,100	$56,465
20%	$3,600	$7,465	$18,575	$46,221	$115,013	$138,015
25%	$3,750	$9,155	$27,940	$85,265	$260,209	$325,261
30%	$3,900	$11,139	$41,358	$153,558	$570,149	$741,194
35%	$4,050	$13,452	$60,320	$270,475	$1,212,821	$1,637,308

	Initial Investment	$4,000				
Years ->	1	5	10	15	20	21
Percent						
1%	$4,040	$4,204	$4,418	$4,644	$4,881	$4,930
5%	$4,200	$5,105	$6,516	$8,316	$10,613	$11,144
10%	$4,400	$6,442	$10,375	$16,709	$26,910	$29,601
15%	$4,600	$8,045	$16,182	$32,548	$65,466	$75,286
20%	$4,800	$9,953	$24,767	$61,628	$153,350	$184,020
25%	$5,000	$12,207	$37,253	$113,687	$346,945	$433,681
30%	$5,200	$14,852	$55,143	$204,744	$760,199	$988,258
35%	$5,400	$17,936	$80,426	$360,634	$1,617,094	$2,183,077

Appendix A (Returns at various rates of return)

	Initial Investment	$1,000				
Years ->	26	27	28	29	30	31
Percent						
1%	$1,295	$1,308	$1,321	$1,335	$1,348	$1,361
5%	$3,556	$3,733	$3,920	$4,116	$4,322	$4,538
10%	$11,918	$13,110	$14,421	$15,863	$17,449	$19,194
15%	$37,857	$43,535	$50,066	$57,575	$66,212	$76,144
20%	$114,475	$137,371	$164,845	$197,814	$237,376	$284,852
25%	$330,872	$413,590	$516,988	$646,235	$807,794	$1,009,742
30%	$917,333	$1,192,533	$1,550,293	$2,015,381	$2,619,996	$3,405,994
35%	$2,447,248	$3,303,785	$4,460,109	$6,021,148	$8,128,550	$10,973,542

	Initial Investment	$2,000				
Years ->	26	27	28	29	30	31
Percent						
1%	$2,591	$2,616	$2,643	$2,669	$2,696	$2,723
5%	$7,111	$7,467	$7,840	$8,232	$8,644	$9,076
10%	$23,836	$26,220	$28,842	$31,726	$34,899	$38,389
15%	$75,714	$87,071	$100,131	$115,151	$132,424	$152,287
20%	$228,951	$274,741	$329,689	$395,627	$474,753	$569,703
25%	$661,744	$827,181	$1,033,976	$1,292,470	$1,615,587	$2,019,484
30%	$1,834,667	$2,385,067	$3,100,587	$4,030,763	$5,239,991	$6,811,989
35%	$4,894,496	$6,607,570	$8,920,219	$12,042,296	$16,257,099	$21,947,084

	Initial Investment	$3,000				
Years ->	26	27	28	29	30	31
Percent						
1%	$3,886	$3,925	$3,964	$4,004	$4,044	$4,084
5%	$10,667	$11,200	$11,760	$12,348	$12,966	$13,614
10%	$35,755	$39,330	$43,263	$47,589	$52,348	$57,583
15%	$113,570	$130,606	$150,197	$172,726	$198,635	$228,431
20%	$343,426	$412,112	$494,534	$593,441	$712,129	$854,555
25%	$992,617	$1,240,771	$1,550,964	$1,938,705	$2,423,381	$3,029,226
30%	$2,752,000	$3,577,600	$4,650,880	$6,046,144	$7,859,987	$10,217,983
35%	$7,341,744	$9,911,354	$13,380,328	$18,063,443	$24,385,649	$32,920,625

	Initial Investment	$4,000				
Years ->	26	27	28	29	30	31
Percent						
1%	$5,181	$5,233	$5,285	$5,338	$5,391	$5,445
5%	$14,223	$14,934	$15,681	$16,465	$17,288	$18,152
10%	$47,673	$52,440	$57,684	$63,452	$69,798	$76,777
15%	$151,427	$174,141	$200,262	$230,302	$264,847	$304,574
20%	$457,902	$549,482	$659,379	$791,254	$949,505	$1,139,406
25%	$1,323,489	$1,654,361	$2,067,952	$2,584,939	$3,231,174	$4,038,968
30%	$3,669,333	$4,770,133	$6,201,173	$8,061,525	$10,479,983	$13,623,977
35%	$9,788,992	$13,215,139	$17,840,438	$24,084,591	$32,514,198	$43,894,167

Appendix A (Returns at various rates of return}

	Initial Investment	$5,000				
Years ->	1	5	10	15	20	21
Percent						
1%	$5,050	$5,255	$5,523	$5,805	$6,101	$6,162
5%	$5,250	$6,381	$8,144	$10,395	$13,266	$13,930
10%	$5,500	$8,053	$12,969	$20,886	$33,637	$37,001
15%	$5,750	$10,057	$20,228	$40,685	$81,833	$94,108
20%	$6,000	$12,442	$30,959	$77,035	$191,688	$230,026
25%	$6,250	$15,259	$46,566	$142,109	$433,681	$542,101
30%	$6,500	$18,565	$68,929	$255,929	$950,248	$1,235,323
35%	$6,750	$22,420	$100,533	$450,792	$2,021,368	$2,728,847

	Initial Investment	$6,000				
Years ->	1	5	10	15	20	21
Percent						
1%	$6,060	$6,306	$6,628	$6,966	$7,321	$7,394
5%	$6,300	$7,658	$9,773	$12,474	$15,920	$16,716
10%	$6,600	$9,663	$15,562	$25,063	$40,365	$44,401
15%	$6,900	$12,068	$24,273	$48,822	$98,199	$112,929
20%	$7,200	$14,930	$37,150	$92,442	$230,026	$276,031
25%	$7,500	$18,311	$55,879	$170,530	$520,417	$650,521
30%	$7,800	$22,278	$82,715	$307,115	$1,140,298	$1,482,387
35%	$8,100	$26,904	$120,639	$540,951	$2,425,642	$3,274,616

	Initial Investment	$7,000				
Years ->	1	5	10	15	20	21
Percent						
1%	$7,070	$7,357	$7,732	$8,127	$8,541	$8,627
5%	$7,350	$8,934	$11,402	$14,552	$18,573	$19,502
10%	$7,700	$11,274	$18,156	$29,241	$47,092	$51,802
15%	$8,050	$14,080	$28,319	$56,959	$114,566	$131,751
20%	$8,400	$17,418	$43,342	$107,849	$268,363	$322,036
25%	$8,750	$21,362	$65,193	$198,952	$607,153	$758,942
30%	$9,100	$25,991	$96,501	$358,301	$1,330,347	$1,729,452
35%	$9,450	$31,388	$140,746	$631,109	$2,829,915	$3,820,385

	Initial Investment	$8,000				
Years ->	1	5	10	15	20	21
Percent						
1%	$8,080	$8,408	$8,837	$9,288	$9,762	$9,859
5%	$8,400	$10,210	$13,031	$16,631	$21,226	$22,288
10%	$8,800	$12,884	$20,750	$33,418	$53,820	$59,202
15%	$9,200	$16,091	$32,364	$65,096	$130,932	$150,572
20%	$9,600	$19,907	$49,534	$123,256	$306,701	$368,041
25%	$10,000	$24,414	$74,506	$227,374	$693,889	$867,362
30%	$10,400	$29,703	$110,287	$409,487	$1,520,397	$1,976,516
35%	$10,800	$35,872	$160,852	$721,268	$3,234,189	$4,366,155

Appendix A (Returns at various rates of return}

Initial Investment	$5,000				
Years ->	26	27	28	29	30	31
Percent						
1%	$6,476	$6,541	$6,606	$6,673	$6,739	$6,807
5%	$17,778	$18,667	$19,601	$20,581	$21,610	$22,690
10%	$59,591	$65,550	$72,105	$79,315	$87,247	$95,972
15%	$189,284	$217,677	$250,328	$287,877	$331,059	$380,718
20%	$572,377	$686,853	$824,223	$989,068	$1,186,882	$1,424,258
25%	$1,654,361	$2,067,952	$2,584,939	$3,231,174	$4,038,968	$5,048,710
30%	$4,586,667	$5,962,666	$7,751,466	$10,076,906	$13,099,978	$17,029,972
35%	$12,236,240	$16,518,924	$22,300,547	$30,105,739	$40,642,748	$54,867,709

Initial Investment	$6,000				
Years ->	26	27	28	29	30	31
Percent						
1%	$7,772	$7,849	$7,928	$8,007	$8,087	$8,168
5%	$21,334	$22,401	$23,521	$24,697	$25,932	$27,228
10%	$71,509	$78,660	$86,526	$95,179	$104,696	$115,166
15%	$227,141	$261,212	$300,394	$345,453	$397,271	$456,861
20%	$686,853	$824,223	$989,068	$1,186,882	$1,424,258	$1,709,109
25%	$1,985,233	$2,481,542	$3,101,927	$3,877,409	$4,846,761	$6,058,452
30%	$5,504,000	$7,155,200	$9,301,760	$12,092,288	$15,719,974	$20,435,966
35%	$14,683,488	$19,822,709	$26,760,657	$36,126,887	$48,771,297	$65,841,251

Initial Investment	$7,000				
Years ->	26	27	28	29	30	31
Percent						
1%	$9,067	$9,157	$9,249	$9,342	$9,435	$9,529
5%	$24,890	$26,134	$27,441	$28,813	$30,254	$31,766
10%	$83,427	$91,770	$100,947	$111,042	$122,146	$134,360
15%	$264,998	$304,747	$350,459	$403,028	$463,482	$533,005
20%	$801,328	$961,594	$1,153,913	$1,384,695	$1,661,634	$1,993,961
25%	$2,316,106	$2,895,132	$3,618,915	$4,523,644	$5,654,555	$7,068,194
30%	$6,421,333	$8,347,733	$10,852,053	$14,107,669	$18,339,970	$23,841,960
35%	$17,130,736	$23,126,494	$31,220,766	$42,148,034	$56,899,847	$76,814,793

Initial Investment	$8,000				
Years ->	26	27	28	29	30	31
Percent						
1%	$10,362	$10,466	$10,570	$10,676	$10,783	$10,891
5%	$28,445	$29,868	$31,361	$32,929	$34,576	$36,304
10%	$95,345	$104,880	$115,368	$126,905	$139,595	$153,555
15%	$302,854	$348,283	$400,525	$460,604	$529,694	$609,148
20%	$915,804	$1,098,964	$1,318,757	$1,582,509	$1,899,011	$2,278,813
25%	$2,646,978	$3,308,722	$4,135,903	$5,169,879	$6,462,349	$8,077,936
30%	$7,338,666	$9,540,266	$12,402,346	$16,123,050	$20,959,965	$27,247,955
35%	$19,577,984	$26,430,278	$35,680,876	$48,169,182	$65,028,396	$87,788,335

Appendix A (Returns at various rates of return}

Initial Investment	$9,000					
Years ->	1	5	10	15	20	21
Percent						
1%	$9,090	$9,459	$9,942	$10,449	$10,982	$11,092
5%	$9,450	$11,487	$14,660	$18,710	$23,880	$25,074
10%	$9,900	$14,495	$23,344	$37,595	$60,547	$66,602
15%	$10,350	$18,102	$36,410	$73,234	$147,299	$169,394
20%	$10,800	$22,395	$55,726	$138,663	$345,038	$414,046
25%	$11,250	$27,466	$83,819	$255,795	$780,626	$975,782
30%	$11,700	$33,416	$124,073	$460,673	$1,710,447	$2,223,581
35%	$12,150	$40,356	$180,959	$811,426	$3,638,462	$4,911,924

Initial Investment	$10,000					
Years ->	1	5	10	15	20	21
Percent						
1%	$10,100	$10,510	$11,046	$11,610	$12,202	$12,324
5%	$10,500	$12,763	$16,289	$20,789	$26,533	$27,860
10%	$11,000	$16,105	$25,937	$41,772	$67,275	$74,002
15%	$11,500	$20,114	$40,456	$81,371	$163,665	$188,215
20%	$12,000	$24,883	$61,917	$154,070	$383,376	$460,051
25%	$12,500	$30,518	$93,132	$284,217	$867,362	$1,084,202
30%	$13,000	$37,129	$137,858	$511,859	$1,900,496	$2,470,645
35%	$13,500	$44,840	$201,066	$901,585	$4,042,736	$5,457,693

Initial Investment	$11,000					
Years ->	1	5	10	15	20	21
Percent						
1%	$11,110	$11,561	$12,151	$12,771	$13,422	$13,556
5%	$11,550	$14,039	$17,918	$22,868	$29,186	$30,646
10%	$12,100	$17,716	$28,531	$45,950	$74,002	$81,403
15%	$12,650	$22,125	$44,501	$89,508	$180,032	$207,037
20%	$13,200	$27,372	$68,109	$169,477	$421,714	$506,056
25%	$13,750	$33,569	$102,445	$312,639	$954,098	$1,192,622
30%	$14,300	$40,842	$151,644	$563,045	$2,090,546	$2,717,710
35%	$14,850	$49,324	$221,172	$991,743	$4,447,009	$6,003,463

Initial Investment	$12,000					
Years ->	1	5	10	15	20	21
Percent						
1%	$12,120	$12,612	$13,255	$13,932	$14,642	$14,789
5%	$12,600	$15,315	$19,547	$24,947	$31,840	$33,432
10%	$13,200	$19,326	$31,125	$50,127	$80,730	$88,803
15%	$13,800	$24,136	$48,547	$97,645	$196,398	$225,858
20%	$14,400	$29,860	$74,301	$184,884	$460,051	$552,061
25%	$15,000	$36,621	$111,759	$341,061	$1,040,834	$1,301,043
30%	$15,600	$44,555	$165,430	$614,231	$2,280,596	$2,964,774
35%	$16,200	$53,808	$241,279	$1,081,902	$4,851,283	$6,549,232

Appendix A (Returns at various rates of return}

Initial Investment $9,000					
Years ->	26	27	28	29	30	31
Percent						
1%	$11,657	$11,774	$11,892	$12,011	$12,131	$12,252
5%	$32,001	$33,601	$35,281	$37,045	$38,897	$40,842
10%	$107,264	$117,990	$129,789	$142,768	$157,045	$172,749
15%	$340,711	$391,818	$450,591	$518,179	$595,906	$685,292
20%	$1,030,279	$1,236,335	$1,483,602	$1,780,322	$2,136,387	$2,563,664
25%	$2,977,850	$3,722,313	$4,652,891	$5,816,114	$7,270,142	$9,087,678
30%	$8,256,000	$10,732,800	$13,952,640	$18,138,431	$23,579,961	$30,653,949
35%	$22,025,232	$29,734,063	$40,140,985	$54,190,330	$73,156,946	$98,761,876

Initial Investment $10,000					
Years ->	26	27	28	29	30	31
Percent						
1%	$12,953	$13,082	$13,213	$13,345	$13,478	$13,613
5%	$35,557	$37,335	$39,201	$41,161	$43,219	$45,380
10%	$119,182	$131,100	$144,210	$158,631	$174,494	$191,943
15%	$378,568	$435,353	$500,656	$575,755	$662,118	$761,435
20%	$1,144,755	$1,373,706	$1,648,447	$1,978,136	$2,373,763	$2,848,516
25%	$3,308,722	$4,135,903	$5,169,879	$6,462,349	$8,077,936	$10,097,420
30%	$9,173,333	$11,925,333	$15,502,933	$20,153,813	$26,199,956	$34,059,943
35%	$24,472,480	$33,037,848	$44,601,095	$60,211,478	$81,285,495	$109,735,418

Initial Investment $11,000					
Years ->	26	27	28	29	30	31
Percent						
1%	$14,248	$14,390	$14,534	$14,680	$14,826	$14,975
5%	$39,112	$41,068	$43,121	$45,277	$47,541	$49,918
10%	$131,100	$144,210	$158,631	$174,494	$191,943	$211,138
15%	$416,425	$478,888	$550,722	$633,330	$728,329	$837,579
20%	$1,259,230	$1,511,076	$1,813,291	$2,175,950	$2,611,139	$3,133,367
25%	$3,639,595	$4,549,493	$5,686,867	$7,108,583	$8,885,729	$11,107,162
30%	$10,090,666	$13,117,866	$17,053,226	$22,169,194	$28,819,952	$37,465,938
35%	$26,919,728	$36,341,633	$49,061,204	$66,232,626	$89,414,045	$120,708,960

Initial Investment $12,000					
Years ->	26	27	28	29	30	31
Percent						
1%	$15,543	$15,699	$15,855	$16,014	$16,174	$16,336
5%	$42,668	$44,801	$47,042	$49,394	$51,863	$54,456
10%	$143,018	$157,320	$173,052	$190,357	$209,393	$230,332
15%	$454,282	$522,424	$600,787	$690,905	$794,541	$913,722
20%	$1,373,706	$1,648,447	$1,978,136	$2,373,763	$2,848,516	$3,418,219
25%	$3,970,467	$4,963,084	$6,203,855	$7,754,818	$9,693,523	$12,116,904
30%	$11,008,000	$14,310,400	$18,603,519	$24,184,575	$31,439,948	$40,871,932
35%	$29,366,976	$39,645,417	$53,521,314	$72,253,773	$97,542,594	$131,682,502

203

Appendix A (Returns at various rates of return}

Initial Investment	$13,000					
Years ->	1	5	10	15	20	21
Percent						
1%	$13,130	$13,663	$14,360	$15,093	$15,862	$16,021
5%	$13,650	$16,592	$21,176	$27,026	$34,493	$36,218
10%	$14,300	$20,937	$33,719	$54,304	$87,457	$96,203
15%	$14,950	$26,148	$52,592	$105,782	$212,765	$244,680
20%	$15,600	$32,348	$80,493	$200,291	$498,389	$598,067
25%	$16,250	$39,673	$121,072	$369,482	$1,127,570	$1,409,463
30%	$16,900	$48,268	$179,216	$665,417	$2,470,645	$3,211,839
35%	$17,550	$58,292	$261,385	$1,172,060	$5,255,557	$7,095,001

Initial Investment	$14,000					
Years ->	1	5	10	15	20	21
Percent						
1%	$14,140	$14,714	$15,465	$16,254	$17,083	$17,253
5%	$14,700	$17,868	$22,805	$29,105	$37,146	$39,003
10%	$15,400	$22,547	$36,312	$58,481	$94,185	$103,603
15%	$16,100	$28,159	$56,638	$113,919	$229,132	$263,501
20%	$16,800	$34,836	$86,684	$215,698	$536,726	$644,072
25%	$17,500	$42,725	$130,385	$397,904	$1,214,306	$1,517,883
30%	$18,200	$51,981	$193,002	$716,603	$2,660,695	$3,458,903
35%	$18,900	$62,776	$281,492	$1,262,219	$5,659,830	$7,640,771

Initial Investment	$15,000					
Years ->	1	5	10	15	20	21
Percent						
1%	$15,150	$15,765	$16,569	$17,415	$18,303	$18,486
5%	$15,750	$19,144	$24,433	$31,184	$39,799	$41,789
10%	$16,500	$24,158	$38,906	$62,659	$100,912	$111,004
15%	$17,250	$30,170	$60,683	$122,056	$245,498	$282,323
20%	$18,000	$37,325	$92,876	$231,105	$575,064	$690,077
25%	$18,750	$45,776	$139,698	$426,326	$1,301,043	$1,626,303
30%	$19,500	$55,694	$206,788	$767,788	$2,850,745	$3,705,968
35%	$20,250	$67,261	$301,598	$1,352,377	$6,064,104	$8,186,540

Initial Investment	$16,000					
Years ->	1	5	10	15	20	21
Percent						
1%	$16,160	$16,816	$17,674	$18,576	$19,523	$19,718
5%	$16,800	$20,421	$26,062	$33,263	$42,453	$44,575
10%	$17,600	$25,768	$41,500	$66,836	$107,640	$118,404
15%	$18,400	$32,182	$64,729	$130,193	$261,865	$301,144
20%	$19,200	$39,813	$99,068	$246,512	$613,402	$736,082
25%	$20,000	$48,828	$149,012	$454,747	$1,387,779	$1,734,723
30%	$20,800	$59,407	$220,574	$818,974	$3,040,794	$3,953,032
35%	$21,600	$71,745	$321,705	$1,442,536	$6,468,377	$8,732,310

Appendix A (Returns at various rates of return}

	Initial Investment $13,000					
Years ->	26	27	28	29	30	31
Percent						
1%	$16,838	$17,007	$17,177	$17,349	$17,522	$17,697
5%	$46,224	$48,535	$50,962	$53,510	$56,185	$58,995
10%	$154,936	$170,430	$187,473	$206,220	$226,842	$249,526
15%	$492,138	$565,959	$650,853	$748,481	$860,753	$989,866
20%	$1,488,181	$1,785,817	$2,142,981	$2,571,577	$3,085,892	$3,703,070
25%	$4,301,339	$5,376,674	$6,720,842	$8,401,053	$10,501,316	$13,126,645
30%	$11,925,333	$15,502,933	$20,153,813	$26,199,956	$34,059,943	$44,277,926
35%	$31,814,224	$42,949,202	$57,981,423	$78,274,921	$105,671,144	$142,656,044

	Initial Investment $14,000					
Years ->	26	27	28	29	30	31
Percent						
1%	$18,134	$18,315	$18,498	$18,683	$18,870	$19,059
5%	$49,779	$52,268	$54,882	$57,626	$60,507	$63,533
10%	$166,854	$183,540	$201,894	$222,083	$244,292	$268,721
15%	$529,995	$609,494	$700,919	$806,056	$926,965	$1,066,010
20%	$1,602,656	$1,923,188	$2,307,825	$2,769,390	$3,323,268	$3,987,922
25%	$4,632,211	$5,790,264	$7,237,830	$9,047,288	$11,309,110	$14,136,387
30%	$12,842,666	$16,695,466	$21,704,106	$28,215,338	$36,679,939	$47,683,921
35%	$34,261,472	$46,252,987	$62,441,533	$84,296,069	$113,799,693	$153,629,586

	Initial Investment $15,000					
Years ->	26	27	28	29	30	31
Percent						
1%	$19,429	$19,623	$19,819	$20,018	$20,218	$20,420
5%	$53,335	$56,002	$58,802	$61,742	$64,829	$68,071
10%	$178,773	$196,650	$216,315	$237,946	$261,741	$287,915
15%	$567,852	$653,030	$750,984	$863,632	$993,177	$1,142,153
20%	$1,717,132	$2,060,558	$2,472,670	$2,967,204	$3,560,645	$4,272,774
25%	$4,963,084	$6,203,855	$7,754,818	$9,693,523	$12,116,904	$15,146,129
30%	$13,760,000	$17,887,999	$23,254,399	$30,230,719	$39,299,935	$51,089,915
35%	$36,708,720	$49,556,772	$66,901,642	$90,317,217	$121,928,243	$164,603,127

	Initial Investment $16,000					
Years ->	26	27	28	29	30	31
Percent						
1%	$20,724	$20,931	$21,141	$21,352	$21,566	$21,781
5%	$56,891	$59,735	$62,722	$65,858	$69,151	$72,609
10%	$190,691	$209,760	$230,736	$253,809	$279,190	$307,109
15%	$605,709	$696,565	$801,050	$921,207	$1,059,388	$1,218,297
20%	$1,831,607	$2,197,929	$2,637,515	$3,165,018	$3,798,021	$4,557,625
25%	$5,293,956	$6,617,445	$8,271,806	$10,339,758	$12,924,697	$16,155,871
30%	$14,677,333	$19,080,533	$24,804,692	$32,246,100	$41,919,930	$54,495,909
35%	$39,155,968	$52,860,557	$71,361,751	$96,338,364	$130,056,792	$175,576,669

Appendix A (Returns at various rates of return)

Initial Investment	$17,000				
Years ->	1	5	10	15	20	21
Percent						
1%	$17,170	$17,867	$18,779	$19,736	$20,743	$20,951
5%	$17,850	$21,697	$27,691	$35,342	$45,106	$47,361
10%	$18,700	$27,379	$44,094	$71,013	$114,367	$125,804
15%	$19,550	$34,193	$68,774	$138,330	$278,231	$319,966
20%	$20,400	$42,301	$105,260	$261,919	$651,739	$782,087
25%	$21,250	$51,880	$158,325	$483,169	$1,474,515	$1,843,144
30%	$22,100	$63,120	$234,359	$870,160	$3,230,844	$4,200,097
35%	$22,950	$76,229	$341,811	$1,532,694	$6,872,651	$9,278,079

Initial Investment	$18,000				
Years ->	1	5	10	15	20	21
Percent						
1%	$18,180	$18,918	$19,883	$20,897	$21,963	$22,183
5%	$18,900	$22,973	$29,320	$37,421	$47,759	$50,147
10%	$19,800	$28,989	$46,687	$75,190	$121,095	$133,204
15%	$20,700	$36,204	$72,820	$146,467	$294,598	$338,787
20%	$21,600	$44,790	$111,451	$277,326	$690,077	$828,092
25%	$22,500	$54,932	$167,638	$511,591	$1,561,251	$1,951,564
30%	$23,400	$66,833	$248,145	$921,346	$3,420,893	$4,447,162
35%	$24,300	$80,713	$361,918	$1,622,852	$7,276,925	$9,823,848

Initial Investment	$19,000				
Years ->	1	5	10	15	20	21
Percent						
1%	$19,190	$19,969	$20,988	$22,058	$23,184	$23,415
5%	$19,950	$24,249	$30,949	$39,500	$50,413	$52,933
10%	$20,900	$30,600	$49,281	$79,368	$127,822	$140,605
15%	$21,850	$38,216	$76,866	$154,604	$310,964	$357,609
20%	$22,800	$47,278	$117,643	$292,733	$728,414	$874,097
25%	$23,750	$57,983	$176,951	$540,012	$1,647,987	$2,059,984
30%	$24,700	$70,546	$261,931	$972,532	$3,610,943	$4,694,226
35%	$25,650	$85,197	$382,025	$1,713,011	$7,681,198	$10,369,618

Initial Investment	$20,000				
Years ->	1	5	10	15	20	21
Percent						
1%	$20,200	$21,020	$22,092	$23,219	$24,404	$24,648
5%	$21,000	$25,526	$32,578	$41,579	$53,066	$55,719
10%	$22,000	$32,210	$51,875	$83,545	$134,550	$148,005
15%	$23,000	$40,227	$80,911	$162,741	$327,331	$376,430
20%	$24,000	$49,766	$123,835	$308,140	$766,752	$920,102
25%	$25,000	$61,035	$186,265	$568,434	$1,734,723	$2,168,404
30%	$26,000	$74,259	$275,717	$1,023,718	$3,800,993	$4,941,291
35%	$27,000	$89,681	$402,131	$1,803,169	$8,085,472	$10,915,387

Appendix A (Returns at various rates of return}

Initial Investment> $17,000					
Years ->	26	27	28	29	30	31
Percent						
1%	$22,019	$22,240	$22,462	$22,687	$22,913	$23,143
5%	$60,446	$63,469	$66,642	$69,974	$73,473	$77,147
10%	$202,609	$222,870	$245,157	$269,673	$296,640	$326,304
15%	$643,566	$740,100	$851,115	$978,783	$1,125,600	$1,294,440
20%	$1,946,083	$2,335,299	$2,802,359	$3,362,831	$4,035,397	$4,842,477
25%	$5,624,828	$7,031,035	$8,788,794	$10,985,993	$13,732,491	$17,165,613
30%	$15,594,666	$20,273,066	$26,354,986	$34,261,481	$44,539,926	$57,901,904
35%	$41,603,216	$56,164,341	$75,821,861	$102,359,512	$138,185,342	$186,550,211

Initial Investment> $18,000					
Years ->	26	27	28	29	30	31
Percent						
1%	$23,315	$23,548	$23,783	$24,021	$24,261	$24,504
5%	$64,002	$67,202	$70,562	$74,090	$77,795	$81,685
10%	$214,527	$235,980	$259,578	$285,536	$314,089	$345,498
15%	$681,422	$783,636	$901,181	$1,036,358	$1,191,812	$1,370,584
20%	$2,060,558	$2,472,670	$2,967,204	$3,560,645	$4,272,774	$5,127,328
25%	$5,955,700	$7,444,626	$9,305,782	$11,632,227	$14,540,284	$18,175,355
30%	$16,511,999	$21,465,599	$27,905,279	$36,276,863	$47,159,922	$61,307,898
35%	$44,050,464	$59,468,126	$80,281,970	$108,380,660	$146,313,891	$197,523,753

Initial Investment> $19,000					
Years ->	26	27	28	29	30	31
Percent						
1%	$24,610	$24,856	$25,105	$25,356	$25,609	$25,865
5%	$67,558	$70,936	$74,482	$78,207	$82,117	$86,223
10%	$226,445	$249,090	$273,999	$301,399	$331,539	$364,693
15%	$719,279	$827,171	$951,247	$1,093,934	$1,258,024	$1,446,727
20%	$2,175,034	$2,610,040	$3,132,049	$3,758,458	$4,510,150	$5,412,180
25%	$6,286,573	$7,858,216	$9,822,770	$12,278,462	$15,348,078	$19,185,097
30%	$17,429,333	$22,658,133	$29,455,572	$38,292,244	$49,779,917	$64,713,892
35%	$46,497,712	$62,771,911	$84,742,080	$114,401,808	$154,442,441	$208,497,295

Initial Investment> $20,000					
Years ->	26	27	28	29	30	31
Percent						
1%	$25,905	$26,164	$26,426	$26,690	$26,957	$27,227
5%	$71,113	$74,669	$78,403	$82,323	$86,439	$90,761
10%	$238,364	$262,200	$288,420	$317,262	$348,988	$383,887
15%	$757,136	$870,706	$1,001,312	$1,151,509	$1,324,235	$1,522,871
20%	$2,289,509	$2,747,411	$3,296,893	$3,956,272	$4,747,526	$5,697,032
25%	$6,617,445	$8,271,806	$10,339,758	$12,924,697	$16,155,871	$20,194,839
30%	$18,346,666	$23,850,666	$31,005,866	$40,307,625	$52,399,913	$68,119,887
35%	$48,944,960	$66,075,696	$89,202,189	$120,422,956	$162,570,990	$219,470,837

Appendix A (Returns at various rates of return}

	Initial Investment	$21,000				
Years ->	1	5	10	15	20	21
Percent						
1%	$21,210	$22,071	$23,197	$24,380	$25,624	$25,880
5%	$22,050	$26,802	$34,207	$43,657	$55,719	$58,505
10%	$23,100	$33,821	$54,469	$87,722	$141,277	$155,405
15%	$24,150	$42,239	$84,957	$170,878	$343,697	$395,252
20%	$25,200	$52,255	$130,026	$323,547	$805,090	$966,108
25%	$26,250	$64,087	$195,578	$596,856	$1,821,460	$2,276,825
30%	$27,300	$77,972	$289,503	$1,074,904	$3,991,042	$5,188,355
35%	$28,350	$94,165	$422,238	$1,893,328	$8,489,745	$11,461,156

	Initial Investment	$22,000				
Years ->	1	5	10	15	20	21
Percent						
1%	$22,220	$23,122	$24,302	$25,541	$26,844	$27,113
5%	$23,100	$28,078	$35,836	$45,736	$58,373	$61,291
10%	$24,200	$35,431	$57,062	$91,899	$148,005	$162,805
15%	$25,300	$44,250	$89,002	$179,015	$360,064	$414,073
20%	$26,400	$54,743	$136,218	$338,954	$843,427	$1,012,113
25%	$27,500	$67,139	$204,891	$625,278	$1,908,196	$2,385,245
30%	$28,600	$81,684	$303,289	$1,126,090	$4,181,092	$5,435,420
35%	$29,700	$98,649	$442,344	$1,983,486	$8,894,019	$12,006,926

	Initial Investment	$23,000				
Years ->	1	5	10	15	20	21
Percent						
1%	$23,230	$24,173	$25,406	$26,702	$28,064	$28,345
5%	$24,150	$29,354	$37,465	$47,815	$61,026	$64,077
10%	$25,300	$37,042	$59,656	$96,077	$154,732	$170,206
15%	$26,450	$46,261	$93,048	$187,152	$376,430	$432,895
20%	$27,600	$57,231	$142,410	$354,361	$881,765	$1,058,118
25%	$28,750	$70,190	$214,204	$653,699	$1,994,932	$2,493,665
30%	$29,900	$85,397	$317,075	$1,177,276	$4,371,142	$5,682,484
35%	$31,050	$103,133	$462,451	$2,073,645	$9,298,293	$12,552,695

	Initial Investment	$24,000				
Years ->	1	5	10	15	20	21
Percent						
1%	$24,240	$25,224	$26,511	$27,863	$29,285	$29,577
5%	$25,200	$30,631	$39,093	$49,894	$63,679	$66,863
10%	$26,400	$38,652	$62,250	$100,254	$161,460	$177,606
15%	$27,600	$48,273	$97,093	$195,289	$392,797	$451,716
20%	$28,800	$59,720	$148,602	$369,769	$920,102	$1,104,123
25%	$30,000	$73,242	$223,517	$682,121	$2,081,668	$2,602,085
30%	$31,200	$89,110	$330,860	$1,228,461	$4,561,191	$5,929,549
35%	$32,400	$107,617	$482,557	$2,163,803	$9,702,566	$13,098,464

Appendix A (Returns at various rates of return}

	Initial Investment $21,000					
Years ->	26	27	28	29	30	31
Percent						
1%	$27,200	$27,472	$27,747	$28,025	$28,305	$28,588
5%	$74,669	$78,403	$82,323	$86,439	$90,761	$95,299
10%	$250,282	$275,310	$302,841	$333,125	$366,437	$403,081
15%	$794,993	$914,242	$1,051,378	$1,209,085	$1,390,447	$1,599,014
20%	$2,403,985	$2,884,782	$3,461,738	$4,154,085	$4,984,903	$5,981,883
25%	$6,948,317	$8,685,396	$10,856,746	$13,570,932	$16,963,665	$21,204,581
30%	$19,263,999	$25,043,199	$32,556,159	$42,323,007	$55,019,909	$71,525,881
35%	$51,392,208	$69,379,481	$93,662,299	$126,444,103	$170,699,540	$230,444,378

	Initial Investment $22,000					
Years ->	26	27	28	29	30	31
Percent						
1%	$28,496	$28,781	$29,068	$29,359	$29,653	$29,949
5%	$78,225	$82,136	$86,243	$90,555	$95,083	$99,837
10%	$262,200	$288,420	$317,262	$348,988	$383,887	$422,276
15%	$832,850	$957,777	$1,101,443	$1,266,660	$1,456,659	$1,675,158
20%	$2,518,460	$3,022,152	$3,626,583	$4,351,899	$5,222,279	$6,266,735
25%	$7,279,189	$9,098,987	$11,373,733	$14,217,167	$17,771,458	$22,214,323
30%	$20,181,333	$26,235,732	$34,106,452	$44,338,388	$57,639,904	$74,931,875
35%	$53,839,456	$72,683,265	$98,122,408	$132,465,251	$178,828,089	$241,417,920

	Initial Investment $23,000					
Years ->	26	27	28	29	30	31
Percent						
1%	$29,791	$30,089	$30,390	$30,694	$31,001	$31,311
5%	$81,780	$85,869	$90,163	$94,671	$99,405	$104,375
10%	$274,118	$301,530	$331,683	$364,851	$401,336	$441,470
15%	$870,706	$1,001,312	$1,151,509	$1,324,235	$1,522,871	$1,751,301
20%	$2,632,936	$3,159,523	$3,791,427	$4,549,713	$5,459,655	$6,551,586
25%	$7,610,062	$9,512,577	$11,890,721	$14,863,402	$18,579,252	$23,224,065
30%	$21,098,666	$27,428,266	$35,656,745	$46,353,769	$60,259,900	$78,337,870
35%	$56,286,704	$75,987,050	$102,582,518	$138,486,399	$186,956,639	$252,391,462

	Initial Investment $24,000					
Years ->	26	27	28	29	30	31
Percent						
1%	$31,086	$31,397	$31,711	$32,028	$32,348	$32,672
5%	$85,336	$89,603	$94,083	$98,787	$103,727	$108,913
10%	$286,036	$314,640	$346,104	$380,714	$418,786	$460,664
15%	$908,563	$1,044,848	$1,201,575	$1,381,811	$1,589,083	$1,827,445
20%	$2,747,411	$3,296,893	$3,956,272	$4,747,526	$5,697,032	$6,836,438
25%	$7,940,934	$9,926,167	$12,407,709	$15,509,636	$19,387,046	$24,233,807
30%	$22,015,999	$28,620,799	$37,207,039	$48,369,150	$62,879,895	$81,743,864
35%	$58,733,952	$79,290,835	$107,042,627	$144,507,547	$195,085,188	$263,365,004

Appendix A (Returns at various rates of return}

	Initial Investment	$22,000				
Years ->	1	5	10	15	20	21
Percent						
1%	$22,220	$23,122	$24,302	$25,541	$26,844	$27,113
5%	$23,100	$28,078	$35,836	$45,736	$58,373	$61,291
10%	$24,200	$35,431	$57,062	$91,899	$148,005	$162,805
15%	$25,300	$44,250	$89,002	$179,015	$360,064	$414,073
20%	$26,400	$54,743	$136,218	$338,954	$843,427	$1,012,113
25%	$27,500	$67,139	$204,891	$625,278	$1,908,196	$2,385,245
30%	$28,600	$81,684	$303,289	$1,126,090	$4,181,092	$5,435,420
35%	$29,700	$98,649	$442,344	$1,983,486	$8,894,019	$12,006,926

	Initial Investment	$23,000				
Years ->	1	5	10	15	20	21
Percent						
1%	$23,230	$24,173	$25,406	$26,702	$28,064	$28,345
5%	$24,150	$29,354	$37,465	$47,815	$61,026	$64,077
10%	$25,300	$37,042	$59,656	$96,077	$154,732	$170,206
15%	$26,450	$46,261	$93,048	$187,152	$376,430	$432,895
20%	$27,600	$57,231	$142,410	$354,361	$881,765	$1,058,118
25%	$28,750	$70,190	$214,204	$653,699	$1,994,932	$2,493,665
30%	$29,900	$85,397	$317,075	$1,177,276	$4,371,142	$5,682,484
35%	$31,050	$103,133	$462,451	$2,073,645	$9,298,293	$12,552,695

	Initial Investment	$24,000				
Years ->	1	5	10	15	20	21
Percent						
1%	$24,240	$25,224	$26,511	$27,863	$29,285	$29,577
5%	$25,200	$30,631	$39,093	$49,894	$63,679	$66,863
10%	$26,400	$38,652	$62,250	$100,254	$161,460	$177,606
15%	$27,600	$48,273	$97,093	$195,289	$392,797	$451,716
20%	$28,800	$59,720	$148,602	$369,769	$920,102	$1,104,123
25%	$30,000	$73,242	$223,517	$682,121	$2,081,668	$2,602,085
30%	$31,200	$89,110	$330,860	$1,228,461	$4,561,191	$5,929,549
35%	$32,400	$107,617	$482,557	$2,163,803	$9,702,566	$13,098,464

	Initial Investment	$25,000				
Years ->	1	5	10	15	20	21
Percent						
1%	$25,250	$26,275	$27,616	$29,024	$30,505	$30,810
5%	$26,250	$31,907	$40,722	$51,973	$66,332	$69,649
10%	$27,500	$40,263	$64,844	$104,431	$168,187	$185,006
15%	$28,750	$50,284	$101,139	$203,427	$409,163	$470,538
20%	$30,000	$62,208	$154,793	$385,176	$958,440	$1,150,128
25%	$31,250	$76,294	$232,831	$710,543	$2,168,404	$2,710,505
30%	$32,500	$92,823	$344,646	$1,279,647	$4,751,241	$6,176,613
35%	$33,750	$112,101	$502,664	$2,253,962	$10,106,840	$13,644,234

Appendix A (Returns at various rates of return}

Initial Investment> $22,000					
Years -> 26	27	28	29	30	31
Percent					
1% $28,496	$28,781	$29,068	$29,359	$29,653	$29,949
5% $78,225	$82,136	$86,243	$90,555	$95,083	$99,837
10% $262,200	$288,420	$317,262	$348,988	$383,887	$422,276
15% $832,850	$957,777	$1,101,443	$1,266,660	$1,456,659	$1,675,158
20% $2,518,460	$3,022,152	$3,626,583	$4,351,899	$5,222,279	$6,266,735
25% $7,279,189	$9,098,987	$11,373,733	$14,217,167	$17,771,458	$22,214,323
30% $20,181,333	$26,235,732	$34,106,452	$44,338,388	$57,639,904	$74,931,875
35% $53,839,456	$72,683,265	$98,122,408	$132,465,251	$178,828,089	$241,417,920

Initial Investment> $23,000					
Years -> 26	27	28	29	30	31
Percent					
1% $29,791	$30,089	$30,390	$30,694	$31,001	$31,311
5% $81,780	$85,869	$90,163	$94,671	$99,405	$104,375
10% $274,118	$301,530	$331,683	$364,851	$401,336	$441,470
15% $870,706	$1,001,312	$1,151,509	$1,324,235	$1,522,871	$1,751,301
20% $2,632,936	$3,159,523	$3,791,427	$4,549,713	$5,459,655	$6,551,586
25% $7,610,062	$9,512,577	$11,890,721	$14,863,402	$18,579,252	$23,224,065
30% $21,098,666	$27,428,266	$35,656,745	$46,353,769	$60,259,900	$78,337,870
35% $56,286,704	$75,987,050	$102,582,518	$138,486,399	$186,956,639	$252,391,462

Initial Investment> $24,000					
Years -> 26	27	28	29	30	31
Percent					
1% $31,086	$31,397	$31,711	$32,028	$32,348	$32,672
5% $85,336	$89,603	$94,083	$98,787	$103,727	$108,913
10% $286,036	$314,640	$346,104	$380,714	$418,786	$460,664
15% $908,563	$1,044,848	$1,201,575	$1,381,811	$1,589,083	$1,827,445
20% $2,747,411	$3,296,893	$3,956,272	$4,747,526	$5,697,032	$6,836,438
25% $7,940,934	$9,926,167	$12,407,709	$15,509,636	$19,387,046	$24,233,807
30% $22,015,999	$28,620,799	$37,207,039	$48,369,150	$62,879,895	$81,743,864
35% $58,733,952	$79,290,835	$107,042,627	$144,507,547	$195,085,188	$263,365,004

Initial Investment> $25,000					
Years -> 26	27	28	29	30	31
Percent					
1% $32,381	$32,705	$33,032	$33,363	$33,696	$34,033
5% $88,892	$93,336	$98,003	$102,903	$108,049	$113,451
10% $297,954	$327,750	$360,525	$396,577	$436,235	$479,859
15% $946,420	$1,088,383	$1,251,640	$1,439,386	$1,655,294	$1,903,588
20% $2,861,886	$3,434,264	$4,121,117	$4,945,340	$5,934,408	$7,121,289
25% $8,271,806	$10,339,758	$12,924,697	$16,155,871	$20,194,839	$25,243,549
30% $22,933,333	$29,813,332	$38,757,332	$50,384,532	$65,499,891	$85,149,858
35% $61,181,200	$82,594,620	$111,502,737	$150,528,694	$203,213,738	$274,338,546

211

Appendix A (Returns at various rates of return}

	Initial Investment	$26,000				
Years ->	1	5	10	15	20	21
Percent						
1%	$26,260	$27,326	$28,720	$30,185	$31,725	$32,042
5%	$27,300	$33,183	$42,351	$54,052	$68,986	$72,435
10%	$28,600	$41,873	$67,437	$108,608	$174,915	$192,406
15%	$29,900	$52,295	$105,185	$211,564	$425,530	$489,359
20%	$31,200	$64,696	$160,985	$400,583	$996,778	$1,196,133
25%	$32,500	$79,346	$242,144	$738,964	$2,255,141	$2,818,926
30%	$33,800	$96,536	$358,432	$1,330,833	$4,941,291	$6,423,678
35%	$35,100	$116,585	$522,770	$2,344,120	$10,511,113	$14,190,003

	Initial Investment	$27,000				
Years ->	1	5	10	15	20	21
Percent						
1%	$27,270	$28,377	$29,825	$31,346	$32,945	$33,275
5%	$28,350	$34,460	$43,980	$56,131	$71,639	$75,221
10%	$29,700	$43,484	$70,031	$112,786	$181,642	$199,807
15%	$31,050	$54,307	$109,230	$219,701	$441,897	$508,181
20%	$32,400	$67,185	$167,177	$415,990	$1,035,115	$1,242,138
25%	$33,750	$82,397	$251,457	$767,386	$2,341,877	$2,927,346
30%	$35,100	$100,249	$372,218	$1,382,019	$5,131,340	$6,670,742
35%	$36,450	$121,069	$542,877	$2,434,279	$10,915,387	$14,735,772

	Initial Investment	$28,000				
Years ->	1	5	10	15	20	21
Percent						
1%	$28,280	$29,428	$30,929	$32,507	$34,165	$34,507
5%	$29,400	$35,736	$45,609	$58,210	$74,292	$78,007
10%	$30,800	$45,094	$72,625	$116,963	$188,370	$207,207
15%	$32,200	$56,318	$113,276	$227,838	$458,263	$527,003
20%	$33,600	$69,673	$173,369	$431,397	$1,073,453	$1,288,143
25%	$35,000	$85,449	$260,770	$795,808	$2,428,613	$3,035,766
30%	$36,400	$103,962	$386,004	$1,433,205	$5,321,390	$6,917,807
35%	$37,800	$125,553	$562,984	$2,524,437	$11,319,660	$15,281,542

	Initial Investment	$29,000				
Years ->	1	5	10	15	20	21
Percent						
1%	$29,290	$30,479	$32,034	$33,668	$35,386	$35,739
5%	$30,450	$37,012	$47,238	$60,289	$76,946	$80,793
10%	$31,900	$46,705	$75,219	$121,140	$195,097	$214,607
15%	$33,350	$58,329	$117,321	$235,975	$474,630	$545,824
20%	$34,800	$72,161	$179,560	$446,804	$1,111,790	$1,334,148
25%	$36,250	$88,501	$270,084	$824,230	$2,515,349	$3,144,186
30%	$37,700	$107,675	$399,790	$1,484,391	$5,511,439	$7,164,871
35%	$39,150	$130,037	$583,090	$2,614,596	$11,723,934	$15,827,311

Appendix A (Returns at various rates of return}

Initial Investment> $26,000						
Years ->	26	27	28	29	30	31
Percent						
1%	$33,677	$34,013	$34,354	$34,697	$35,044	$35,395
5%	$92,447	$97,070	$101,923	$107,020	$112,371	$117,989
10%	$309,873	$340,860	$374,946	$412,440	$453,684	$499,053
15%	$984,277	$1,131,918	$1,301,706	$1,496,962	$1,721,506	$1,979,732
20%	$2,976,362	$3,571,634	$4,285,961	$5,143,153	$6,171,784	$7,406,141
25%	$8,602,678	$10,753,348	$13,441,685	$16,802,106	$21,002,633	$26,253,291
30%	$23,850,666	$31,005,866	$40,307,625	$52,399,913	$68,119,887	$88,555,853
35%	$63,628,448	$85,898,405	$115,962,846	$156,549,842	$211,342,287	$285,312,087

Initial Investment> $27,000						
Years ->	26	27	28	29	30	31
Percent						
1%	$34,972	$35,322	$35,675	$36,032	$36,392	$36,756
5%	$96,003	$100,803	$105,843	$111,136	$116,692	$122,527
10%	$321,791	$353,970	$389,367	$428,304	$471,134	$518,247
15%	$1,022,133	$1,175,454	$1,351,772	$1,554,537	$1,787,718	$2,055,876
20%	$3,090,837	$3,709,005	$4,450,806	$5,340,967	$6,409,160	$7,690,993
25%	$8,933,551	$11,166,938	$13,958,673	$17,448,341	$21,810,426	$27,263,033
30%	$24,767,999	$32,198,399	$41,857,919	$54,415,294	$70,739,882	$91,961,847
35%	$66,075,696	$89,202,189	$120,422,956	$162,570,990	$219,470,837	$296,285,629

Initial Investment> $28,000						
Years ->	26	27	28	29	30	31
Percent						
1%	$36,267	$36,630	$36,996	$37,366	$37,740	$38,117
5%	$99,559	$104,537	$109,764	$115,252	$121,014	$127,065
10%	$333,709	$367,080	$403,788	$444,167	$488,583	$537,442
15%	$1,059,990	$1,218,989	$1,401,837	$1,612,113	$1,853,930	$2,132,019
20%	$3,205,313	$3,846,375	$4,615,651	$5,538,781	$6,646,537	$7,975,844
25%	$9,264,423	$11,580,529	$14,475,661	$18,094,576	$22,618,220	$28,272,775
30%	$25,685,332	$33,390,932	$43,408,212	$56,430,675	$73,359,878	$95,367,841
35%	$68,522,944	$92,505,974	$124,883,065	$168,592,138	$227,599,386	$307,259,171

Initial Investment> $29,000						
Years ->	26	27	28	29	30	31
Percent						
1%	$37,562	$37,938	$38,317	$38,701	$39,088	$39,478
5%	$103,115	$108,270	$113,684	$119,368	$125,336	$131,603
10%	$345,627	$380,190	$418,209	$460,030	$506,033	$556,636
15%	$1,097,847	$1,262,524	$1,451,903	$1,669,688	$1,920,141	$2,208,163
20%	$3,319,788	$3,983,746	$4,780,495	$5,736,594	$6,883,913	$8,260,696
25%	$9,595,295	$11,994,119	$14,992,649	$18,740,811	$23,426,013	$29,282,517
30%	$26,602,666	$34,583,465	$44,958,505	$58,446,057	$75,979,874	$98,773,836
35%	$70,970,192	$95,809,759	$129,343,175	$174,613,286	$235,727,936	$318,232,713

213

Appendix A (Returns at various rates of return}

	Initial Investment	$30,000				
Years ->	1	5	10	15	20	21
Percent						
1%	$30,300	$31,530	$33,139	$34,829	$36,606	$36,972
5%	$31,500	$38,288	$48,867	$62,368	$79,599	$83,579
10%	$33,000	$48,315	$77,812	$125,317	$201,825	$222,007
15%	$34,500	$60,341	$121,367	$244,112	$490,996	$564,646
20%	$36,000	$74,650	$185,752	$462,211	$1,150,128	$1,380,154
25%	$37,500	$91,553	$279,397	$852,651	$2,602,085	$3,252,607
30%	$39,000	$111,388	$413,575	$1,535,577	$5,701,489	$7,411,936
35%	$40,500	$134,521	$603,197	$2,704,754	$12,128,208	$16,373,080

	Initial Investment	$31,000				
Years ->	1	5	10	15	20	21
Percent						
1%	$31,310	$32,581	$34,243	$35,990	$37,826	$38,204
5%	$32,550	$39,565	$50,496	$64,447	$82,252	$86,365
10%	$34,100	$49,926	$80,406	$129,495	$208,552	$229,408
15%	$35,650	$62,352	$125,412	$252,249	$507,363	$583,467
20%	$37,200	$77,138	$191,944	$477,618	$1,188,466	$1,426,159
25%	$38,750	$94,604	$288,710	$881,073	$2,688,821	$3,361,027
30%	$40,300	$115,101	$427,361	$1,586,763	$5,891,539	$7,659,000
35%	$41,850	$139,005	$623,303	$2,794,913	$12,532,481	$16,918,850

	Initial Investment	$32,000				
Years ->	1	5	10	15	20	21
Percent						
1%	$32,320	$33,632	$35,348	$37,151	$39,046	$39,437
5%	$33,600	$40,841	$52,125	$66,526	$84,906	$89,151
10%	$35,200	$51,536	$83,000	$133,672	$215,280	$236,808
15%	$36,800	$64,363	$129,458	$260,386	$523,729	$602,289
20%	$38,400	$79,626	$198,136	$493,025	$1,226,803	$1,472,164
25%	$40,000	$97,656	$298,023	$909,495	$2,775,558	$3,469,447
30%	$41,600	$118,814	$441,147	$1,637,949	$6,081,588	$7,906,065
35%	$43,200	$143,489	$643,410	$2,885,071	$12,936,755	$17,464,619

	Initial Investment	$33,000				
Years ->	1	5	10	15	20	21
Percent						
1%	$33,330	$34,683	$36,453	$38,312	$40,266	$40,669
5%	$34,650	$42,117	$53,754	$68,605	$87,559	$91,937
10%	$36,300	$53,147	$85,594	$137,849	$222,007	$244,208
15%	$37,950	$66,375	$133,503	$268,523	$540,096	$621,110
20%	$39,600	$82,115	$204,327	$508,432	$1,265,141	$1,518,169
25%	$41,250	$100,708	$307,336	$937,916	$2,862,294	$3,577,867
30%	$42,900	$122,527	$454,933	$1,689,134	$6,271,638	$8,153,129
35%	$44,550	$147,973	$663,516	$2,975,229	$13,341,028	$18,010,388

Appendix A (Returns at various rates of return}

	Initial Investment	$30,000				
Years ->	26	27	28	29	30	31
Percent						
1%	$38,858	$39,246	$39,639	$40,035	$40,435	$40,840
5%	$106,670	$112,004	$117,604	$123,484	$129,658	$136,141
10%	$357,545	$393,300	$432,630	$475,893	$523,482	$575,830
15%	$1,135,704	$1,306,059	$1,501,968	$1,727,264	$1,986,353	$2,284,306
20%	$3,434,264	$4,121,117	$4,945,340	$5,934,408	$7,121,289	$8,545,547
25%	$9,926,167	$12,407,709	$15,509,636	$19,387,046	$24,233,807	$30,292,259
30%	$27,519,999	$35,775,999	$46,508,798	$60,461,438	$78,599,869	$102,179,830
35%	$73,417,440	$99,113,544	$133,803,284	$180,634,433	$243,856,485	$329,206,255

	Initial Investment	$31,000				
Years ->	26	27	28	29	30	31
Percent						
1%	$40,153	$40,554	$40,960	$41,370	$41,783	$42,201
5%	$110,226	$115,737	$121,524	$127,600	$133,980	$140,679
10%	$369,463	$406,410	$447,051	$491,756	$540,931	$595,025
15%	$1,173,561	$1,349,595	$1,552,034	$1,784,839	$2,052,565	$2,360,450
20%	$3,548,739	$4,258,487	$5,110,185	$6,132,221	$7,358,666	$8,830,399
25%	$10,257,040	$12,821,299	$16,026,624	$20,033,280	$25,041,601	$31,302,001
30%	$28,437,332	$36,968,532	$48,059,092	$62,476,819	$81,219,865	$105,585,824
35%	$75,864,688	$102,417,328	$138,263,393	$186,655,581	$251,985,035	$340,179,797

	Initial Investment	$32,000				
Years ->	26	27	28	29	30	31
Percent						
1%	$41,448	$41,863	$42,281	$42,704	$43,131	$43,562
5%	$113,782	$119,471	$125,444	$131,716	$138,302	$145,217
10%	$381,382	$419,520	$461,472	$507,619	$558,381	$614,219
15%	$1,211,417	$1,393,130	$1,602,100	$1,842,415	$2,118,777	$2,436,593
20%	$3,663,215	$4,395,858	$5,275,029	$6,330,035	$7,596,042	$9,115,250
25%	$10,587,912	$13,234,890	$16,543,612	$20,679,515	$25,849,394	$32,311,743
30%	$29,354,666	$38,161,065	$49,609,385	$64,492,200	$83,839,861	$108,991,819
35%	$78,311,936	$105,721,113	$142,723,503	$192,676,729	$260,113,584	$351,153,338

	Initial Investment	$33,000				
Years ->	26	27	28	29	30	31
Percent						
1%	$42,743	$43,171	$43,603	$44,039	$44,479	$44,924
5%	$117,337	$123,204	$129,364	$135,832	$142,624	$149,755
10%	$393,300	$432,630	$475,893	$523,482	$575,830	$633,413
15%	$1,249,274	$1,436,665	$1,652,165	$1,899,990	$2,184,988	$2,512,737
20%	$3,777,690	$4,533,228	$5,439,874	$6,527,849	$7,833,418	$9,400,102
25%	$10,918,784	$13,648,480	$17,060,600	$21,325,750	$26,657,188	$33,321,485
30%	$30,271,999	$39,353,599	$51,159,678	$66,507,582	$86,459,856	$112,397,813
35%	$80,759,184	$109,024,898	$147,183,612	$198,697,877	$268,242,134	$362,126,880

Appendix A (Returns at various rates of return}

	Initial Investment	$34,000				
Years ->	1	5	10	15	20	21
Percent						
1%	$34,340	$35,734	$37,557	$39,473	$41,486	$41,901
5%	$35,700	$43,394	$55,382	$70,684	$90,212	$94,723
10%	$37,400	$54,757	$88,187	$142,026	$228,735	$251,608
15%	$39,100	$68,386	$137,549	$276,660	$556,462	$639,932
20%	$40,800	$84,603	$210,519	$523,839	$1,303,478	$1,564,174
25%	$42,500	$103,760	$316,650	$966,338	$2,949,030	$3,686,287
30%	$44,200	$126,240	$468,719	$1,740,320	$6,461,688	$8,400,194
35%	$45,900	$152,457	$683,623	$3,065,388	$13,745,302	$18,556,158

	Initial Investment	$35,000				
Years ->	1	5	10	15	20	21
Percent						
1%	$35,350	$36,785	$38,662	$40,634	$42,707	$43,134
5%	$36,750	$44,670	$57,011	$72,762	$92,865	$97,509
10%	$38,500	$56,368	$90,781	$146,204	$235,462	$259,009
15%	$40,250	$70,398	$141,595	$284,797	$572,829	$658,753
20%	$42,000	$87,091	$216,711	$539,246	$1,341,816	$1,610,179
25%	$43,750	$106,812	$325,963	$994,760	$3,035,766	$3,794,708
30%	$45,500	$129,953	$482,505	$1,791,506	$6,651,737	$8,647,259
35%	$47,250	$156,941	$703,729	$3,155,546	$14,149,576	$19,101,927

	Initial Investment	$36,000				
Years ->	1	5	10	15	20	21
Percent						
1%	$36,360	$37,836	$39,766	$41,795	$43,927	$44,366
5%	$37,800	$45,946	$58,640	$74,841	$95,519	$100,295
10%	$39,600	$57,978	$93,375	$150,381	$242,190	$266,409
15%	$41,400	$72,409	$145,640	$292,934	$589,195	$677,575
20%	$43,200	$89,580	$222,903	$554,653	$1,380,154	$1,656,184
25%	$45,000	$109,863	$335,276	$1,023,182	$3,122,502	$3,903,128
30%	$46,800	$133,665	$496,291	$1,842,692	$6,841,787	$8,894,323
35%	$48,600	$161,425	$723,836	$3,245,705	$14,553,849	$19,647,696

	Initial Investment	$37,000				
Years ->	1	5	10	15	20	21
Percent						
1%	$37,370	$38,887	$40,871	$42,956	$45,147	$45,599
5%	$38,850	$47,222	$60,269	$76,920	$98,172	$103,081
10%	$40,700	$59,589	$95,968	$154,558	$248,917	$273,809
15%	$42,550	$74,420	$149,686	$301,071	$605,562	$696,396
20%	$44,400	$92,068	$229,094	$570,060	$1,418,491	$1,702,189
25%	$46,250	$112,915	$344,589	$1,051,603	$3,209,238	$4,011,548
30%	$48,100	$137,378	$510,076	$1,893,878	$7,031,837	$9,141,388
35%	$49,950	$165,909	$743,943	$3,335,863	$14,958,123	$20,193,466

216

Appendix A (Returns at various rates of return}

Initial Investment	$34,000				
Years ->	26	27	28	29	30	31
Percent						
1%	$44,039	$44,479	$44,924	$45,373	$45,827	$46,285
5%	$120,893	$126,938	$133,284	$139,949	$146,946	$154,293
10%	$405,218	$445,740	$490,314	$539,345	$593,280	$652,608
15%	$1,287,131	$1,480,201	$1,702,231	$1,957,565	$2,251,200	$2,588,880
20%	$3,892,166	$4,670,599	$5,604,719	$6,725,662	$8,070,795	$9,684,954
25%	$11,249,656	$14,062,070	$17,577,588	$21,971,985	$27,464,981	$34,331,227
30%	$31,189,332	$40,546,132	$52,709,972	$68,522,963	$89,079,852	$115,803,807
35%	$83,206,432	$112,328,683	$151,643,722	$204,719,024	$276,370,683	$373,100,422

Initial Investment	$35,000				
Years ->	26	27	28	29	30	31
Percent						
1%	$45,334	$45,787	$46,245	$46,708	$47,175	$47,646
5%	$124,449	$130,671	$137,205	$144,065	$151,268	$158,831
10%	$417,136	$458,850	$504,735	$555,208	$610,729	$671,802
15%	$1,324,988	$1,523,736	$1,752,296	$2,015,141	$2,317,412	$2,665,024
20%	$4,006,641	$4,807,969	$5,769,563	$6,923,476	$8,308,171	$9,969,805
25%	$11,580,529	$14,475,661	$18,094,576	$22,618,220	$28,272,775	$35,340,969
30%	$32,106,666	$41,738,665	$54,260,265	$70,538,344	$91,699,848	$119,209,802
35%	$85,653,680	$115,632,468	$156,103,831	$210,740,172	$284,499,233	$384,073,964

Initial Investment	$36,000				
Years ->	26	27	28	29	30	31
Percent						
1%	$46,629	$47,096	$47,566	$48,042	$48,523	$49,008
5%	$128,004	$134,404	$141,125	$148,181	$155,590	$163,369
10%	$429,054	$471,960	$519,156	$571,071	$628,178	$690,996
15%	$1,362,845	$1,567,271	$1,802,362	$2,072,716	$2,383,624	$2,741,167
20%	$4,121,117	$4,945,340	$5,934,408	$7,121,289	$8,545,547	$10,254,657
25%	$11,911,401	$14,889,251	$18,611,564	$23,264,455	$29,080,568	$36,350,711
30%	$33,023,999	$42,931,199	$55,810,558	$72,553,726	$94,319,843	$122,615,796
35%	$88,100,928	$118,936,252	$160,563,941	$216,761,320	$292,627,782	$395,047,506

Initial Investment	$37,000				
Years ->	26	27	28	29	30	31
Percent						
1%	$47,924	$48,404	$48,888	$49,377	$49,870	$50,369
5%	$131,560	$138,138	$145,045	$152,297	$159,912	$167,907
10%	$440,973	$485,070	$533,577	$586,934	$645,628	$710,191
15%	$1,400,701	$1,610,807	$1,852,428	$2,130,292	$2,449,836	$2,817,311
20%	$4,235,592	$5,082,710	$6,099,253	$7,319,103	$8,782,924	$10,539,508
25%	$12,242,273	$15,302,841	$19,128,552	$23,910,690	$29,888,362	$37,360,452
30%	$33,941,332	$44,123,732	$57,360,851	$74,569,107	$96,939,839	$126,021,790
35%	$90,548,176	$122,240,037	$165,024,050	$222,782,468	$300,756,332	$406,021,048

217

Appendix A (Returns at various rates of return}

	Initial Investment▶	$38,000				
Years ->	1	5	10	15	20	21
Percent						
1%	$38,380	$39,938	$41,976	$44,117	$46,367	$46,831
5%	$39,900	$48,499	$61,898	$78,999	$100,825	$105,867
10%	$41,800	$61,199	$98,562	$158,735	$255,645	$281,209
15%	$43,700	$76,432	$153,731	$309,208	$621,928	$715,218
20%	$45,600	$94,556	$235,286	$585,467	$1,456,829	$1,748,195
25%	$47,500	$115,967	$353,903	$1,080,025	$3,295,975	$4,119,968
30%	$49,400	$141,091	$523,862	$1,945,064	$7,221,886	$9,388,452
35%	$51,300	$170,393	$764,049	$3,426,022	$15,362,396	$20,739,235

	Initial Investment▶	$39,000				
Years ->	1	5	10	15	20	21
Percent						
1%	$39,390	$40,989	$43,080	$45,278	$47,587	$48,063
5%	$40,950	$49,775	$63,527	$81,078	$103,479	$108,653
10%	$42,900	$62,810	$101,156	$162,913	$262,372	$288,610
15%	$44,850	$78,443	$157,777	$317,345	$638,295	$734,039
20%	$46,800	$97,044	$241,478	$600,874	$1,495,166	$1,794,200
25%	$48,750	$119,019	$363,216	$1,108,447	$3,382,711	$4,228,388
30%	$50,700	$144,804	$537,648	$1,996,250	$7,411,936	$9,635,517
35%	$52,650	$174,877	$784,156	$3,516,180	$15,766,670	$21,285,004

	Initial Investment▶	$40,000				
Years ->	1	5	10	15	20	21
Percent						
1%	$40,400	$42,040	$44,185	$46,439	$48,808	$49,296
5%	$42,000	$51,051	$65,156	$83,157	$106,132	$111,439
10%	$44,000	$64,420	$103,750	$167,090	$269,100	$296,010
15%	$46,000	$80,454	$161,822	$325,482	$654,661	$752,861
20%	$48,000	$99,533	$247,669	$616,281	$1,533,504	$1,840,205
25%	$50,000	$122,070	$372,529	$1,136,868	$3,469,447	$4,336,809
30%	$52,000	$148,517	$551,434	$2,047,436	$7,601,986	$9,882,581
35%	$54,000	$179,361	$804,262	$3,606,339	$16,170,944	$21,830,774

	Initial Investment▶	$41,000				
Years ->	1	5	10	15	20	21
Percent						
1%	$41,410	$43,091	$45,290	$47,600	$50,028	$50,528
5%	$43,050	$52,328	$66,785	$85,236	$108,785	$114,224
10%	$45,100	$66,031	$106,343	$171,267	$275,827	$303,410
15%	$47,150	$82,466	$165,868	$333,620	$671,028	$771,682
20%	$49,200	$102,021	$253,861	$631,688	$1,571,842	$1,886,210
25%	$51,250	$125,122	$381,842	$1,165,290	$3,556,183	$4,445,229
30%	$53,300	$152,230	$565,220	$2,098,622	$7,792,035	$10,129,646
35%	$55,350	$183,845	$824,369	$3,696,497	$16,575,217	$22,376,543

Appendix A (Returns at various rates of return}

Initial Investment	$38,000				
Years ->	26	27	28	29	30	31
Percent						
1%	$49,220	$49,712	$50,209	$50,711	$51,218	$51,730
5%	$135,116	$141,871	$148,965	$156,413	$164,234	$172,446
10%	$452,891	$498,180	$547,998	$602,798	$663,077	$729,385
15%	$1,438,558	$1,654,342	$1,902,493	$2,187,867	$2,516,047	$2,893,454
20%	$4,350,067	$5,220,081	$6,264,097	$7,516,917	$9,020,300	$10,824,360
25%	$12,573,145	$15,716,432	$19,645,540	$24,556,924	$30,696,156	$38,370,194
30%	$34,858,665	$45,316,265	$58,911,145	$76,584,488	$99,559,834	$129,427,785
35%	$92,995,424	$125,543,822	$169,484,160	$228,803,616	$308,884,881	$416,994,589

Initial Investment	$39,000				
Years ->	26	27	28	29	30	31
Percent						
1%	$50,515	$51,020	$51,530	$52,046	$52,566	$53,092
5%	$138,671	$145,605	$152,885	$160,529	$168,556	$176,984
10%	$464,809	$511,290	$562,419	$618,661	$680,527	$748,579
15%	$1,476,415	$1,697,877	$1,952,559	$2,245,443	$2,582,259	$2,969,598
20%	$4,464,543	$5,357,452	$6,428,942	$7,714,730	$9,257,676	$11,109,211
25%	$12,904,018	$16,130,022	$20,162,527	$25,203,159	$31,503,949	$39,379,936
30%	$35,775,999	$46,508,798	$60,461,438	$78,599,869	$102,179,830	$132,833,779
35%	$95,442,672	$128,847,607	$173,944,269	$234,824,763	$317,013,431	$427,968,131

Initial Investment	$40,000				
Years ->	26	27	28	29	30	31
Percent						
1%	$51,810	$52,328	$52,852	$53,380	$53,914	$54,453
5%	$142,227	$149,338	$156,805	$164,645	$172,878	$181,522
10%	$476,727	$524,400	$576,840	$634,524	$697,976	$767,774
15%	$1,514,272	$1,741,413	$2,002,624	$2,303,018	$2,648,471	$3,045,742
20%	$4,579,018	$5,494,822	$6,593,786	$7,912,544	$9,495,053	$11,394,063
25%	$13,234,890	$16,543,612	$20,679,515	$25,849,394	$32,311,743	$40,389,678
30%	$36,693,332	$47,701,332	$62,011,731	$80,615,251	$104,799,826	$136,239,773
35%	$97,889,920	$132,151,392	$178,404,379	$240,845,911	$325,141,980	$438,941,673

Initial Investment	$41,000				
Years ->	26	27	28	29	30	31
Percent						
1%	$53,106	$53,637	$54,173	$54,715	$55,262	$55,814
5%	$145,783	$153,072	$160,725	$168,762	$177,200	$186,060
10%	$488,645	$537,510	$591,261	$650,387	$715,425	$786,968
15%	$1,552,129	$1,784,948	$2,052,690	$2,360,594	$2,714,683	$3,121,885
20%	$4,693,494	$5,632,193	$6,758,631	$8,110,357	$9,732,429	$11,678,915
25%	$13,565,762	$16,957,203	$21,196,503	$26,495,629	$33,119,536	$41,399,420
30%	$37,610,665	$48,893,865	$63,562,024	$82,630,632	$107,419,821	$139,645,768
35%	$100,337,168	$135,455,176	$182,864,488	$246,867,059	$333,270,530	$449,915,215

Appendix A (Returns at various rates of return}

Initial Investment▷		$42,000			
Years -> 1	5	10	15	20	21
Percent					
1%	$42,420	$44,142	$46,394	$48,761	$51,248	$51,760
5%	$44,100	$53,604	$68,414	$87,315	$111,439	$117,010
10%	$46,200	$67,641	$108,937	$175,444	$282,555	$310,810
15%	$48,300	$84,477	$169,913	$341,757	$687,395	$790,504
20%	$50,400	$104,509	$260,053	$647,095	$1,610,179	$1,932,215
25%	$52,500	$128,174	$391,155	$1,193,712	$3,642,919	$4,553,649
30%	$54,600	$155,943	$579,006	$2,149,808	$7,982,085	$10,376,710
35%	$56,700	$188,329	$844,475	$3,786,656	$16,979,491	$22,922,312

Initial Investment▷		$43,000			
Years -> 1	5	10	15	20	21
Percent					
1%	$43,430	$45,193	$47,499	$49,922	$52,468	$52,993
5%	$45,150	$54,880	$70,042	$89,394	$114,092	$119,796
10%	$47,300	$69,252	$111,531	$179,622	$289,282	$318,211
15%	$49,450	$86,488	$173,959	$349,894	$703,761	$809,325
20%	$51,600	$106,998	$266,245	$662,502	$1,648,517	$1,978,220
25%	$53,750	$131,226	$400,469	$1,222,134	$3,729,655	$4,662,069
30%	$55,900	$159,656	$592,792	$2,200,993	$8,172,134	$10,623,775
35%	$58,050	$192,813	$864,582	$3,876,814	$17,383,764	$23,468,082

Initial Investment▷		$44,000			
Years -> 1	5	10	15	20	21
Percent					
1%	$44,440	$46,244	$48,603	$51,083	$53,688	$54,225
5%	$46,200	$56,156	$71,671	$91,473	$116,745	$122,582
10%	$48,400	$70,862	$114,125	$183,799	$296,010	$325,611
15%	$50,600	$88,500	$178,005	$358,031	$720,128	$828,147
20%	$52,800	$109,486	$272,436	$677,909	$1,686,854	$2,024,225
25%	$55,000	$134,277	$409,782	$1,250,555	$3,816,392	$4,770,490
30%	$57,200	$163,369	$606,577	$2,252,179	$8,362,184	$10,870,839
35%	$59,400	$197,297	$884,688	$3,966,973	$17,788,038	$24,013,851

Initial Investment▷		$45,000			
Years -> 1	5	10	15	20	21
Percent					
1%	$45,450	$47,295	$49,708	$52,244	$54,909	$55,458
5%	$47,250	$57,433	$73,300	$93,552	$119,398	$125,368
10%	$49,500	$72,473	$116,718	$187,976	$302,737	$333,011
15%	$51,750	$90,511	$182,050	$366,168	$736,494	$846,968
20%	$54,000	$111,974	$278,628	$693,316	$1,725,192	$2,070,230
25%	$56,250	$137,329	$419,095	$1,278,977	$3,903,128	$4,878,910
30%	$58,500	$167,082	$620,363	$2,303,365	$8,552,234	$11,117,904
35%	$60,750	$201,782	$904,795	$4,057,131	$18,192,312	$24,559,621

Appendix A (Returns at various rates of return}

	Initial Investment $42,000					
Years ->	26	27	28	29	30	31
Percent						
1%	$54,401	$54,945	$55,494	$56,049	$56,610	$57,176
5%	$149,338	$156,805	$164,645	$172,878	$181,522	$190,598
10%	$500,563	$550,620	$605,682	$666,250	$732,875	$806,162
15%	$1,589,985	$1,828,483	$2,102,756	$2,418,169	$2,780,894	$3,198,029
20%	$4,807,969	$5,769,563	$6,923,476	$8,308,171	$9,969,805	$11,963,766
25%	$13,896,634	$17,370,793	$21,713,491	$27,141,864	$33,927,330	$42,409,162
30%	$38,527,999	$50,086,398	$65,112,318	$84,646,013	$110,039,817	$143,051,762
35%	$102,784,416	$138,758,961	$187,324,598	$252,888,207	$341,399,079	$460,888,757

	Initial Investment $43,000					
Years ->	26	27	28	29	30	31
Percent						
1%	$55,696	$56,253	$56,816	$57,384	$57,958	$58,537
5%	$152,894	$160,539	$168,566	$176,994	$185,844	$195,136
10%	$512,482	$563,730	$620,103	$682,113	$750,324	$825,357
15%	$1,627,842	$1,872,019	$2,152,821	$2,475,745	$2,847,106	$3,274,172
20%	$4,922,445	$5,906,934	$7,088,320	$8,505,985	$10,207,181	$12,248,618
25%	$14,227,507	$17,784,383	$22,230,479	$27,788,099	$34,735,123	$43,418,904
30%	$39,445,332	$51,278,932	$66,662,611	$86,661,394	$112,659,813	$146,457,756
35%	$105,231,664	$142,062,746	$191,784,707	$258,909,354	$349,527,629	$471,862,299

	Initial Investment $44,000					
Years ->	26	27	28	29	30	31
Percent						
1%	$56,991	$57,561	$58,137	$58,718	$59,305	$59,898
5%	$156,450	$164,272	$172,486	$181,110	$190,165	$199,674
10%	$524,400	$576,840	$634,524	$697,976	$767,774	$844,551
15%	$1,665,699	$1,915,554	$2,202,887	$2,533,320	$2,913,318	$3,350,316
20%	$5,036,920	$6,044,304	$7,253,165	$8,703,798	$10,444,558	$12,533,469
25%	$14,558,379	$18,197,973	$22,747,467	$28,434,334	$35,542,917	$44,428,646
30%	$40,362,665	$52,471,465	$68,212,904	$88,676,776	$115,279,808	$149,863,751
35%	$107,678,912	$145,366,531	$196,244,816	$264,930,502	$357,656,178	$482,835,840

	Initial Investment $45,000					
Years ->	26	27	28	29	30	31
Percent						
1%	$58,287	$58,869	$59,458	$60,053	$60,653	$61,260
5%	$160,005	$168,006	$176,406	$185,226	$194,487	$204,212
10%	$536,318	$589,950	$648,945	$713,839	$785,223	$863,745
15%	$1,703,556	$1,959,089	$2,252,953	$2,590,895	$2,979,530	$3,426,459
20%	$5,151,396	$6,181,675	$7,418,010	$8,901,612	$10,681,934	$12,818,321
25%	$14,889,251	$18,611,564	$23,264,455	$29,080,568	$36,350,711	$45,438,388
30%	$41,279,999	$53,663,998	$69,763,198	$90,692,157	$117,899,804	$153,269,745
35%	$110,126,160	$148,670,316	$200,704,926	$270,951,650	$365,784,728	$493,809,382

Appendix A (Returns at various rates of return}

Initial Investment> $46,000						
Years ->	1	5	10	15	20	21
Percent						
1%	$46,460	$48,346	$50,813	$53,405	$56,129	$56,690
5%	$48,300	$58,709	$74,929	$95,631	$122,052	$128,154
10%	$50,600	$74,083	$119,312	$192,153	$309,465	$340,411
15%	$52,900	$92,522	$186,096	$374,305	$752,861	$865,790
20%	$55,200	$114,463	$284,820	$708,723	$1,763,530	$2,116,236
25%	$57,500	$140,381	$428,408	$1,307,399	$3,989,864	$4,987,330
30%	$59,800	$170,795	$634,149	$2,354,551	$8,742,283	$11,364,968
35%	$62,100	$206,266	$924,902	$4,147,290	$18,596,585	$25,105,390

Initial Investment> $47,000						
Years ->	1	5	10	15	20	21
Percent						
1%	$47,470	$49,397	$51,917	$54,566	$57,349	$57,922
5%	$49,350	$59,985	$76,558	$97,710	$124,705	$130,940
10%	$51,700	$75,694	$121,906	$196,331	$316,192	$347,812
15%	$54,050	$94,534	$190,141	$382,442	$769,227	$884,611
20%	$56,400	$116,951	$291,012	$724,130	$1,801,867	$2,162,241
25%	$58,750	$143,433	$437,722	$1,335,820	$4,076,600	$5,095,750
30%	$61,100	$174,508	$647,935	$2,405,737	$8,932,333	$11,612,033
35%	$63,450	$210,750	$945,008	$4,237,448	$19,000,859	$25,651,159

Initial Investment> $48,000						
Years ->	1	5	10	15	20	21
Percent						
1%	$48,480	$50,448	$53,022	$55,727	$58,569	$59,155
5%	$50,400	$61,262	$78,187	$99,789	$127,358	$133,726
10%	$52,800	$77,304	$124,500	$200,508	$322,920	$355,212
15%	$55,200	$96,545	$194,187	$390,579	$785,594	$903,433
20%	$57,600	$119,439	$297,203	$739,537	$1,840,205	$2,208,246
25%	$60,000	$146,484	$447,035	$1,364,242	$4,163,336	$5,204,170
30%	$62,400	$178,221	$661,721	$2,456,923	$9,122,383	$11,859,097
35%	$64,800	$215,234	$965,115	$4,327,607	$19,405,132	$26,196,929

Initial Investment> $49,000						
Years ->	1	5	10	15	20	21
Percent						
1%	$49,490	$51,499	$54,126	$56,887	$59,789	$60,387
5%	$51,450	$62,538	$79,816	$101,867	$130,012	$136,512
10%	$53,900	$78,915	$127,093	$204,685	$329,647	$362,612
15%	$56,350	$98,557	$198,232	$398,716	$801,960	$922,254
20%	$58,800	$121,928	$303,395	$754,944	$1,878,542	$2,254,251
25%	$61,250	$149,536	$456,348	$1,392,664	$4,250,073	$5,312,591
30%	$63,700	$181,934	$675,507	$2,508,109	$9,312,432	$12,106,162
35%	$66,150	$219,718	$985,221	$4,417,765	$19,809,406	$26,742,698

Appendix A (Returns at various rates of return}

	Initial Investment> $46,000					
Years ->	26	27	28	29	30	31
Percent						
1%	$59,582	$60,178	$60,779	$61,387	$62,001	$62,621
5%	$163,561	$171,739	$180,326	$189,342	$198,809	$208,750
10%	$548,236	$603,060	$663,366	$729,702	$802,673	$882,940
15%	$1,741,413	$2,002,624	$2,303,018	$2,648,471	$3,045,742	$3,502,603
20%	$5,265,871	$6,319,045	$7,582,854	$9,099,425	$10,919,310	$13,103,173
25%	$15,220,123	$19,025,154	$23,781,443	$29,726,803	$37,158,504	$46,448,130
30%	$42,197,332	$54,856,531	$71,313,491	$92,707,538	$120,519,800	$156,675,739
35%	$112,573,408	$151,974,100	$205,165,035	$276,972,798	$373,913,277	$504,782,924

	Initial Investment> $47,000					
Years ->	26	27	28	29	30	31
Percent						
1%	$60,877	$61,486	$62,101	$62,722	$63,349	$63,982
5%	$167,117	$175,472	$184,246	$193,458	$203,131	$213,288
10%	$560,154	$616,170	$677,787	$745,565	$820,122	$902,134
15%	$1,779,269	$2,046,160	$2,353,084	$2,706,046	$3,111,953	$3,578,746
20%	$5,380,347	$6,456,416	$7,747,699	$9,297,239	$11,156,687	$13,388,024
25%	$15,550,996	$19,438,744	$24,298,430	$30,373,038	$37,966,298	$47,457,872
30%	$43,114,665	$56,049,065	$72,863,784	$94,722,919	$123,139,795	$160,081,734
35%	$115,020,656	$155,277,885	$209,625,145	$282,993,946	$382,041,827	$515,756,466

	Initial Investment> $48,000					
Years ->	26	27	28	29	30	31
Percent						
1%	$62,172	$62,794	$63,422	$64,056	$64,697	$65,344
5%	$170,672	$179,206	$188,166	$197,575	$207,453	$217,826
10%	$572,072	$629,280	$692,208	$761,428	$837,571	$921,328
15%	$1,817,126	$2,089,695	$2,403,149	$2,763,622	$3,178,165	$3,654,890
20%	$5,494,822	$6,593,786	$7,912,544	$9,495,053	$11,394,063	$13,672,876
25%	$15,881,868	$19,852,335	$24,815,418	$31,019,273	$38,774,091	$48,467,614
30%	$44,031,998	$57,241,598	$74,414,077	$96,738,301	$125,759,791	$163,487,728
35%	$117,467,904	$158,581,670	$214,085,254	$289,015,093	$390,170,376	$526,730,008

	Initial Investment> $49,000					
Years ->	26	27	28	29	30	31
Percent						
1%	$63,468	$64,102	$64,743	$65,391	$66,045	$66,705
5%	$174,228	$182,939	$192,086	$201,691	$211,775	$222,364
10%	$583,991	$642,390	$706,629	$777,292	$855,021	$940,523
15%	$1,854,983	$2,133,230	$2,453,215	$2,821,197	$3,244,377	$3,731,033
20%	$5,609,298	$6,731,157	$8,077,388	$9,692,866	$11,631,439	$13,957,727
25%	$16,212,740	$20,265,925	$25,332,406	$31,665,508	$39,581,885	$49,477,356
30%	$44,949,332	$58,434,131	$75,964,371	$98,753,682	$128,379,787	$166,893,723
35%	$119,915,152	$161,885,455	$218,545,364	$295,036,241	$398,298,926	$537,703,550

Appendix A (Returns at various rates of return}

	Initial Investment	$50,000				
Years ->	1	5	10	15	20	21
Percent						
1%	$50,500	$52,551	$55,231	$58,048	$61,010	$61,620
5%	$52,500	$63,814	$81,445	$103,946	$132,665	$139,298
10%	$55,000	$80,526	$129,687	$208,862	$336,375	$370,012
15%	$57,500	$100,568	$202,278	$406,853	$818,327	$941,076
20%	$60,000	$124,416	$309,587	$770,351	$1,916,880	$2,300,256
25%	$62,500	$152,588	$465,661	$1,421,085	$4,336,809	$5,421,011
30%	$65,000	$185,647	$689,292	$2,559,295	$9,502,482	$12,353,226
35%	$67,500	$224,202	$1,005,328	$4,507,923	$20,213,679	$27,288,467

	Initial Investment	$51,000				
Years ->	1	5	10	15	20	21
Percent						
1%	$51,510	$53,602	$56,336	$59,209	$62,230	$62,852
5%	$53,550	$65,090	$83,074	$106,025	$135,318	$142,084
10%	$56,100	$82,136	$132,281	$213,040	$343,102	$377,413
15%	$58,650	$102,579	$206,323	$414,990	$834,693	$959,897
20%	$61,200	$126,904	$315,779	$785,758	$1,955,218	$2,346,261
25%	$63,750	$155,640	$474,975	$1,449,507	$4,423,545	$5,529,431
30%	$66,300	$189,359	$703,078	$2,610,481	$9,692,532	$12,600,291
35%	$68,850	$228,686	$1,025,434	$4,598,082	$20,617,953	$27,834,237

	Initial Investment	$52,000				
Years ->	1	5	10	15	20	21
Percent						
1%	$52,520	$54,653	$57,440	$60,370	$63,450	$64,084
5%	$54,600	$66,367	$84,703	$108,104	$137,971	$144,870
10%	$57,200	$83,747	$134,875	$217,217	$349,830	$384,813
15%	$59,800	$104,591	$210,369	$423,127	$851,060	$978,719
20%	$62,400	$129,393	$321,970	$801,165	$1,993,555	$2,392,266
25%	$65,000	$158,691	$484,288	$1,477,929	$4,510,281	$5,637,851
30%	$67,600	$193,072	$716,864	$2,661,666	$9,882,581	$12,847,356
35%	$70,200	$233,170	$1,045,541	$4,688,240	$21,022,227	$28,380,006

	Initial Investment	$53,000				
Years ->	1	5	10	15	20	21
Percent						
1%	$53,530	$55,704	$58,545	$61,531	$64,670	$65,317
5%	$55,650	$67,643	$86,331	$110,183	$140,625	$147,656
10%	$58,300	$85,357	$137,468	$221,394	$356,557	$392,213
15%	$60,950	$106,602	$214,415	$431,264	$867,426	$997,540
20%	$63,600	$131,881	$328,162	$816,572	$2,031,893	$2,438,271
25%	$66,250	$161,743	$493,601	$1,506,351	$4,597,017	$5,746,272
30%	$68,900	$196,785	$730,650	$2,712,852	$10,072,631	$13,094,420
35%	$71,550	$237,654	$1,065,647	$4,778,399	$21,426,500	$28,925,775

Appendix A (Returns at various rates of return}

	Initial Investment	$50,000				
Years ->	26	27	28	29	30	31
Percent						
1%	$64,763	$65,410	$66,065	$66,725	$67,392	$68,066
5%	$177,784	$186,673	$196,006	$205,807	$216,097	$226,902
10%	$595,909	$655,500	$721,050	$793,155	$872,470	$959,717
15%	$1,892,840	$2,176,766	$2,503,281	$2,878,773	$3,310,589	$3,807,177
20%	$5,723,773	$6,868,528	$8,242,233	$9,890,680	$11,868,816	$14,242,579
25%	$16,543,612	$20,679,515	$25,849,394	$32,311,743	$40,389,678	$50,487,098
30%	$45,866,665	$59,626,665	$77,514,664	$100,769,063	$130,999,782	$170,299,717
35%	$122,362,400	$165,189,239	$223,005,473	$301,057,389	$406,427,475	$548,677,091

	Initial Investment	$51,000				
Years ->	26	27	28	29	30	31
Percent						
1%	$66,058	$66,719	$67,386	$68,060	$68,740	$69,428
5%	$181,339	$190,406	$199,927	$209,923	$220,419	$231,440
10%	$607,827	$668,610	$735,471	$809,018	$889,920	$978,911
15%	$1,930,697	$2,220,301	$2,553,346	$2,936,348	$3,376,800	$3,883,320
20%	$5,838,248	$7,005,898	$8,407,078	$10,088,493	$12,106,192	$14,527,430
25%	$16,874,484	$21,093,106	$26,366,382	$32,957,978	$41,197,472	$51,496,840
30%	$46,783,998	$60,819,198	$79,064,957	$102,784,444	$133,619,778	$173,705,711
35%	$124,809,648	$168,493,024	$227,465,583	$307,078,537	$414,556,025	$559,650,633

	Initial Investment	$52,000				
Years ->	26	27	28	29	30	31
Percent						
1%	$67,353	$68,027	$68,707	$69,394	$70,088	$70,789
5%	$184,895	$194,140	$203,847	$214,039	$224,741	$235,978
10%	$619,745	$681,720	$749,892	$824,881	$907,369	$998,106
15%	$1,968,553	$2,263,836	$2,603,412	$2,993,924	$3,443,012	$3,959,464
20%	$5,952,724	$7,143,269	$8,571,922	$10,286,307	$12,343,568	$14,812,282
25%	$17,205,357	$21,506,696	$26,883,370	$33,604,212	$42,005,265	$52,506,582
30%	$47,701,332	$62,011,731	$80,615,251	$104,799,826	$136,239,773	$177,111,706
35%	$127,256,896	$171,796,809	$231,925,692	$313,099,684	$422,684,574	$570,624,175

	Initial Investment	$53,000				
Years ->	26	27	28	29	30	31
Percent						
1%	$68,649	$69,335	$70,028	$70,729	$71,436	$72,150
5%	$188,451	$197,873	$207,767	$218,155	$229,063	$240,516
10%	$631,663	$694,830	$764,313	$840,744	$924,818	$1,017,300
15%	$2,006,410	$2,307,372	$2,653,477	$3,051,499	$3,509,224	$4,035,608
20%	$6,067,199	$7,280,639	$8,736,767	$10,484,121	$12,580,945	$15,097,134
25%	$17,536,229	$21,920,286	$27,400,358	$34,250,447	$42,813,059	$53,516,324
30%	$48,618,665	$63,204,265	$82,165,544	$106,815,207	$138,859,769	$180,517,700
35%	$129,704,144	$175,100,594	$236,385,802	$319,120,832	$430,813,124	$581,597,717

Appendix A (Returns at various rates of return}

	Initial Investment	$54,000				
Years ->	1	5	10	15	20	21
Percent						
1%	$54,540	$56,755	$59,650	$62,692	$65,890	$66,549
5%	$56,700	$68,919	$87,960	$112,262	$143,278	$150,442
10%	$59,400	$86,968	$140,062	$225,571	$363,285	$399,613
15%	$62,100	$108,613	$218,460	$439,401	$883,793	$1,016,362
20%	$64,800	$134,369	$334,354	$831,979	$2,070,230	$2,484,276
25%	$67,500	$164,795	$502,914	$1,534,772	$4,683,753	$5,854,692
30%	$70,200	$200,498	$744,436	$2,764,038	$10,262,680	$13,341,485
35%	$72,900	$242,138	$1,085,754	$4,868,557	$21,830,774	$29,471,545

	Initial Investment	$55,000				
Years ->	1	5	10	15	20	21
Percent						
1%	$55,550	$57,806	$60,754	$63,853	$67,110	$67,782
5%	$57,750	$70,195	$89,589	$114,341	$145,931	$153,228
10%	$60,500	$88,578	$142,656	$229,749	$370,012	$407,014
15%	$63,250	$110,625	$222,506	$447,538	$900,160	$1,035,183
20%	$66,000	$136,858	$340,546	$847,386	$2,108,568	$2,530,282
25%	$68,750	$167,847	$512,227	$1,563,194	$4,770,490	$5,963,112
30%	$71,500	$204,211	$758,222	$2,815,224	$10,452,730	$13,588,549
35%	$74,250	$246,622	$1,105,861	$4,958,716	$22,235,047	$30,017,314

	Initial Investment	$56,000				
Years ->	1	5	10	15	20	21
Percent						
1%	$56,560	$58,857	$61,859	$65,014	$68,331	$69,014
5%	$58,800	$71,472	$91,218	$116,420	$148,585	$156,014
10%	$61,600	$90,189	$145,250	$233,926	$376,740	$414,414
15%	$64,400	$112,636	$226,551	$455,675	$916,526	$1,054,005
20%	$67,200	$139,346	$346,737	$862,793	$2,146,906	$2,576,287
25%	$70,000	$170,898	$521,541	$1,591,616	$4,857,226	$6,071,532
30%	$72,800	$207,924	$772,008	$2,866,410	$10,642,780	$13,835,614
35%	$75,600	$251,106	$1,125,967	$5,048,874	$22,639,321	$30,563,083

	Initial Investment	$57,000				
Years ->	1	5	10	15	20	21
Percent						
1%	$57,570	$59,908	$62,963	$66,175	$69,551	$70,246
5%	$59,850	$72,748	$92,847	$118,499	$151,238	$158,800
10%	$62,700	$91,799	$147,843	$238,103	$383,467	$421,814
15%	$65,550	$114,647	$230,597	$463,813	$932,893	$1,072,827
20%	$68,400	$141,834	$352,929	$878,200	$2,185,243	$2,622,292
25%	$71,250	$173,950	$530,854	$1,620,037	$4,943,962	$6,179,952
30%	$74,100	$211,637	$785,793	$2,917,596	$10,832,829	$14,082,678
35%	$76,950	$255,590	$1,146,074	$5,139,033	$23,043,595	$31,108,853

226

Appendix A (Returns at various rates of return}

Initial Investment>	$54,000				
Years ->	26	27	28	29	30	31
Percent						
1%	$69,944	$70,643	$71,350	$72,063	$72,784	$73,512
5%	$192,006	$201,607	$211,687	$222,271	$233,385	$245,054
10%	$643,582	$707,940	$778,734	$856,607	$942,268	$1,036,494
15%	$2,044,267	$2,350,907	$2,703,543	$3,109,075	$3,575,436	$4,111,751
20%	$6,181,675	$7,418,010	$8,901,612	$10,681,934	$12,818,321	$15,381,985
25%	$17,867,101	$22,333,877	$27,917,346	$34,896,682	$43,620,853	$54,526,066
30%	$49,535,998	$64,396,798	$83,715,837	$108,830,588	$141,479,765	$183,923,694
35%	$132,151,392	$178,404,379	$240,845,911	$325,141,980	$438,941,673	$592,571,259

Initial Investment>	$55,000				
Years ->	26	27	28	29	30	31
Percent						
1%	$71,239	$71,951	$72,671	$73,398	$74,132	$74,873
5%	$195,562	$205,340	$215,607	$226,387	$237,707	$249,592
10%	$655,500	$721,050	$793,155	$872,470	$959,717	$1,055,689
15%	$2,082,124	$2,394,442	$2,753,609	$3,166,650	$3,641,647	$4,187,895
20%	$6,296,150	$7,555,380	$9,066,456	$10,879,748	$13,055,697	$15,666,837
25%	$18,197,973	$22,747,467	$28,434,334	$35,542,917	$44,428,646	$55,535,808
30%	$50,453,332	$65,589,331	$85,266,130	$110,845,970	$144,099,760	$187,329,689
35%	$134,598,640	$181,708,163	$245,306,021	$331,163,128	$447,070,223	$603,544,800

Initial Investment>	$56,000				
Years ->	26	27	28	29	30	31
Percent						
1%	$72,534	$73,260	$73,992	$74,732	$75,480	$76,234
5%	$199,118	$209,074	$219,527	$230,504	$242,029	$254,130
10%	$667,418	$734,160	$807,576	$888,333	$977,167	$1,074,883
15%	$2,119,981	$2,437,978	$2,803,674	$3,224,225	$3,707,859	$4,264,038
20%	$6,410,626	$7,692,751	$9,231,301	$11,077,561	$13,293,074	$15,951,688
25%	$18,528,846	$23,161,057	$28,951,321	$36,189,152	$45,236,440	$56,545,550
30%	$51,370,665	$66,781,864	$86,816,424	$112,861,351	$146,719,756	$190,735,683
35%	$137,045,888	$185,011,948	$249,766,130	$337,184,276	$455,198,772	$614,518,342

Initial Investment>	$57,000				
Years ->	26	27	28	29	30	31
Percent						
1%	$73,830	$74,568	$75,314	$76,067	$76,827	$77,596
5%	$202,673	$212,807	$223,447	$234,620	$246,351	$258,668
10%	$679,336	$747,270	$821,997	$904,196	$994,616	$1,094,078
15%	$2,157,837	$2,481,513	$2,853,740	$3,281,801	$3,774,071	$4,340,182
20%	$6,525,101	$7,830,121	$9,396,146	$11,275,375	$13,530,450	$16,236,540
25%	$18,859,718	$23,574,647	$29,468,309	$36,835,387	$46,044,233	$57,555,292
30%	$52,287,998	$67,974,398	$88,366,717	$114,876,732	$149,339,752	$194,141,677
35%	$139,493,136	$188,315,733	$254,226,240	$343,205,423	$463,327,322	$625,491,884

Appendix A (Returns at various rates of return}

Initial Investment	$58,000				
Years -> 1	5	10	15	20	21
Percent					
1% $58,580	$60,959	$64,068	$67,336	$70,771	$71,479
5% $60,900	$74,024	$94,476	$120,578	$153,891	$161,586
10% $63,800	$93,410	$150,437	$242,280	$390,195	$429,214
15% $66,700	$116,659	$234,642	$471,950	$949,259	$1,091,648
20% $69,600	$144,323	$359,121	$893,607	$2,223,581	$2,668,297
25% $72,500	$177,002	$540,167	$1,648,459	$5,030,698	$6,288,373
30% $75,400	$215,350	$799,579	$2,968,782	$11,022,879	$14,329,743
35% $78,300	$260,074	$1,166,180	$5,229,191	$23,447,868	$31,654,622

Initial Investment	$59,000				
Years -> 1	5	10	15	20	21
Percent					
1% $59,590	$62,010	$65,173	$68,497	$71,991	$72,711
5% $61,950	$75,301	$96,105	$122,657	$156,545	$164,372
10% $64,900	$95,020	$153,031	$246,458	$396,922	$436,615
15% $67,850	$118,670	$238,688	$480,087	$965,626	$1,110,470
20% $70,800	$146,811	$365,312	$909,014	$2,261,918	$2,714,302
25% $73,750	$180,054	$549,480	$1,676,881	$5,117,434	$6,396,793
30% $76,700	$219,063	$813,365	$3,019,968	$11,212,929	$14,576,807
35% $79,650	$264,558	$1,186,287	$5,319,350	$23,852,142	$32,200,391

Initial Investment	$60,000				
Years -> 1	5	10	15	20	21
Percent					
1% $60,600	$63,061	$66,277	$69,658	$73,211	$73,944
5% $63,000	$76,577	$97,734	$124,736	$159,198	$167,158
10% $66,000	$96,631	$155,625	$250,635	$403,650	$444,015
15% $69,000	$120,681	$242,733	$488,224	$981,992	$1,129,291
20% $72,000	$149,299	$371,504	$924,421	$2,300,256	$2,760,307
25% $75,000	$183,105	$558,794	$1,705,303	$5,204,170	$6,505,213
30% $78,000	$222,776	$827,151	$3,071,154	$11,402,978	$14,823,872
35% $81,000	$269,042	$1,206,393	$5,409,508	$24,256,415	$32,746,161

Initial Investment	$61,000				
Years -> 1	5	10	15	20	21
Percent					
1% $61,610	$64,112	$67,382	$70,819	$74,432	$75,176
5% $64,050	$77,853	$99,363	$126,815	$161,851	$169,944
10% $67,100	$98,241	$158,218	$254,812	$410,377	$451,415
15% $70,150	$122,693	$246,779	$496,361	$998,359	$1,148,113
20% $73,200	$151,788	$377,696	$939,828	$2,338,594	$2,806,312
25% $76,250	$186,157	$568,107	$1,733,724	$5,290,907	$6,613,633
30% $79,300	$226,489	$840,937	$3,122,339	$11,593,028	$15,070,936
35% $82,350	$273,526	$1,226,500	$5,499,667	$24,660,689	$33,291,930

Appendix A (Returns at various rates of return}

	Initial Investment $58,000					
Years ->	26	27	28	29	30	31
Percent						
1%	$75,125	$75,876	$76,635	$77,401	$78,175	$78,957
5%	$206,229	$216,540	$227,367	$238,736	$250,673	$263,206
10%	$691,254	$760,380	$836,418	$920,059	$1,012,065	$1,113,272
15%	$2,195,694	$2,525,048	$2,903,805	$3,339,376	$3,840,283	$4,416,325
20%	$6,639,577	$7,967,492	$9,560,990	$11,473,189	$13,767,826	$16,521,391
25%	$19,190,590	$23,988,238	$29,985,297	$37,481,622	$46,852,027	$58,565,034
30%	$53,205,332	$69,166,931	$89,917,010	$116,892,113	$151,959,747	$197,547,672
35%	$141,940,384	$191,619,518	$258,686,349	$349,226,571	$471,455,871	$636,465,426

	Initial Investment $59,000					
Years ->	26	27	28	29	30	31
Percent						
1%	$76,420	$77,184	$77,956	$78,736	$79,523	$80,318
5%	$209,785	$220,274	$231,288	$242,852	$254,995	$267,744
10%	$703,172	$773,490	$850,839	$935,922	$1,029,515	$1,132,466
15%	$2,233,551	$2,568,584	$2,953,871	$3,396,952	$3,906,495	$4,492,469
20%	$6,754,052	$8,104,863	$9,725,835	$11,671,002	$14,005,203	$16,806,243
25%	$19,521,462	$24,401,828	$30,502,285	$38,127,856	$47,659,820	$59,574,776
30%	$54,122,665	$70,359,464	$91,467,304	$118,907,495	$154,579,743	$200,953,666
35%	$144,387,632	$194,923,303	$263,146,458	$355,247,719	$479,584,421	$647,438,968

	Initial Investment $60,000					
Years ->	26	27	28	29	30	31
Percent						
1%	$77,715	$78,493	$79,277	$80,070	$80,871	$81,680
5%	$213,340	$224,007	$235,208	$246,968	$259,317	$272,282
10%	$715,091	$786,600	$865,260	$951,786	$1,046,964	$1,151,661
15%	$2,271,408	$2,612,119	$3,003,937	$3,454,527	$3,972,706	$4,568,612
20%	$6,868,528	$8,242,233	$9,890,680	$11,868,816	$14,242,579	$17,091,095
25%	$19,852,335	$24,815,418	$31,019,273	$38,774,091	$48,467,614	$60,584,518
30%	$55,039,998	$71,551,998	$93,017,597	$120,922,876	$157,199,739	$204,359,660
35%	$146,834,880	$198,227,087	$267,606,568	$361,268,867	$487,712,970	$658,412,510

	Initial Investment $61,000					
Years ->	26	27	28	29	30	31
Percent						
1%	$79,011	$79,801	$80,599	$81,405	$82,219	$83,041
5%	$216,896	$227,741	$239,128	$251,084	$263,638	$276,820
10%	$727,009	$799,710	$879,681	$967,649	$1,064,414	$1,170,855
15%	$2,309,265	$2,655,654	$3,054,002	$3,512,103	$4,038,918	$4,644,756
20%	$6,983,003	$8,379,604	$10,055,524	$12,066,629	$14,479,955	$17,375,946
25%	$20,183,207	$25,229,009	$31,536,261	$39,420,326	$49,275,408	$61,594,259
30%	$55,957,331	$72,744,531	$94,567,890	$122,938,257	$159,819,734	$207,765,655
35%	$149,282,128	$201,530,872	$272,066,677	$367,290,015	$495,841,520	$669,386,051

Appendix A (Returns at various rates of return}

	Initial	$10,000				
Years ->	1	5	10	15	20	21
Percent						
1%	$10,100	$10,510	$11,046	$11,610	$12,202	$12,324
5%	$10,500	$12,763	$16,289	$20,789	$26,533	$27,860
10%	$11,000	$16,105	$25,937	$41,772	$67,275	$74,002
15%	$11,500	$20,114	$40,456	$81,371	$163,665	$188,215
20%	$12,000	$24,883	$61,917	$154,070	$383,376	$460,051
25%	$12,500	$30,518	$93,132	$284,217	$867,362	$1,084,202
30%	$13,000	$37,129	$137,858	$511,859	$1,900,496	$2,470,645
35%	$13,500	$44,840	$201,066	$901,585	$4,042,736	$5,457,693

	Initial	$50,000				
Years ->	1	5	10	15	20	21
Percent						
1%	$50,500	$52,551	$55,231	$58,048	$61,010	$61,620
5%	$52,500	$63,814	$81,445	$103,946	$132,665	$139,298
10%	$55,000	$80,526	$129,687	$208,862	$336,375	$370,012
15%	$57,500	$100,568	$202,278	$406,853	$818,327	$941,076
20%	$60,000	$124,416	$309,587	$770,351	$1,916,880	$2,300,256
25%	$62,500	$152,588	$465,661	$1,421,085	$4,336,809	$5,421,011
30%	$65,000	$185,647	$689,292	$2,559,295	$9,502,482	$12,353,226
35%	$67,500	$224,202	$1,005,328	$4,507,923	$20,213,679	$27,288,467

	Initial	$100,000				
Years ->	1	5	10	15	20	21
Percent						
1%	$101,000	$105,101	$110,462	$116,097	$122,019	$123,239
5%	$105,000	$127,628	$162,889	$207,893	$265,330	$278,596
10%	$110,000	$161,051	$259,374	$417,725	$672,750	$740,025
15%	$115,000	$201,136	$404,556	$813,706	$1,636,654	$1,882,152
20%	$120,000	$248,832	$619,174	$1,540,702	$3,833,760	$4,600,512
25%	$125,000	$305,176	$931,323	$2,842,171	$8,673,617	$10,842,022
30%	$130,000	$371,293	$1,378,585	$5,118,589	$19,004,964	$24,706,453
35%	$135,000	$448,403	$2,010,656	$9,015,847	$40,427,359	$54,576,935

	Initial	$150,000				
Years ->	1	5	10	15	20	21
Percent						
1%	$151,500	$157,652	$165,693	$174,145	$183,029	$184,859
5%	$157,500	$191,442	$244,334	$311,839	$397,995	$417,894
10%	$165,000	$241,577	$389,061	$626,587	$1,009,125	$1,110,037
15%	$172,500	$301,704	$606,834	$1,220,559	$2,454,981	$2,823,228
20%	$180,000	$373,248	$928,760	$2,311,053	$5,750,640	$6,900,768
25%	$187,500	$457,764	$1,396,984	$4,263,256	$13,010,426	$16,263,033
30%	$195,000	$556,940	$2,067,877	$7,677,884	$28,507,446	$37,059,679
35%	$202,500	$672,605	$3,015,983	$13,523,770	$60,641,038	$81,865,402

Appendix A (Returns at various rates of return}

Initial Investment	$10,000				
Years ->	26	27	28	29	30	31
Percent						
1%	$12,953	$13,082	$13,213	$13,345	$13,478	$13,613
5%	$35,557	$37,335	$39,201	$41,161	$43,219	$45,380
10%	$119,182	$131,100	$144,210	$158,631	$174,494	$191,943
15%	$378,568	$435,353	$500,656	$575,755	$662,118	$761,435
20%	$1,144,755	$1,373,706	$1,648,447	$1,978,136	$2,373,763	$2,848,516
25%	$3,308,722	$4,135,903	$5,169,879	$6,462,349	$8,077,936	$10,097,420
30%	$9,173,333	$11,925,333	$15,502,933	$20,153,813	$26,199,956	$34,059,943
35%	$24,472,480	$33,037,848	$44,601,095	$60,211,478	$81,285,495	$109,735,418

Initial Investment	$50,000				
Years ->	26	27	28	29	30	31
Percent						
1%	$64,763	$65,410	$66,065	$66,725	$67,392	$68,066
5%	$177,784	$186,673	$196,006	$205,807	$216,097	$226,902
10%	$595,909	$655,500	$721,050	$793,155	$872,470	$959,717
15%	$1,892,840	$2,176,766	$2,503,281	$2,878,773	$3,310,589	$3,807,177
20%	$5,723,773	$6,868,528	$8,242,233	$9,890,680	$11,868,816	$14,242,579
25%	$16,543,612	$20,679,515	$25,849,394	$32,311,743	$40,389,678	$50,487,098
30%	$45,866,665	$59,626,665	$77,514,664	$100,769,063	$130,999,782	$170,299,717
35%	$122,362,400	$165,189,239	$223,005,473	$301,057,389	$406,427,475	$548,677,091

Initial Investment	$100,000				
Years ->	26	27	28	29	30	31
Percent						
1%	$129,526	$130,821	$132,129	$133,450	$134,785	$136,133
5%	$355,567	$373,346	$392,013	$411,614	$432,194	$453,804
10%	$1,191,818	$1,310,999	$1,442,099	$1,586,309	$1,744,940	$1,919,434
15%	$3,785,680	$4,353,531	$5,006,561	$5,757,545	$6,621,177	$7,614,354
20%	$11,447,546	$13,737,055	$16,484,466	$19,781,359	$23,737,631	$28,485,158
25%	$33,087,225	$41,359,031	$51,698,788	$64,623,485	$80,779,357	$100,974,196
30%	$91,733,330	$119,253,329	$155,029,328	$201,538,126	$261,999,564	$340,599,434
35%	$244,724,799	$330,378,479	$446,010,947	$602,114,778	$812,854,950	$1,097,354,183

Initial Investment	$150,000				
Years ->	26	27	28	29	30	31
Percent						
1%	$194,288	$196,231	$198,194	$200,176	$202,177	$204,199
5%	$533,351	$560,018	$588,019	$617,420	$648,291	$680,706
10%	$1,787,726	$1,966,499	$2,163,149	$2,379,464	$2,617,410	$2,879,151
15%	$5,678,519	$6,530,297	$7,509,842	$8,636,318	$9,931,766	$11,421,531
20%	$17,171,319	$20,605,583	$24,726,699	$29,672,039	$35,606,447	$42,727,736
25%	$49,630,837	$62,038,546	$77,548,182	$96,935,228	$121,169,035	$151,461,294
30%	$137,599,995	$178,879,994	$232,543,992	$302,307,190	$392,999,347	$510,899,151
35%	$367,087,199	$495,567,718	$669,016,420	$903,172,167	$1,219,282,425	$1,646,031,274

Index

Author Bio

Jim Vickery is the Editor and founder of InvestProfits.com, a website with interactive tools and investment research for investors and traders. A review of the website has been published in *Technical Analysis of Stocks and Commodities* Magazine. He writes an investing blog that covers investing techniques using stock charts to find investments with momentum and stocks that are oversold.

He has been an active investor in the market for more than 12 years. He uses technical analysis and fundamental analysis to find stocks. He holds an M.B.A. in Finance from Tourou University graduating with honors, Magna Cum Laude.